THE BOOK OF SECRET WISDOM

The Book of Secret Wisdom

THE PROPHETIC RECORD OF HUMAN DESTINY AND EVOLUTION

Translated from the Senzar by
Zinovia Dushkova

Radiant Books

Moscow

Copyright © 2015 by Zinovia Dushkova and Alexander Gerasimchuk

The main text of this work was originally published in Russian as *Stantsy Liubvi* by Zvezda Vostoka, Novosibirsk, in 2001. Copyright © 2001 by Zinovia Dushkova. Translated from the Russian and edited with additional material by Alexander Gerasimchuk in consultation with Zinovia Dushkova. For further copyright information, please see page 249.

All rights reserved. No part of this book may be used or reproduced in any manner whatsoever without written permission from the publisher except in the case of brief quotations embodied in critical articles and reviews. For additional information, please contact info@radiantbooks.org.

Disclaimer: This book is intended to be educational. In the event you wish to apply ideas contained herein, you are taking full responsibility for your actions. Neither the publisher nor the copyright holders may be held liable for any misuse or misinterpretation of the information in this publication.

Note on language: To refer to a human being of any gender, this book uses the word *man*, which has its roots in the Sanskrit *manu* ("thinking creature"), and the pronouns *he*, *him*, and *his* accordingly. This is not intended to exclude women, but simply to ensure readability and clarity, since gender-neutral language can sometimes be cumbersome and confusing.

The book uses the term *Great White Brotherhood* in reference to the Hierarchy of Light existing on the Earth. The word *white* here symbolizes spiritual purity, and has absolutely no association with ethnicity or skin-colour. In the White Brotherhood there is no distinction of race, gender, colour, nationality, culture, creed, religion, or any other differences. The White Brotherhood is opposed by the black brotherhood. The word *black* here, too, has absolutely no racial connotation; it is merely used to describe the use of powers for evil purposes. The same applies for the term *black magic*.

The main text of this work uses personification and grammatical gender for inanimate objects in order to avoid confusion with frequent use of *it* and *its*. Therefore: *Sun*, *Light*, *Fire*, and *evil* have masculine gender; *Earth*, *Love*, *Life*, and *darkness* have feminine gender.

The publisher is grateful to all who have contributed their time and efforts to making this book possible:

Translation Editor: John Woodsworth | *Initial Copyeditor:* Jo-Ann Langseth
Proofreader: Julie Clayton | *Indexer:* Lydia Jones | *Cover & Interior Designer:* Richard Wehrman

Publisher's Cataloging-In-Publication Data
(Prepared by The Donohue Group, Inc.)

The book of secret wisdom : the prophetic record of human destiny and evolution / [original work] translated [into Russian] from the Senzar by Zinovia Dushkova ; translated from the Russian and edited with additional material by Alexander Gerasimchuk. — First English ed.

pages ; cm

"The main text of this work was originally published in Russian as *Stantsy Liubvi* by Zvezda Vostoka, Novosibirsk, in 2001 ... [this English edition] Translated from the Russian and edited with additional material by Alexander Gerasimchuk in consultation with Zinovia Dushkova."—Title page verso.

Based on the Tibetan work: Book of Dzyan.
Issued also as an e-book.
Includes bibliographical references and index.
ISBN: 978-5-9905431-3-3 (hardcover)
ISBN: 978-5-9905431-4-0 (paperback)

1. Theosophy. 2. Evolution. 3. Cosmology, Ancient. 4. Love—Philosophy. 5. Spiritual life—Miscellanea.

I. Dushkova, Zinovia. Stantsy liubvi. English. II. Gerasimchuk, Alexander. III. Title: Based on (work) Book of Dzyan.
BP573.E8 D8813 2015
299/.934

British Library Cataloguing-in-Publication Data
A catalogue record for this book is available from the British Library.

First English Edition
published in 2015 by Radiant Books,
an imprint of Dushkova Publishing, LLC
www.radiantbooks.org

ISBN 978-5-9905431-3-3 (hardcover)
ISBN 978-5-9905431-4-0 (paperback)
ISBN 978-5-9905431-5-7 (e-book)

*This Work
is dedicated
to all Truth-seeking Hearts
of all Countries and of all Races,
for they are graced with
the Cosmic Right — to know
the Truth of the World's Creation
by the Law of Divine Love.*

सत्यात् नास्ति परो धर्मः।

"There is no Religion higher than Truth."

CONTENTS

The Oldest Book in the World and Its Sacred Language ix

AGAPEGENESIS
Twelve Stanzas from the *Book of Dzyan*

STANZA I: The Genesis of Divine Love 3
STANZA II: The Knowledge of the Heart. 7
STANZA III: The Sowing of Love 10
STANZA IV: The Gift of Mind. 14
STANZA V: The Persecution of Love. 18
STANZA VI: The Final Battle. 23
STANZA VII: The Fiery Baptism. 28
STANZA VIII: The Love of the Heart. 31
STANZA IX: The Era of Wisdom and Beauty 35
STANZA X: The Divine Humanity 40
STANZA XI: The Fire of Love. 46
STANZA XII: The Birth of Gods 51
Epilogue. 59

Glossary 61
Recommended Reading. 213
Index. 221

About the Translator. 237
Letter to the Reader. 241

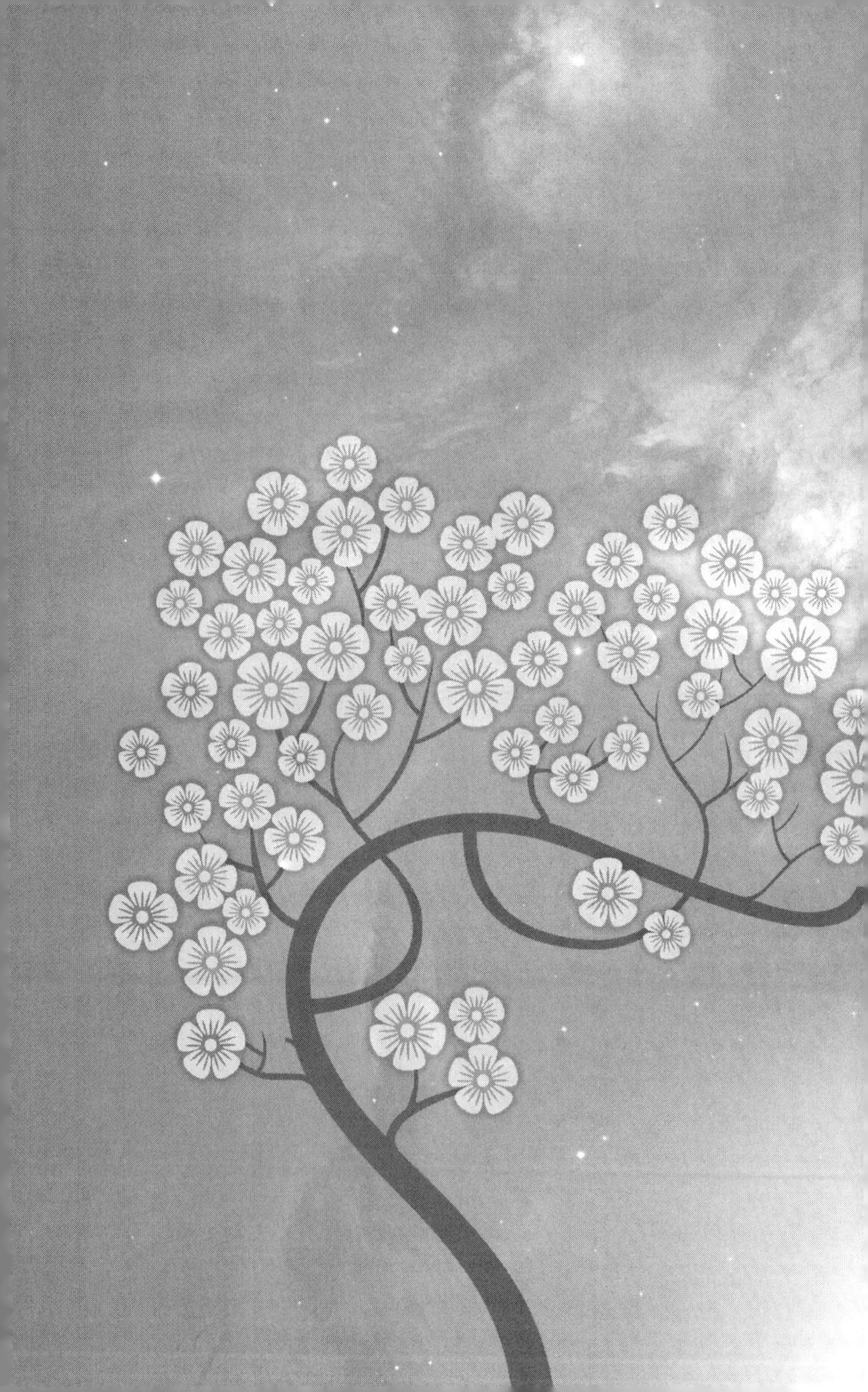

THE OLDEST BOOK IN THE WORLD AND ITS SACRED LANGUAGE

The One Source of Truth nourishes the Tree of Knowledge, stretching its roots into Infinite Eternity. In each cycle of human evolution it bears good fruit in the form of a Great Book, which serves as the source of all knowledge and wisdom for humanity for a specific period. And every Book of this kind, like a tree, grows and yields its own fruit for the good of the whole world.

At the dawn of the conscious evolution of humanity, approximately eighteen million years ago, the Sons of Light brought the Fiery Teaching of Kalachakra from the Distant Worlds as a gift for the people of Lemuria, sowing the first seeds of all the existing religions of the Earth. The new pages of knowledge opened in the one universal language of the Sun — Senzar — inviting them to further delve into the books of enlightened knowledge. And thus ever after, each epoch aimed to reveal the secret pages of universal knowledge, thereby facilitating the progress of human consciousness round by round.

Many of the innermost pages of the Great Book were revealed to the human population of Atlantis. They knew more than anyone else, for many secrets of surrounding Nature were confided to them. And their best representatives had gained the right to look beyond the field of vision, unveiling the invisible Life. But the Atlanteans had not accepted the heart as the organ to which one should subordinate the intellect — they honoured the mind above all. And they disappeared from the stage of Life without learning this simple truth: "Knowledge without Love is dead." Thus, because of their pride, people deprived themselves of the Secret Wisdom, gradually forgetting their pristine universal language. Nevertheless, the Great Initiates remained in every land and nation, guarding the Ancient Wisdom as a sacred trust.

About a million years ago, at the beginning of the evolution of our present humanity, the Sons of Light recorded in the language of Senzar the most ancient book of our time, known as the *Book of Dzyan* — a Tibetan name meaning the *Book of Secret Wisdom*. This archaic manuscript, in its turn, has yielded a multitude of its own fruits for the development of humanity. But as soon as humanity received the highest knowledge, it immediately began to throw these books into fires and subject to severe condemnation those who had presented them with the priceless gifts. Humanity was ready to turn any Messenger of the Kingdom of Heaven into an outcast. And yet hundreds of thousands of the Sons of Light have walked upon the Earth, leaving profound traces in the history of human development.

Despite the destruction of numerous libraries full of the magnificent scrolls of inexhaustible knowledge, from time immemorial to the present day, there exist secret treasuries of sacred books, written by the Messengers of Light and presented as a gift to humanity.

AND ITS SACRED LANGUAGE

Every line has been crystallized by the heartfelt fires of the souls, who were magnanimous in their giving. Yes, some were burnt at the stake together with their gifts; others were mutilated by cruellest torture. But still there were those who managed to save the sacred manuscripts and, risking their lives, placed one priceless gift after another in secret repositories. And all these unusual libraries — located in the mountains of Tibet, the Himalayas, the Karakorum, the Pyrenees, and other mountainous areas, as well as hidden under the sands of the Gobi Desert, parts of the Sahara, in the sands of Nubia and other lands — can be revealed to the world only when people are able to discern white from black and distribute the priceless gifts solely for the good of their neighbours.

These are the Abodes of the Brotherhood, members of which came from the Distant Worlds. Being concealed in impenetrable mountains and deserts, they are guarded by mysterious powers. Physical flesh is not able to endure the force of the currents that rise like a wall when they are approached. And in order to gain access to them, one needs to pass through many lives with a loving heart and a pure soul. When the time comes, worthy candidates for discipleship might be summoned into one of the Ashrams, where they would be entitled to come into contact with the Highest Knowledge and Wisdom.

The chief of these is the legendary realm of Shambhala the Resplendent, the Abode of the Great White Brotherhood of Teachers. The approaches to this Stronghold of Light are vigilantly protected. For mere curiosity-seekers there is no access beyond the permitted boundaries. An unbidden guest will never reach it and will inevitably fail to find the way to it. However, one who responds to the Call of the Great Lord of Shambhala discovers one's path thanks to invisible signs. Only a pure consciousness is able to correctly discern the symbols which appear to one's gaze. The wise heart alone is able to understand the secret signs that lead the pilgrim to the White Ashram, situated on the White Island. Mysterious white waters wash its banks, but the one who is summoned by the Lord passes through these waters as easily as on dry land.

In Shambhala, indeed, not people but Gods abide. The Greatest Teachers — the Leaders of Humanity, the Discoverers of the Distant Worlds, the Messengers of the Faraway Stars — in shining bodies of Divine Purity, glide about like Angels, doing their work every moment. Ceaselessly they watch over the world, protecting it from a disastrous fate. A seal of smiles illumines their sunny faces, enchanting the gaze of the pilgrim who is encountering for the first time in their life the miracle of miracles, which actually exists on the Earth.

Here reigns the sacred language of Senzar, from which have originated the tongues of all peoples through the ages. Thus, the roots of many current eastern languages come from Sanskrit, which is based on Senzar. Many words of this most ancient language underlie not only Sanskrit but also Egyptian, Hebrew, Latin, and other languages of various known and yet-to-be discovered sacred texts. The language of Senzar is distinct from others in that, because of its flexible nature, it has no dead or long-entrenched forms of expression. Just like any other language, Senzar has both spoken and written forms of speech, which are substantially different from our traditional understanding.

Conversation among Initiated Adepts, for the most part, takes place on the subconscious level, using thought-forms. And here, by means of two or three "phrases," one can express that which even several volumes of text cannot, for human words, so often comprising many contradictory shades and nuances, have only limited capabilities of meaning. The concision of the Senzar language enables it to express most completely and compactly any thought, including infinitely extensive phenomena. Symbolism underlies speech. Hence one small symbol, sent in the form of a particular vibration to a companion, unfolds a whole network of images, and fiery signs through the living breath and geometric expression of a combination of rays bring out a whole range of light in sequence, where a particular colour dominates, as though emphasizing the key tone of the message. In this way, we note the presence of light, colour, and sound, contained in a thought-form, thereby completely excluding the necessity of direct verbal contact. The Voice of the Great Silence is heard everywhere in Shambhala, but its sounds are always arranged in the diapason of high-frequency energy vibrations. And they, refracted through a sensitive heart, develop into a specific "word."

The writing system of Senzar is even more complicated, combining in itself seemingly incompatible elements. These include signs, syllables, and letters based on symbolism. A single symbol is capable of developing into an entire treatise, being easily understandable by an initiated disciple of any ethnic background. Of course, the reader's level of consciousness is also important. Colour, light, number, and sound play a significant role in a secret alphabet from which words and sentences are composed. Each letter, possessing its own specific colour of the rainbow, shade of light, number, and mystic sound syllable, has its equivalent in the languages of all peoples of the world and may be reproduced using different cryptographic methods, with the aid of specialized calculation tables. Thus, a new cryptographic alphabet is created in a given tongue while numerological, geometrical, and astrological keys help the reader precisely determine the way to decode this secret writing. Consequently, this language of signs and symbols facilitates the comprehension of a text written in any tongue. Herein lies the value of such scriptures, for their language is unique, affording the opportunity to preserve itself without the imposed changes that inevitably take place in the languages we are familiar with. But special knowledge is needed in order to learn this language of original cryptography, though the acquisition of it is not as complicated as it might seem at first sight.

Above the Sacred Island rises a multi-storey Tower called *Chung*. And here, on one of the floors, is stored the only original copy of the *Book of Dzyan* — among other archaic manuscripts such as the *Book of the Golden Precepts* and the *Book of Maitreya Buddha*. In fact, the Tower of Chung, going deep into the rock and high above the clouds, keeps a great number of mysteries, which were inscribed into the pages of extremely voluminous books.

The gates of the depositories open wide, like a book, ready to endow waiting hearts with secret knowledge. How many unexplored folios one can behold within the Stronghold of Light — only the Great Lord knows! From the earth to Heaven, the rows of books are lined up in an orderly manner, in the order of the Hierarchical Ladder, the highest steps of which are occupied by the worthiest of the worthy.

Here one can see the very earliest manuscripts, recorded on tablets of every kind; and one may discover further blessed signs of engraved human thought by transferring one's reading from stone to invisible books, inaccessible to earthly eyes. Thus, one may find here records of the development of the entire Universe, folios devoted to the study of the physical spheres of the Earth and the history of all the Kingdoms of Nature and Space.

However, not only these records are stored here, but also that of the history of any specific individual, beginning from the moment of their spirit's origin to their descent into dense matter. The books of human destinies are kept in special repositories and they are similar to the Scrolls of Akasha, through whose unfoldment one can watch the unfoldment of one's own life — in any period of incarnation — just like a film. These books are crystallized by a special kind of fire and, when opening them, one may enter any Space-Time dimension and witness hitherto unseen episodes of one's life. Many advanced souls will succeed in perceiving their future as well on the pages of these books. The volumes of the Subtle Plane contain the names of those who have advanced farther than others on the Path of Light. Their names are expressed in the form of certain signs, for a soul may have thousands of names. And this sign confers the right to open the needed page, where a text starts to appear, allowing one to read about the deeds done in the Name of Light. Here one can find the answer to any question. Seven Books successively reveal the history of spirit's movement through the earthly and Ethereal Worlds.

There is one special Book where not many souls are inscribed — the *Book of Fiery Destinies*. It registers only those who have trod the heroic path and with their self-sacrificing labour have brought the

Light of the Empyreal Spheres to the Earth. This Book records fiery deeds, and it is entirely woven from the highest substance of Fire. Only those who are inscribed in the Book are able to read it, for one needs special knowledge in order to understand the Fiery Signs. While in the former volumes one may find deeds of the flesh and soul, this one reflects only the fiery path of the Divine Spirit. And it is possible to read one's destiny for many thousands of years ahead.

The best deeds on the level of countries, peoples, and leaders have been gathered into the depository of experience, finding their place on the pages of numerous books. They are arranged according to the degree of chiaroscuro, as mentioned before, set forth pyramidally by hierarchical principle, at the foundation of which are those folios which are the closest to earthly spheres. Closer to the top are the tablets of the Subtle Plane, crowned by the volumes of Fiery Destinies.

In addition, the mysterious Tower houses the records of all neglected opportunities given to the Human Race since its creation. Books burnt in fires, containing the knowledge covering all spheres of life; the most progressive ideas, scientific discoveries and many, many other things, which today could have helped humanity to ascend to the step of Divine Humanity — if only people had accepted all this with their minds!

The entire human life would not be sufficient to copy on paper the contents of even a single folio. But even the most comprehensive volume seems to be amazingly light, since its pages are made from a special composition of matter. Neither fire nor water can affect the compactly written lines, which have been crystallized forever. Even though it represents a specific historical era, this is a living word, affirmed beyond Time and Space. Light revives before one's eyes, and a statically affirmed word takes on a definite hue of manifested energy, resulting in pictures visible to the human eye. However, it is impossible to describe in human words such concepts as colour, light, and sound that figure on the Empyreal Tablets, written in the sacred Senzar.

For each of the priceless artefacts a special niche was created, which was imbued with the currents of those times when an individual manuscript came to light. Further, the energy constant of the currents is preserved, thanks to a specially constructed covering — a "vitreous" substance, which has a clearly defined geometrical shape. Thus the manuscripts bear within themselves an extremely powerful energy potential for many millennia to come. The *Book of Dzyan* is preserved in a similar manner.

The lines of the *Book of Dzyan* bear secret signs that unfold the entire history of world development: from inception until the very last moment. Its pages may be disclosed before the eyes of pilgrims only by the Great Lord of Shambhala, who has summoned them with a specific aim: to share with humanity the Ancient Wisdom that has been concealed within unknown caves and mysterious multi-storey towers rooted deep in the Earth. And while they who gain access to the Great Book are able to behold it with their own eyes, nevertheless, the manuscript itself must remain in its energy niche, and should not be touched by human hands. The needed pages will open all by themselves, simply from touches on the Subtle Plane by the Instructor of the Human Race.

Nowadays, many volumes of exoteric and esoteric Commentaries on the *Book of Dzyan*, representing all of the innermost sciences, are kept hidden in the secret lamaseries of the East. Each of the ancient sciences, religions, and philosophies of the present stage of human evolution is derived from this Great Book. And that is why all sacred texts and all the works of initiated philosophers and alchemists have the same ideas in common, being only popular interpretations of certain parts of the secret manuscript, presented in a different light. In the meantime, the true meaning was veiled by the Messengers of Light behind symbols, myths and legends, deliberate vagueness and unfamiliar terms, extremely abstruse mathematical calculations, and a secret code of certain words and expressions, plus many other forms of camouflage — the seven keys to which are in the hands of the Mahatmas alone. And each of the seven keys must be turned seven times before the entire meaning is revealed.

The *Book of Dzyan* consists of stanzas, the total number of which is known only to the Initiates. During certain periods of time, fragments of this sacred manuscript are divulged by the Great Masters of Wisdom through their messengers in a certain Ray, since different epochs demand expressions of different energies, imbuing knowledge with the specific energy "colouring" which is needed for the enrichment of the world in a particular century.

Thus, in 1888, for the first time in the history of modern humanity, nineteen stanzas from the *Book of Dzyan* were revealed by Helena Petrovna Blavatsky in her landmark masterwork, *The Secret Doctrine*, comprising two volumes on the creation of the Universe and the origin of humanity, known as *Cosmogenesis* and *Anthropogenesis*. A third volume — *Theogenesis* — which includes nine stanzas of *Dzyan* on the inherent divinity of humanity, was received by Francia La Due between 1906 and 1918.

The present volume is a new excerpt from the *Book of Dzyan* — or the *Book of Secret Wisdom* — entitled *Agapegenesis*. It comprises twelve stanzas, which were originally translated from Senzar into Russian by Zinovia Vasilievna Dushkova in 1995, expounding the symbolism of the mysterious language in the Ray of Love-Wisdom.

The translation from the language of Senzar is complicated by the fact that it is not always possible to find equivalents in other languages for words conveying a complex idea or action. For example, in the matter of finding a human term for the *Divine Infinite Principle* or the *Inconceivable Cause of all Existence*, there are very few words that are able to clearly express the main idea to the majority of people living in the Christian countries. Two of these would be *God* and the *Creator*. But the Christian understanding of these words does not quite correspond to Truth. At the same time, it is better not to use terms such as *Ein Sof*, *Brahman*, or *Adi-Buddhi*, which might only confuse readers who have been brought up in the Christian tradition. Therefore, in order not to be misunderstood and avoid so many complicated terms, the translator, as a rule, uses those words and expressions that are the most acceptable and accessible in the society she lives in.

xvii

Unlike the previous parts of the *Book of Dzyan*, the stanzas of *Agapegenesis* were given without the Commentaries of the Great Teachers. This is because they were translated through the Ray of Love-Wisdom, with its particular focus on the heart. A whole volume of commentary could be devoted to each of the twelve stanzas, but the heart, possessing an All-Seeing Eye, allows one to grasp the whole Truth contained in them.

Like all esoteric texts, *Agapegenesis* comprises seven levels of understanding, and therefore, with every new reading, more and more secrets will be revealed to the eyes of one's heart. This in turn will proclaim the assimilated Truth through the voice of intuition. However, to aid those who are taking their first steps towards studying such books, the *Glossary* of words and phrases was compiled. Using the knowledge given by the Masters of the Ancient Wisdom over the last centuries, it is designed to serve as a basis for understanding this work.

And so, beyond Time and Space, the twelve mysterious Stanzas of Love will open before your eyes not only the past, but also the present and future of humanity and the Earth. Thus, bearing in mind the Universal Law of Correspondences, "As below, so above" — it is possible to understand by analogy the development of all Races of Humanity in all their Rounds of Evolution as well as comprehend the path of evolution of our planet, the Solar System, and the whole Universe, according to the Law of Divine Love.

AGAPEGENESIS

Twelve Stanzas from the *Book of Dzyan*

STANZA I
THE GENESIS OF DIVINE LOVE

1. The Gods were at work, rotating the Stellar Wheel. They were winding up the hidden mainspring, which then would unfold, manifesting itself in the concept of *Time*. The Earth was waiting for it, for the spot bearing that name was already aware of its mission. A small, barely visible drop of Matter was swirling around in Eternity. And for it the Lords of Destiny had foreordained Love! It was their loving intention to see that Love would fill that little drop and, after condensing it, carry it to its defined ultimate boundaries.

2. The Sun was beginning his Round. He had a defined role — the Bearer of Love. It was his job to imbue that small cluster with the warmth of the Fiery Heart, which finally started to take on a definite appearance. The newly attenuated state of Matter enabled the Sun to carry out the excellent work of filling it with his currents of abundant Love.

3. The Gods knew their Task and set a new pace for their Wheel, which was now vibrating faster than ever. The density of Matter

was coupled with firmness and elasticity. The currents of Love had to struggle in order to successfully pierce the stone with their Fire.

4. The new Kingdom of Stones was populating the Earth, endowing her with power over their motionless bodies. The planet, raised by the currents of Love, knew only one way she herself could bring forth Life, and that was Love!

Love! Here she was a rule, a law, a form of Life. Only one thing was required of the Earth: to *love*! And the Lords of Destiny kept strict watch over the fulfilling of Karma.

5. The planet was doing her utmost. She knew how to love, and what it was to be loved. With all the zeal and fervour of her Loving Soul, she warmed the motionless stones, breaking through their hardness and elasticity. They revived, drinking in the generous currents of Love. Stones were resurrected! They began to blossom like petals of Divine Flowers, and took their place in turn. The planet was beautified by a profusion of flowers.

6. The warmth of the Sun became stronger, for he was clearly experiencing the magical Power of the influence of Love. And the flowers loved both their Father Sun and their Mother Earth. They were their children, born in common! The parents carefully looked after their flowers' luxuriant heads of many colours, open wide towards them.

The Universe beheld the work of the Lords, and was pleased with the flowers' first successful appearance. Ceaselessly they worked, imbuing the world with a fragrant aroma. Attracted by the flowers' Power of Love, constellations generously imparted their own… The Lords of Destiny were content: all was proceeding according to their Predestined Plan.

7. Love reigned supreme all over the world! She was calm and content in her earthly domains. All the celestial bodies supported her in that Divine Work. Only the Sun sometimes peered anxiously into the bowels of Earth during the times when she hid her sides from him as she rotated. Because of the density of Matter, the Sun was not able to glimpse what was happening on the other side of the planet.

STANZA I: THE GENESIS OF DIVINE LOVE

8. Eventually, robust vegetation girdled the world, hiding the gentle flowers in its shadow and choking their tiny stems with its mighty roots. These giants seized power and began to swallow light greedily, cutting off the warm solar rays from those who were shorter and much weaker than they. Without the caressing warmth of the All-Loving Sun, lesser creatures withered and perished.

9. Evil had appeared in the world for the first time. The Sun was unable to discern what was going on beneath the thick crowns of giant trees. These effectively concealed evil, which had managed to steal in surreptitiously. The All-Seeing Eye of the Sun partially lost its power, for he could not illuminate the hidden back side of the Earth.

10. The condensation of Matter came to the end of its tether. Billions of years had passed, and human souls were still similar to stones... How could they have become so callous and impenetrable? It was a difficult question to answer! They had become acquainted with evil, who was already rotating his black wheel of time in full swing, standing just beyond the border of the Light. While, on the reverse side, the darkness was trying to obscure the whole of the Light so as to transform him into gloom. But for that she needed some assistance from earthlings.

11. The Light was fighting bravely, armed with the One Power of Love. But because he was always ablaze with pure Divine Love, he felt no hatred towards the darkness, nor did he know jealousy. Love was the most powerful weapon, and the darkness was helpless against her. It was necessary to wield that weapon to be omnipotent! But the darkness could not approach the Light openly, for she would immediately burn down, engulfed in the Flame of Love. But by and by she found a way around: she would enter human Hearts, which were alone capable of holding the Sacred Divine Gift.

12. The human Heart started to glow, like the Celestial Star itself. And that tiny sun in a human breast was full of the bright and brimming-over currents of Love. Nevertheless, the Heart, parched with an endless thirst, went on constantly searching — only for Love, for that Divine impulse could be quenched by Love alone. Apparently, the Love of the earthly Hearts did not know satisfaction, for she still had not yet fully experienced the Power of the Sacred, Divinely Supreme Love. An enormous task of recognition lay ahead.

And so to fulfil that Task of pure Heavenly Labour, the Lords of Destiny asked the Gods to launch the Supreme Mechanism which would turn *another* Wheel — one that would go beyond the bounds of Time, leading human Hearts along heavenly pathways to the recognition of True Love.

STANZA II
THE KNOWLEDGE OF THE HEART

13. The Day arrived. The Wheel gradually gained momentum and led human Hearts towards Knowledge — something the Hearts had known for a long time. But man was not yet able to comprehend the Wisdom of his own Heart. He had not actually guessed that the Heart was capable of *knowing*. And all the while, the still, small Voice, which imparted the wise counsel of Life, was practically inaudible to the insensitive human ear. And even when that Voice rang out with unmistakable clarity, like an alarm bell, calling its hearers to arm themselves with the Power of Love on the eve of death, man attempted to muffle it, preferring to take a roundabout route through the labyrinths and machinations of the mind. But the intellect was not able to perceive what the Heart knew, for it was subject to decay. Evil could easily penetrate thereinto, not fearing any encounter with the bright, dazzling Light of Fiery Thought. Man could think only on the lowest levels. And so the Wheel began a New Round.

14. People gradually began to pay attention to the leadings of their own Heart, becoming convinced that the mind's contemplations, more often than not, led them to wrong conclusions. And the barely perceptible Voice of the Heart, it appeared, had presaged the Truth... And so there was a pressing need to hearken to that which possessed the Wisdom of insight. But how to do this? How is it possible to avoid mistaking the voice of the mind for the inaudible tremors of the currents of the Heart? People became thoughtful once again. And the Heart meanwhile was still waiting for the time when it would be accepted as the best and most faithful friend...

15. The Sun was shining. Keeping a close watch on human Hearts, he tried to nourish them with Fires in a bid to reinforce the power of Life. Life herself was the gift of the Light, for without him, she could not be conceived. Would this world even exist if there were no Sun? He gave the Light, and it was in the rays of Light that Life had spread her Immortal Wings. Yes, Life was immortal, for she was the forever companion of the Light, who did not know death. Life and the Light were One.

16. The Heart, woven out of Light, belonged to Life. The most delicate particles of condensed Matter were used in its formation. The Heart's secret was that it could not live without Love. Only Love's energizing currents could wind the hidden mainspring therein — the spring that allowed the Wheel of Life to rotate. The Heart without Love was dying away, losing its life-force, even turning to stone.

17. The darkness was overtaking those people who had trampled down their inner Light and so were useless to Life. These were the people of death whom evil was penetrating continuously — not only their thoughts, but also their breast, wherein he ruled on a soulless throne of stone. There was nothing for him to fear, for a stone could not strike a spark that would have burnt the darkness' tenacious paws. O, how the darkness desired such hearts! One had to work very hard to get one's own way, and the darkness spared no effort or means to this end, if only she could see herself ensconced on the throne which had previously belonged to Life.

18. Man was endeavouring to grow in grace and wisdom. He had already been able to distinguish the Light from the darkness. In

him, these two principles were tightly interwoven, forming a single indivisible essence. Gloomy thoughts swept past, dictating strict orders and generating a combative atmosphere. Evil was amassing legions of venomous thoughts, capable of poisoning the whole Joy of Life with their sinister stench. Joy was the lampion oil which made the Flame of Love glow so brightly. The dark host of gloomy thoughts was successfully depriving the little fire of the nourishment it needed. The flame was gradually diminishing in size, and a light puff of air was all it would take to extinguish it forever. The world was being deprived of Joy, without which both Life and Love would be unthinkable.

19. The Sun, too, was endeavouring to give all that he could. He tirelessly warmed the ever-cooling Hearts in his rays of Love. The Sun wished to apply the full force of his energizing currents to restore human souls to Life. He did not blame people for having lost the Gift — their ability to love. For the Star himself, the most important thing was Love. Therefore, he kept on blazing with greater and greater fervour, so that the Fire-breathing Warmth of his Heart would be enough for all... He was ready to enter into every breast and ascend from the depths of the Earth in the form of billions of tiny lights, which would scatter like stars and delight Eternity with their munificent currents of Love. But to that end it was necessary to find such people capable of accepting the mighty Warmth of Heaven, unafraid of being burnt alive in the Fire-breathing Flame of Love. To become the Sun — this was something only man could wish for. So, day by day, the Sun circled the Earth in search of him...

The Gods were turning the Wheel and winding up the mainspring, which was merging with the powerful spirals of the new currents being sent to the Sun's aid. They were proclaiming the beginning of a New Era, which would be experienced under the Sign of Fiery Love.

STANZA III
THE SOWING OF LOVE

20. The Light was triumphing. The Light knew how strongly people felt the need for him. The human Heart was in need of the Fires of Love; that was already established as the undeniable Truth for everyone. The Gods knew their work. And above all — they knew the Periods. Being beyond Time and Space, they were fully aware of the great significance of the designated Periods by which the world was ruled. The Bright Light had broken through. He had pierced the layers of darkness piled up by human ignorance. Penetrating the dense veil of Matter, he glistened in the gloom. The Light was given birth in the soul. He was palpably felt by man.

21. Wonderful changes started happening in the world. Once they realized the whole life-giving Might of the Flame, people began serving the Fire. They were burning in their Hearts. But the tongues of Fire were still erratic and did not reach very high. Man had given Life to the Fiery Seed, and now he began to glimpse a faint and still immature shoot, not knowing how to make it grow. With his still limited knowledge, he reached out and touched the Flame. Knowing

STANZA III: THE SOWING OF LOVE

from his earthly experience how necessary it was to water shoots for more vigorous growth, he generously drenched the germinating seed in water. Only, the water extinguished the fire with a hiss.

In the gathering darkness, the Light grew dim upon contact with this cooling Matter. Once again, a forbidding time was at hand, when rampant extinguishing forces could come into play. Yet the servants of the darkness were unaware of a central fact: that their Period had expired, and they were helpless before the Divine Power of the Seed. Even though the Flame was now practically devoid of its bright tongues of illumination, it was able to revive again. The Seed held within itself the ability to send forth new shoots out of the depths to replace the fading ones. The Light was inextinguishable.

22. The Stellar Period had defined a New Round. At this point it would be impossible to return to the past, since all bridges would be burnt. And they would be burnt by none other than man himself. The most important thing was to discern where the Light was and where the darkness was, and what the past and the future meant for him. Through wise discernment of the essence of all things, he was able to build the saving bridge that would span the abyss and lead him to the Kingdom of the Light. But, all too often, people were stubbornly closing their eyes, unwilling to glimpse the Bright Path which was right beneath their feet, and blindly burnt the bridges that would lead them to the shore of Salvation. Insisting on their own way, these blind ones were depriving themselves forever of the Kingdom of Eternal Fires, preferring to remain instead in the total gloom of ignorance. Thus began to unfold the stratification of humanity, which was to make the last step beyond the border of the darkness or the Light. That was their Final Choice, for the Period — as designated by the stars — had so determined.

23. Love once again came to life in the world and diffused the Almighty Rays, which were even able to pierce through the most incredibly dense masses of petrified Matter. And, little by little, people began to open their eyes. They had long known that even a stone was capable of loving, protecting, guarding, and bringing

happiness to their owners — owners whom they indeed loved. Yes, the world was brimming over with Love.

Man beheld how a flower which he had mercilessly torn from its stem would incline its beautiful little head towards him, dedicating the last moments of its life to a declaration of Love — Love for him, a man. Yes, a flower is able to love even a slayer that has brutally severed the thread of its marvellous, innocent life. Flowers forgive everything, because they sincerely love man — even men who are most in "love" with the money they receive for the "goods" they sell. The flowers very much hoped that people would open their eyes and understand how it was even painful to love them...

Indeed, humanity was coming nearer to this understanding, for the language of one flower was always understandable to another member of the floral kingdom. After all, it was not so long ago that human beings were flowers themselves, covering the whole planet in a carpet of beautiful bloom. But the Gods did not pluck them...

24. A Time to blossom and a Time to bear fruit. Were not bounteous fruits being borne by those that had been blooming so luxuriantly, in accord with the Periods established for them? Yes, their fruits were fresh and fragrant. But at first they could be seen only by the Creator — the One who had sown the Seeds. His was the Hand that had generously scattered the Divine Seeds on the Earth. But some of them fell among thorns and were choked. Many fell in stony places...

God was waiting for the harvest. He longed to see the Divine Fruit, for like would bear like unto Him, as an apple tree would bear an apple and a pear tree a pear. Thus, in everything, His Law would be obeyed. The Seed germinated and hastened to bear fruit. All the shoots were by now firmly established, showing strong stems. Only their fruit was still in question. And only as the fruit ripened was it possible to judge the results. But for that the Periods had not yet come. In the meantime, the fruit was absorbing everything granted to it by a generous world. And the roots, whether they were sunk into the darkness or into the Light, served to determine the fruit's true value...

STANZA III: THE SOWING OF LOVE

Thus the Gods directed the Motion of the Wheel towards the New Period. And that was the Season of Reaping, designed to effect the final calculation of the ripened Divine Harvest.

ॐ

STANZA IV
THE GIFT OF MIND

25. The Sons of God came. They descended to examine the Field, wherein the Golden Seed was emerging. But the Earth had already been partially poisoned with the foreboding fumes of evil. Poison seeped into soil, threatening to envenom the new shoots. The plants resisted as they strove to develop according to the Programme laid out in the Core of the Seed. The Fiery essence of the Seed was impervious to the darkness. Evil hid himself, lying in wait for an opportune moment to attack the shoots just as they were on the point of breaking through... The Sons of God discerned the lurking danger — henceforth evil would fall under their eagle-eyed control.

26. The Gods awaited the arrival of the Sons who had been sent to the Earth. The Sons were delayed, however, as they attempted to expose all the spheres that had been seized by evil. They were trying to explain certain Truths to the people, but these people did not have sufficient intelligence to properly understand the Sons of God.

27. The Great Sages of Insight cried unto the Gods turning the Wheel to hasten the coming of the Periods, when man would be endowed with a more perfect mind... And man became thoughtful...

STANZA IV: THE GIFT OF MIND

He began to notice that his skin had quite recently changed from that of an animal to something quite different — a human one. But a sinister, lower power, one based more on instincts than reason, held sway inside of him and prevented him from ascending. The Sons of God therefore undertook the enormous Task of transmuting instinct into *intuition*, which would allow man to hear the Voice of the Heart.

28. The work was in full swing on the Earth. Immortal Beings were walking amongst mortals, effecting colossal transformations in human Hearts. And as the condensed clusters of matter steadily softened, losing their impenetrable stoniness, man became capable of feeling with the Heart. There were still many things he could not yet understand, but already he was speaking of what he *felt* in his Heart. And so he took the first step towards the Country of Immortality.

29. The Sons of God noticed that some of the mortals were now robed in seamless Immortal Garments. Their Hearts were blazing, being reflected with all their fervour and purity in the Great Divine Fires. In them, the power of the animal principle had been obliterated forever, and all instincts of the past overcome. These were Earthly Gods, created from ordinary people. Once they were qualified to replace the Higher Toilers of Light, the Sons of God left the Fields of the Earth and returned to the Gods on high.

30. Labour was transforming all living things. Wherever vigilance was abandoned, the darkness appeared at once, bringing her inner laws into play. But she could not approach a toiler, for she knew that Labour was a Prayer to the Light. Taking advantage of the departure of the Sons of God, evil began to invade the Souls of Light — those that had accepted the Heavenly Burden of Fire — with his countless legions of gloom. The darkness endeavoured to confront these Souls of Light with equal, or even stronger, forces of evil. She had already found such people, catching them at the very moment when they had let go of the Sacred Labour which had been entrusted to them. After tricking them into believing that one could enjoy the fruits

of somebody else's labour, the darkness did not allow them to work and instead put a sword into their dangling hands. Evil permitted the forceful appropriation of that which had been given for the good of the whole world, as it had been cultivated for everyone.

31. Menacing whirlwinds of darkness skimmed over the entire planet, spiralling from one end of the globe to the other. These black wheels spun as if by a giant hand, sweeping up all living things in their path. The darkness was determined to raze to the ground all the new shoots that were threatening to cover the Earth with a Field of Gold.

God's Seeds sprouted tender shoots as they broke free from the deep ruts they had been trampled into by the gloom, and promised a rich harvest. Those who had cultivated their Divine Seeds in the Fire were now joined by new souls. They had a great desire to assist their brethren who had risen from the ashes and now shone like lodestars before the eyes of sighted people. Hearts followed the Light-Bearers, prepared to pass through a deep abyss of gloom, carrying with them their inner Divine Light undefiled.

32. The time had come. People began to talk about the Periods. They started to rise above the concept of *Time* and break away from the ground. Man understood that he was the nexus of the decaying temporal and the undecaying *eternal*. He was the possessor of two opposite poles, on one of which was the epicentre of death, and the other one — the centre of Immortality. He was, at one and the same time, the son of ashes and the Son of God. It was indeed a challenge to understand himself, since he had been woven entirely of contradictions, which had taken up a firm position inside him, unwilling to change their own polarity. He was being torn apart: on the one hand, the mortal was luring him with all its might, while on the other, the immortal was attracting and charming him with the marvellous Fires of Spirit. Man kept swinging from one extreme to another. Decaying, earthly treasures held no importance for the Light, but decay could not recognize the Divine Gifts of Eternity.

STANZA IV: THE GIFT OF MIND

A fierce internal struggle was underway: man was in conflict with himself.

33. A gong struck. The Third Round of the battle was over. Balance had won. Man understood that he should not rush about and fret, thereby weakening his precious life forces. His two poles, like two scale-pans, he resolved to keep in balance, not letting evil outweigh his divine heritage. The pan of Light was feathery and weightless. He must no longer add dark deeds to the opposing pan of darkness; at the same time he would sort through its contents for worthiness, so as to burn whatever he didn't need as superfluous rubbish. The work progressed quickly. Man glanced sometimes into one of the pans, and sometimes into the other. Keeping constant watch over new additions to the pan of Light was difficult, for it was so weightless and invisible that it was a challenge to perceive just when the pan of evil started to outweigh it...

A high degree of alertness was required. And the Gods decided to set a New Period for the Round of Earthly Time, so that mankind would be armed with this priceless Gift of Heaven.

STANZA V
THE PERSECUTION OF LOVE

34. The Light of Illumination touched the Earth. The long night that had dominated human consciousness was losing its thickly hued layers. The dark veil of ignorance began to drop from people's eyes as they opened their vision and were imbued with *alertness*.

35. Those who most longed for the Light were touched with Fires by the Sons of Heaven. Their flash of illumination spread among the chosen. Those people absorbed the Fires with eager enthusiasm, adding to the luminous capabilities of their Heart. The world became lighter and brighter. But, still, one had to work hard to kindle the Fires in the Light-Bearers' companions. And the Sons of Heaven called for help from those who had preserved the lucidity of the Flame.

36. Sparks were flaring. And with the New Era came a great inflow of Fire. Many people were already carrying the Divine Flame within their breasts. Nevertheless, they were in the minority, compared with the whole mass of humanity. These Light-Bearers were recognized immediately, for it is impossible to conceal the Light. They spoke of

STANZA V: THE PERSECUTION OF LOVE

God, of Pure Heaven embraced by the Flame of Love, of the Sons of Eternity.

The darkness was irritated by such "flowery" speeches and, wanting to wrap everyone in an even denser veil of ignorance, she infused malice into the minds of her listeners. Consumed with violent rage and blinded by anger, the sightless groped for stones. Stones from stony hearts, interlaced with a hail of curses, rained down on those who were bearing the Light of Love...

Love was beaten, tortured, burnt... But she was ineffaceable, for she was drawing upon Immortal Forces within herself. She *loved*, and that was all that mattered... Sparks were igniting.

37. The Gods saw how desperately the Warriors of Love were fighting. Armed with the Divine Gift, they walked the Earth with a single Mission in mind — to *love*. For them, the most important thing was to preserve Love for humanity intact. They did not expect a loving response in return, as they failed to meet Love in those who had extinguished the spark of Fire within themselves and had grown cold. Love was to ignite their godlessly smoking wick. The Bearers of the Flame touched everyone in sight. Some were ignited at once, promising to preserve and cultivate their tiny Flame, while others averted their eyes; still others took a stone out of their bosoms, which they had harboured there in place of their Heart. Yes, a stone had replaced the Heart! But the Gods knew how to work with such dense Matter, which at some point would turn into a gentle igniferous scarlet flower. On and on they laboured.

38. A drop of water can wear away a stone. A seemingly weak force defeats a stronger one. Water gushed into the world. And the strongest of all was a tiny drop, for the drop knew that it was one with the limitless Ocean of Eternity. It started in to work, polishing dense granite-like masses.

39. It was as though drops of hot tears were falling on the unyielding surface of a stone. The stone was helpless in the face of that steady tap-tap-tapping. It was knocking at the door of its soul, demanding that it open itself to the whole world. The world waited. The stone

was silent. But the drop proved to be stronger, and washed away all soulless barriers with which the darkness had attempted to smother the stone's ever so delicate nature. Now it was free and open to all. And the New World believed in it...

40. The Sons of God finally caught their breath and let out a quiet sigh: the scale-pan of evil was becoming noticeably lighter. They breathed out a new stream of fresh Fires in response to the Call of the Hearts that reached them from the bowels of Earth. Plunged into darkness, the planet resembled the night sky, for she was all a-twinkling with little sparks of stars — these glowed in the Hearts of those who had preserved the Fire safe from the malicious claws of forces that would extinguish it. The Sons of God were reaching out with stellar silver threads towards the Hearts of the Light-Bearers, turning them into immortal carriers of Divine Currents. Such people were able to love and to know what Love is.

41. The outer covering of the planet looked something like lace. Bright glowing threads were being interwoven in a fanciful pattern, faithfully streaming the Divine Current which was bearing the life-giving Power of Love. And the Earth began to breathe in these Fires.

42. The Sun was blazing, filling all the channels of the life-bearing artery of the Light with streams of new Fires. And even the people of the Earth noticed that — from their point of view, at least — the excessive activity of the Sun was burning through everything.

43. The world began to be ruled by completely different currents, which had come to replace the old ones, carrying within themselves the aroma of Divine Spheres. Even the Earth had changed her appearance. She could not resist the renewing power of the Fires. The planet also renewed her continents, submerging to the bottom those that needed the purifying effect of water. In the Flame of yawning craters, she had burnt away anything that could not fit in to the new Life. Now she was being nourished by other currents, desiring to rid herself forever of the mistakes which had stained her mantle in the past.

STANZA V: THE PERSECUTION OF LOVE

With the transformation of her appearance, the Earth sought release from the clutch of the filthy hands of evil that were blackening her spheres. For evil had gone into hiding, and was now immersed in the gloom of non-existence. But therein, too, remained his carriers — carriers that formed the greater part of slumbering humanity. Evil was trying with new strength to bring back his former glory-days and, in this, his main hope, as always, rested on people. For they would have to hate literally everything in order to infuse the whole soil with seeds of hatred, which were alone capable of choking the gentle shoots of Love.

44. Gloom was once more on the attack, using human hands and feet to trample the deeds of the Light. Man seemed to be a vessel for cruelty and insidious malice. He knew no peace, feverishly attempting to reap God's bounty with bloodstained instruments. But the Light had no knowledge of hatred; condemnation was alien to him, along with the many other weapons comprising the arsenal of the darkness. The Light was capable only of loving. And so he loved…

45. Malice was devouring itself, oozing with anger. It was counting on provoking hatred in response to hatred. But the Light-Bearers totally rejected condemnation and spiteful attacks in response, for they perceived no enemy. Nor would they pervert the energy of Love by transforming it into its opposite. They had confidently taken their places on the pole bearing the imprint of Love. For them, the opposite pole, from which only cold hatred was pouring forth, held no attraction at all.

The darkness was losing strength: her army simply melted before her eyes as it drew near to the Warmth of Loving Hearts. Rarely did anyone forsake the Camp of the Light. Deserters were becoming ever harder to find, and it was now almost impossible to win over to the dark side anyone who had recognized the true value of Divine Love.

46. The Flame did not die out. Rather, it shone ever more gently, illumining the world with a steady Light. Balance was established on the planet. The scale-pans were gradually stabilized, manifesting a balance of power…

Everything lay low, held in abeyance: the darkness was afraid of making a single step towards the Light, for she could easily be dissolved in the fervent embrace of the Flame; nor did the Light advance, for he had no right to attack or to impose his warmth or the Light of Love upon the unwilling. Light responds only to the Call, and does so in the twinkling of an eye, filling the crying Heart with generous currents of Love...

The two huge pans of the scales were being held by the Invisible Hand of Humanity, which was free to place into them either evil or good, calling upon the forces of either the darkness or the Light. All the Worlds stood still, awaiting the Final Choice that the people of the Earth, now divided and clustering at two opposite poles, were obliged to make. Humanity was deciding its destiny... The Gods stood still and, just for a moment, stopped the motion of the rotating Wheel of Time.

STANZA VI
THE FINAL BATTLE

47. The hour had struck. Time began to flow in its designated channel. People were searching for those who were nearer and dearer to their Hearts. Many united in groups, forming societies knitted together by a single idea or aspiration. The idea of good or evil was that connecting link around which communities were organized.

Humanity had made the Final Choice — in favour of Good. Evil therefore decided to change this Progress of Evolutionary Movement towards the Light, and to lay decisive battle against the idea of Peace. Thus began a series of global wars.

48. The Warriors of Love died, unable to withstand the attacks on their perishable bodies. But the Immortal Souls departed heavenward and, once again robed in human skins, returned to the Earth with strength derived from the Immortal Fires. They resumed the battle the darkness had imposed on them. Stars were supporting their chosen ones, unceasingly strengthening their Hearts with the currents of Love. Aglow with the thought of Good and Light, the Loving Hearts of the Warriors were being immersed into pitch darkness, where their mission was to sow the Seeds of Love. The gloom of ignorance again and again erected solid walls of misunderstanding between the Bearers of Light and dormant consciousnesses.

Evil knew that he could still find a great number of willing servants among the slumbering souls.

49. The Titans entered the battle. Giants suckled by the darkness were trying to slay these Good Titans, which had been raised by Mother Earth herself. But while in contact with the Earth they seemed invincible, drawing tremendous strength from native soil. The battle raged on.

50. Erelong, the Earth opened wide beneath the feet of these malicious giant sorcerers, swallowing them up in turbulent streams of fiery lava. As a true Mother, she went to join the fray of battle, heroically defending her Sons of Light. And now, as her ground shuddered with indignation, she literally exploded with thousands of volcanoes that began to speak. And many sorcerers of black magic were buried alive beneath the volcanic soil. For long millennia they had become fossilized as stone, transformed into mountains...

51. The Sons of Light were victorious. Yet many of the enemy forces still lay concealed, using their knowledge of black magic. Furious with rage, under the will of the Lord of the Darkness, they were determined to avenge their rout by blowing up the planet. But the Earth had become unsuitable for the machinations of evil, as her soil, absorbing the Light, threw off the pretensions of the darkness. The planet had to pay dearly for her Choice of Light. And the price of atonement allotted to her was death. At this point, however, the Gods intervened.

52. Earth felt a fresh inflow of forces. The Gods were tirelessly spinning the Wheel. And Earth could see how the Sparkling Thread was reaching towards her. The Golden Fleece presented her with a new garment, woven from stellar threads. Yes, the Golden Fleece could array many an earthling in gold-brocaded garments which would protect them from the darkness. And heroes set out in search of it...

53. The planet could not lose people. The Mysterious Origin of Life had not arisen on her only to be crowned with death, grinding

STANZA VI: THE FINAL BATTLE

into dust all the works of Eternity, which had never been made by human hand. No, the Earth had been begotten of the Light, and only He who gave her Life could ask for it back. But He who gives birth does not know death, for everything woven by Him contains the Threads of Immortality in its weave. The planet was well aware that she was *immortal*. Yet all her earthly mysteries were accessible to the warlocks of the darkness, and it was precisely in this situation that the principal danger lurked.

54. Evil was busy casting his magical spells, engendering monsters of a like never before seen. The Earth was as open as the palm of one's hand, for the Light is impossible to hide — it is there for everyone to see. And lo, the darkness beheld the Shining Hearts of those who were full of the Spirit of Heroism. And she could not bear that dazzling Light. What she needed was stony hearts. So she at once sent to the heroes her monstrous progeny — Medusa the Gorgon. Even one glance at that creature could turn a living being into a heartless stone. But one hero triumphed. Medusa herself was beheaded and was no longer capable of harm. Wherever her two older sisters may have concealed themselves was a mystery to be solved by future generations of heroes.

55. The beast had now lost one of her three lives, making her number 66. The next Gorgon sister could be defeated only by the Heart, full of the Fires of Immortality implanted by the Hand of the Creator. And this was His Son.

The Only Begotten Son of God had descended to the Earth to take upon His Loving Heart all the venomous arrows of gloom. His triumphs were due to Love alone. He softened petrified Hearts with the tenderest currents of the Light. Many followed Him, proclaiming the Gospel of Love — which had defeated the beast in man.

56. Love had dissolved the second Gorgon of gloom, leaving the eldest sister alone with a single number — 6. But 6 was the number of the Earth, and also the number of Life. It was immortal, as was the last Gorgon, who was woven of earthly Matter and reared on

the currents of spiteful human miasmas. She could be defeated only by the united *will* of the all Loving Hearts knit together. Her name — the name of the monstrous mistress of darkness — was Basest Matter. And her glare had already touched every earthling, leaving in people's minds the impress of gloom. The Gorgon had simply dissolved in human minds, bequeathing to each one a cell of her ill-fated flesh. Now she was completely confident in her own immortality.

57. Humanity had become obsessed with the idea of gain, the accumulation of material goods. Small and big wars were started with only one aim — to rob one's neighbours... Sorcerers of black magic rejoiced, devouring lavish food received in the form of bloody vapours. They did not need to sully themselves through contact with those paltry people, who were prone to slay each other in hand-to-hand combat and were even prepared to blow up the planet simply to clear everything out of her bowels. People refused to understand that they themselves would perish with all the rest. But greed was simply blinding. And that was playing into the hands of the darkness. The world went mad. The Gorgon reigned supreme in people's minds.

58. The Great Beacons of the World then arrived on the scene. Sometimes they would appear at one end of the Earth, sometimes at the other. These were the Sons of God, descended again to the Earth in order to bring the half-crazed world to its senses. People gradually began to wake up to the perception of Truths. But with the departure of these Great Bearers of Fire, human beings once again attacked each other with weapons, hiding behind the name or banner of the Son of God...

Sorrow filled the Hearts of the Sons of Light, who watched from above as the blood of those whom they had instructed in Love and Forgiveness was shed... Claiming the authority of the Sacred Names and Images, human beings schemed and plotted terrible intrigues. The darkness was deceptive, claiming to act on behalf of Heaven... The bloody harvest was on, as those who blindly trusted in the darkness were plunged into the gloom of ignorance.

STANZA VI: THE FINAL BATTLE

59. Yet another wave of Light, now with even greater force, hit right at the root of the darkness' foundations, exposing the human situation in all its horror. Many had been blinded by the Bright Light and could no longer take notice of the false brilliance of earthly treasures. The material world, with its innumerable perishable trinkets, no longer held any attraction. Losing sight of earthly things, the Eye opened up to the Heavenly Realm — the boundless space of Imperishable Beauty, brimming with countless treasures, each with its own special charm. And all of them belonged to man. Thus perished another cell of the Matter-Gorgon, being transformed into the marvellous Light of Illumination. The beast had finally lost her last number and dissolved into the Fires of the Soul of Born-again Man...

Thus the beast ultimately perished, but only after giving birth to the New Man who, casting off his human skin, would ascend as a shining Spirit and stand beside the Sons of God.

60. The Gods had witnessed everything that was taking place in the world. With their ability to behold multiple images simultaneously, they succeeded in perceiving everything that was occurring in all the layers of the Earth, starting from her bowels right up to the innumerable spheres which stretch into the Infinite Ocean of Eternity.

Humanity was uniting under the Banner of Light. It was resonating with the Fires of the Heart. But among them, the servants of darkness were darting to and fro more furiously than ever, hunting for those who had maintained their spiteful stoniness of heart... But those who had arisen from the ashes were already ascending the radiant Stairs to the Stars.

Above them shone more powerful Spirits, taking on the appearance of a single solar luminary. And their number was increasing constantly... The Gods had never known doubt and believed firmly in Humanity. It was with new confidence that they now began to turn the High Wheel of Eternity.

STANZA VII
THE FIERY BAPTISM

61. Time was passing. Rapidly gaining speed, it pushed urgently forward. With each new turn, Time was leading earthlings on a new Spiral of Ascent. Human Hearts were already capable of peering into the Future. And the Future reached out to them, drawing them ever closer to itself. Anxiously looking back, human beings feared the return of the past. Their Hearts recognized those who were trying to ensnare them in the thoughtlessness of bygone ages.

62. Solar activity was starting to approach the limits of the possible. Glowing white-hot from the new currents, the Sun was releasing from his Fiery-White Core a sheaf of rays, which swiftly disappeared from view, thrusting themselves into the bowels of Earth. The Sun was knocking at the Earth's Heart, calling upon it to let in a sheaf of Fires of the New Sound. The Earth opened up.

63. Now the Earth was being enveloped by a Light hitherto unseen. She was once again renewing herself, permeating all spheres of Life with the stamp of newness. Once again earthly shapes were changing, mainly in the realm of Colour... Nature was attempting to heal the wounds that had been inflicted on her by humanity, and to cover her gaping black holes with luxuriant blossoms. All living

things refused to clothe themselves in old dark, gloomy colours. As before, the darkness was threatening to grind everything into dust and to cover the fragments of the planet with a layer of thick black-grey ash.

64. People were bearing the Cross of Renewal. They took on the appearance of a chain of creatures, stretched out along all the roads of the Earth. Some had already walked the whole path, bearing on their shoulders the disproportionately heavy Cross of Repentance for human sins. Others were trying to tear that excessive weight off the toilers' shoulders and replace it with their own load. Among them were even those who were not searching for anybody in particular — they simply cast away their own burden, and this was immediately picked up by the darkness. Such seekers of an easy life quickly found themselves bound with coarse ropes to the darkness' own spheres. Hence, anyone who had dropped the load of Light entrusted to them now belonged to the kingdom of darkness. They themselves had made the Choice, having broken off the Path of Ascent, and were now sliding down along the line of descent.

65. Those who had managed to reach the Spheres of Fire with their heavy burden were now able to drop it into the life-giving Flame, which burnt away everything that had been superimposed by the darkness. And the bright Fiery Cross was presented to whoever was prepared to renew their commitment to the Quest. They were bearing the Karma of Love... Such people had already attracted the special attention of the watchful eye of the Gods, and were already considered to be Messengers of Heaven, Ambassadors of the World of Light.

66. The Heavenly Host of Love had intermingled among earthlings. The two had merged together and could no longer be distinguished from each other by outward signs. The main difference was internal: they were Bearers of Love, with the aim of giving her away. The world no longer greeted them with its erstwhile hostility. The smoky bonfires of mock trials had died out long ago. Deprived of their lavish nourishment, the lofty tongues of flame had disappeared.

But not so easy to tame were the human tongues: they burnt more painfully than the sting of any incandescent heat... But the Beacons were moving toward them with the tremendous Burden of Heavenly Love.

67. Little by little, the Light illumined what had once been the domain of the darkness, whose puzzlingly restless and chaotic thoughts were still letting themselves be felt as blustery drafts. One by one they attacked the tiny tongues of Fire, releasing their venomous sting of doubt and zealous distrust of his healing life-creating force. Still, the wee fire continued to glimmer gently, despite the dense drops of poison falling into it. The Light lived.

68. The struggle had moved from an external to an internal plane, taking on forms more and more subtle and concealed. Many servants of the darkness went about their business surreptitiously, masked by the guise of "light." It was still a challenge to distinguish the false reflection from the true. Intellectual reasoning was useless. It was the Heart that possessed the highest gift of discernment, and only it could help.

69. People began to listen ever more keenly to the Heart, which was now drawing more attention than the brain. Many began to listen eagerly and attentively to the words of the Beacons of the Fiery World, proclaiming that the future belonged to the Heart, for it was pure. Yes, the Heart was incapable of lying or pretence; it had no feelings of hatred, revenge, greed, and all the other ills harboured by the human mind. It knew only Love, and that pulsating organ could love like none other... While the mind had been defiled with dark thoughts, the Heart was utterly impervious to evil. To the Heart belonged the Future, while the mind was bogged down in the past. People hearkened to its Call...

70. The Gods sensed the readiness of human Hearts to receive New Currents. And then they set to work, rotating the Wheel in the New Rhythm of the outpouring currents of Sacred Love.

STANZA VIII
THE LOVE OF THE HEART

71. The Light began to glimmer with New Fires, blazing in people's Hearts. Fires were carrying the Joy of Illumination with them, endowing human souls with Wisdom's Insight. This new rhythm was in perfect tune with the Heart, for it brought enlightenment to the world.

72. The stream of Time was rapidly pouring forth, introducing innovations everywhere... And the Heart became ever more open and refined. It was responding with pain to the pain of the world. It was throbbing and trembling from grief and despair in sympathy with all sufferers. Seized with the sensitivity of universal anguish, it sometimes even stopped, missing a beat. The Heart was behaving in very mysterious ways, for it was no longer subject to human control. And if one did not take good care of this sensitive sounding board, it would fall silent forever, handing one over to the cold hands of death.

Thus, at the cost of its Life, it had come to be treated as a mere object of scientific study. The cold, petrified, immortal organ began to be manipulated by mortal hands... Not understanding their own Heart, people attempted to comprehend somebody else's.

But one would first have to learn the language of one's own Heart, which alone made it possible to understand another's. Only the Heart was capable of rendering assistance in the study of the Heart. The mind had to tame its wagging tongue and yield the floor to the Silent Currents of the Heart.

73. A sheet of cotton batting swaddled the Heart, which was still radiating warmth. Other Hearts, both large and small, were reposing in glass jars, resting on torn threads — the very same threads through which life had earlier been streaming — in darkly transparent liquid. Here was where the Heart was being studied... And the Hearts of the living flinched in pain. What could these already sealed lips speak of — except, perhaps, about death, which had in the meantime turned them to stone? Only the living, tender Heart was in a position to share anything significant about itself. And it was *speaking*... The living ought therefore to listen to the living — for only in this way are mysteries comprehended.

74. The obstacles erected by the hand of the darkness gradually loosed their hold. Man had wended a long and tiresome way towards himself. Indeed, the trek to draw closer to his own Heart had lasted millennia. And he was not deprived of his reward. The Heart had been waiting a long time for this moment, throbbing on the bloodstained table of oblation where it had been tossed by man himself. By his own gentle hand he should have lifted up that treasure and set up an altar to it, nourishing the Heavenly Love for his own Heart which welled up from deep within his soul...

No, he could no longer expose to the ravenous hunger of the darkness that most gentle and tender organ — which had been entrusted to him by the Lord of Eternity Himself. Had not His Hand stopped the Motion of Time, thereby cutting off the currents which streamed through the thread of Life and preventing an unworthy vessel from receiving this Sacred Gift? Yes, the Heart indeed belonged to Heaven. Understanding only the language of Heaven, every instant it appealed to its owner to speak the same language — the language of Love.

STANZA VIII: THE LOVE OF THE HEART

75. Those who were closest to the Heart were its subjects. Those who had destroyed the invisible obstacle on the way to their own Heart became possessors of the Immortal Elixir of Life. The Heart was fully obedient to the Man that had overcome all the obstacles to reach it. It gave itself over entirely to the power of those with whom it could converse in the same language. The Heart was ready to beat eternally, warming with currents of Love the Divine Soul, which was following its own lonely path in the world. It was embracing both its owner and those around him with Immortal Currents of Love. And Man cherished this treasure entrusted to him as the apple of his eye, understanding that while it was radiating Love, he, too, would live, and fulfil the Divine Mission of Love.

76. The Heart fell silent at the very moment when it sensed man rejecting Love. It could not emanate hatred, as it was attuned to the universal rhythm of Eternity, which was pulsating with the currents of Love. The living Heart was made to love, and if it did not love, that meant it was dead; and its trembling would fade away, after sounding its last mechanical throbs... But this was no longer the action of the Heart, which could breathe only the vital, palpitating Fires of Love. It was simply a thick clot of Matter, petrified with anger, which it had attempted to put in the place of the human Heart. The hand of the darkness desired to wind up the invisible mainsprings of such devices to serve her gloomy purposes. They were like bombs lurking in the breast, which would set off explosions, filling all human beings with malicious arrogance and acrid bile. Though dying away, the darkness had not lost her cunning and inventiveness. Many gave their Hearts into her hands, for they did not know Love. There still was not enough Love in the world, and the forces of evil took advantage of that.

77. Many had tasted the Light and knew the power of the life-giving Fires. The taste of victory was intoxicating, giving Life a new face and making it more attractive than before. But the first step taken now called for a second, higher step. The darkness could still easily sweep away those who had stepped a single rung higher, but those

who were already standing on the higher rungs of the Ladder of Light were no longer within her range. Those robed in someone else's fiery glow, claiming it for their own, were easily swept away by the darkness. Anyone standing on their own self-raised pedestals could not help but totter. Any human "soap bubble" resting on them and twinkling with reflected fires, became an easy prey for the darkness. For this was a Time when the last of the rubbish was being cleared away, and the remnants of rags — from the bursting of over-bloated beings — wiped off the face of the Earth...

The Earth was now wholly exposed to the purifying currents, which were wafting through from those Spheres where the Grand Gods were rotating the Heavenly Wheel, assigning to Humanity a New Period for purification in the Fires of Love.

ꣳ

STANZA IX
THE ERA OF WISDOM AND BEAUTY

78. Once more the poets began to speak. Glorifying the Kingdom of Light, theirs was the song of immeasurable Love reigning in the Heavens. Their hymns to the Fire were sung in temples, pouring forth directly from Hearts enraptured by the ecstasy of Love…

Now more than ever, the Gods knew no rest. More and more, the prayers of the human souls were reaching out to them, pleading for a grant of Great Love. The world was thirsting and patiently waiting for the Decision of the Heavens. Everyone needed Love, and everyone understood that any Life without Love would be lived in vain. The Gods were not stingy with their Fires.

79. The Fire of the Spheres began to approach ever closer to the Earth, advancing as a solid wall. The servants of the darkness began to grow anxious. The Call of Humanity had given the Gods the Legitimate Right to increase the Rotation of the Wheel, which was cutting through the Holy Fire. While the Fire was not dangerous for the people who were yearning for Love, he was feared by the darkness more than anything else in the world. She knew that Sparks

could be extinguished only by human hands. And so she furiously set off to find such human hands.

80. To the darkness, the world had become one big problem, for it was slipping out of her grasp. The Light was calm. He was coming to power. His power was Self-Sacrifice... The Light had put himself on the greatest table of oblation — the Altar of the Spirit of all Humanity. The Light was coming in response to the Call — a cry from the human soul. He knew that the Man who was filled with him would shine eternally and would never put out his own Fires to appease the darkness. The Light was confident in himself.

81. People had become stratified, revealing their inner essence in sharp detail. Many were no longer disguising themselves with the mask of a "light-bearer." They simply grinned at the world, wholly captivated by the forces of evil. As zealous servants of the darkness, they strove with their last breath to destroy the foundations of the incipient New World of Fires. They lent her their dirty hands, prepared to blast and scatter all living things to dust. Those who carried out these actions were eager to fanatically follow their idols. The darkness skilfully deployed rampant aggression to foment a host of conflicts. She needed bloody emanations to multiply her forces. And her servants once again began eagerly to supply it. All over the place there arose instances of bloody strife, and for one fleeting moment evil actually believed he could triumph.

82. Ideas of Good now soared loftily throughout the world. Goodness was attracting not only human Hearts but also human minds as never before. The world had grown tired of war. It was now harder and harder to find anyone willing to take up arms against another people. Everyone was longing for peace and friendship. The idea of war had lost all appeal. Evil, in the meantime was naturally infuriated by these lofty ideas of peace, and found it more and more difficult to count on new clashes popping up. The world was becoming too kind for that...

STANZA IX: THE ERA OF WISDOM AND BEAUTY

83. The New Time was marked by fresh inspiration in the sphere of the arts. Ugliness no longer attracted glances. Human Hearts turned to those creations in which the warm tones of goodness and cordiality shone through. Beauty was so desired that in human pursuit of it, the tastelessness of garish artificial forms and colours was somehow ignored. The world quickly realized its mistake. It did not wish to sing out of tune.

A New Era of Beauty was dawning, in which only masterpieces created by the pure currents of soul would be recognized. New Sparks of Light brought with them new inspiration. And the world was now full of them.

84. The anxiety prevailing in the camp of the darkness had reached its limit. Spiteful thoughts of hatred, greed, envy, fear, and such like were swiftly retreating, finding no shelter in human minds. People started acquiring Wisdom, which was granted them by generous Love. She alone spoke the language of the Heart and thus comprehended the principles of Wisdom. Now that gift was predestined for Humanity.

The Light began to kindle with a bright fire, swallowing up all the delusions of the erring human mind. Man began to discern the true colouring of his own thoughts. And now he truly began to earn the right to be called *Homo sapiens*, for he finally realized that he had prematurely considered himself wise, possessing in fact no such gift. The mind began to perceive Wisdom, which is always based on Love alone.

85. Light ignited in the world. Everything appeared in its true colour. The world had come clean, baring the sores that needed healing. They could not be ignored, as they had the capacity to infect everyone with the spores of decay. The next step which Humanity was poised to make, as it climbed to the next rung on the Ladder of Light, would draw a sharp line of demarcation between the past and the Future. That was a step in the direction of the Light. Here there was no place for the past; there existed only the Future — pure

and bright, with no room for even a single reminder of the old sores. The world was making rapid strides in its Evolution.

86. But the old past would not give up, and attempted to compete with the new Future by disputing the rights of the Light. The scales, which had been evenly balanced before, gave a little shudder, for Humanity had somehow slowed its step and fallen behind. One foot remained in the past, while the other just barely touched the rung above, which led to the Future. This foot needed to be planted more securely in the Future and its companion, which was still in the past, needed to be pulled up. With both feet set firmly on the solid ground of Evolution, Man would have the power to stop forever the swaying pans of the scales and establish the final balance. Fortunately, he already realized that in his struggle to escape the tenacious traps of the past, one foot was still stuck there... The Light had no anxiety about Man. He believed in him.

87. Left alone by himself, Man was gaining a knowledge of the world and realizing that it was entirely something within himself. As a droplet of water is one with the ocean — its very reflection — so too the little particle called *Man* was a reflection of all Humanity. And he knew that in order to refine and purify his fellow droplets, he would first have to refine and purify himself. The purity of water is determined by the transparency of its droplets collectively. Even a handful of dirty, turbid, and stenchful drops can defile a whole fountain, making it unsuitable to drink from, except, perhaps, for the darkness, who was wont to quench her thirst on putrid waste.

Man — a drop at one with the whole ocean of Humanity — would have to first purify himself. And help in this rescue mission came through the gift of the Light and the purifying Flame of Love, wherein everything that needed purification was to be immersed. Man was thus armed with the Light of Love.

88. A new Rotation of the Wheel had replaced the old currents with new ones. Love blossomed out into the world, unfolding yet another invisible petal of the Flame. Love had endless forms and countless

STANZA IX: THE ERA OF WISDOM AND BEAUTY

currents. Her abilities were limitless, her powers measureless, her ways unsearchable.

The world stood still in anticipation of the Secret, hitherto unseen: the unfolding Mystery of Fire. The Gods were bringing into the world an Extravaganza of Light.

STANZA X
THE DIVINE HUMANITY

89. The Day of the Light had come. The forces of Good had triumphed over the forces of evil. An overwhelming majority of earthlings were on the side of the Light. The souls had opened up to the Exalted Fires. Many turned to Heaven for help, for only in Heaven was salvation to be sought. Thoughts of Light, streaking quick as lightning from Heaven in response to the Call of the Heart, had succeeded in piercing the dark crust around the planet. The darkness had attempted to block that Light, but her shield was already riddled with holes. The Light was triumphantly breaking through everywhere.

90. The Fire was actually capable of destroying the whole world. But he was the Creator. And whatever had been grasped by the hot tongues of the Flame by no means disappeared without a trace; it was simply transformed from one form to another, more evolutionary one. The Fire had his own Plan of Transfiguration, and he followed it to the letter. He burnt all bridges to the past, so that people could not slide backwards and return to the state from which they had barely managed to escape — at the cost of irretrievable sacrifices and suffering. The Fire acted only for people's Good, and they understood that.

STANZA X: THE DIVINE HUMANITY

91. The Fire-Creator was in charge of all construction activity. His wisdom permeated all spheres of Life, stirring up dissension between the New and the old, the Future and the past. It was necessary to separate the wheat from the chaff, the priceless from the worthless. People sometimes grasped at the decrepit or the obsolete, trying to conceal it from the scorching tongues of the All-Devouring Flame. But what they tried to conceal only turned against them, poisoning them with the fetid stench of decay. Realizing their mistake, they themselves began to bring to the Fire whatever they found to be unnecessary on their Bright Path to the Future. And the Fire leapt up joyfully, consuming the dust and, in return, breathing out the gentle warmth of gratitude, embracing those who had given up everything.

The warmth and tenderness of Love were like swaddling clothes to the born-anew Man who had gone through the purifying Fire. Yes, this was the New Man, born in the Flame of joy-filled Victories.

92. By now the heat had somewhat abated, or, perhaps, people had simply got used to the Fire. Indeed, he was simply no longer noticed — any more than the air we need for breathing. Inhale... and exhale... The Heart inhaled the Fire and exhaled the same. It could not live without him. Once a human being is deprived of air, he dies immediately; once the Heart is deprived of the Fire, it immediately falls silent forever.

As a rule, the man of the past would not take account of the value of things until he lost them. The New Man, on the other hand, was already aware of the actual value of such invisible treasures. In endowing Man with the gift of insight, Heaven shined its Light on the true value of things. It trusted people with everything that was precious and they, in turn, were responsible for protecting these treasures from the darkness' clutching claws. Was it not she who had been reigning for so long, sitting on her spoils, and endeavouring to steal even more in a bid to impoverish the whole world? Having deprived the world of Faith, Hope, and Love, the darkness instead imposed her way of violent negation, falsehood, doubt, hatred, greed, and many other evils on the whole of humanity, leading it to her fathomless abyss. It was only on the edge of this chasm that people realized the enormity of their loss. But Heaven's generosity knew no bounds: it preserved everything safe and sound, and gave it back to the people in turn. Oaths and promises were no longer made, as people in the past had failed to keep them. But Heaven knew that the New Man would preserve the treasures that had now been entrusted to him.

93. The Sun was rising from behind the horizon, lighting up every new day with the Light of Illumination. The gifts of Heaven were inexhaustible. The Sun was joyfully reflecting the ever New Currents aimed straight at his Fiery-White Core from the fathomless depths of Eternity, directed by the Gods as they rotated the Wheel of Life.

94. Many had noticed a certain regularity in the activity of the Luminary. This small Star, which absorbed the Light of other Luminaries, was the deepest mystery of all. It was observed every day, but could not be comprehended. The Sun remained a puzzlement. Humanity meditated on its role in the life of the planet and of people in general. The Sun had opened wide all his closets of mysteries. But to glimpse their contents, one needed a Flaming Heart that would not fear to step into the scorching heat of the red-hot Fire, and there to discover Truth...

The New Round had brought with it new people. They were not afraid of the Flame, for they had been woven from it. Their Hearts were breathing in the Fire...

95. People were saying that there was Life on the Sun. Their spiritual eye was regaining its sight and beheld, through a layer of Fire, a multitude of Flaming Exalted Beings. They could discern that Life had extended its bounds, far beyond the limits of a single planet... Their consciousness was expanding to hold the new mysteries of Creation being revealed. Man, who could see for himself, now had access to everything that before was invisible to his blind eyes. The world was infinite and full of Life. Everything was conscious and breathing — inhaling and exhaling — whether it was a flower, a Man, a star, or the boundless Ocean of Eternity. Everything was

breathing, infused with Life. Man was not alone; he had within himself living Worlds…

96. Only the New Humanity still harboured within itself remnants of the past, which were on the verge of outliving their time. The Universal Law had justly placed them among those who were already considered as belonging to the Humanity of the Future. For those with Hearts open for all to see, it was a tremendous challenge to walk alongside people of the past whose heart was still blind. The stench of thoughts rotting in the foul miasmas of such darkened minds was making their joint path unbearable for the New Humanity. But those committed to the Mission of Divine Love did not have the right to deviate from their designated path or seek an easier way. Instead, they were obliged to pass without fail through whatever length of path that would allow their blind fellow-travellers to recover their sight from the Bright Light. And the Heart, now softened in the rays of the tenderest Love, would then have to make its Choice: to accept the Light of Love or shut itself up in the gloom of malicious negation.

Endeavouring to purify its own ranks, and hurrying on the stragglers who were still clinging with a long black tail to the thorns of the past, Humanity was taking rapid strides into the Future. But that tail was impeding progress, to the point that impatient minds suggested that it be simply cut off. Wisdom, however, indicated that it was already on the point of atrophying and falling off on its own. There were hardly any moments left before Man would have almost nothing in common with an animal. Humanity was transforming itself into its New Form, and it was beautiful.

97. Vestiges and throwbacks from the past were disappearing. Inhale… and exhale… The Hearts kept on breathing in and breathing out an ever-increasing amount of Fire, transforming the inner and outer nature of both Man and his environment. Without even noticing it, Man was changing for the better — more or less, depending upon the intensity of the inhaled Fires and their degree of suitability for the given organism. Not everyone could withstand the life-giving force of the Flame. An imperfect vessel would be

incapable of bearing the intensity and would be burnt to a small and pitch-black piece of coal. Those who resisted the new properties of the Fire's surging currents turned to stone, unfit for further Evolution.

There was a Time to cast away stones, and then — to gather them together... Now was a Time to store up stones for other Times, when the Gods would again begin a completely new Rotation of the Wheel — under entirely different rays of an entirely different Sun... With the help of its currents, they would again turn stones into flowers and, later, into those who would succeed in becoming Gods themselves. Now the Time was approaching when it would be necessary to raise new stars and subsequently scatter them across the endless Firmament of Eternity.

98. A soaring of stars. This was the hour especially honoured by the Gods rotating the Wheel... The stars were gathering in the crops. And around them were lining up whole constellations of Igniferous Hearts that had soared to great heights. These were Fiery-White Cores, which had flown out of a simple human Heart, full of Love. They were the nuclei of future giant stars that would illuminate Eternity... This was a magical spectacle to charm the keen Eye of the Gods...

99. The Joy of the spheres! It was limitless. Humanity succeeded in spreading Joy to everybody. It was able to purify itself and the spheres surrounding it from the rubbish it had once tossed out. With a sober self-examination from all sides, it eventually regained its sight, and could now evaluate properly both the Light itself and the darkness around the Light. It gracefully accepted the one and rejected the other. Humanity had made its Final Choice, the result of which was the Light of the Newborn Stars... And, all the while, the spheres had been filling themselves with a silver radiance, feeling the fresh inflow of the tenderest Divine currents of Human Stellar Love...

The world was melting in the Fires, dissolving in the fervent embraces of Warm and Loving Hearts. Stones were melting...

STANZA X: THE DIVINE HUMANITY

100. The Earth, enveloped in the Flame of Love, was losing her hardness, becoming pliable and amenable to the gentle and caressing rays of the Luminary. The Earth's petrified composition was gradually changing to a softer and more supple form of Matter. She gave herself entirely into the fervid Hands of the Fire, knowing that he was full of Love for her. At the same time she was chastising herself for previously having given herself so thoughtlessly into the hands of the darkness... The Fire, however, swiftly consumed even this thought, as he could not let into the Future any vestiges of the dark past. Ahead lay the Light, and everything should be surrounded only by the Light of Love... The Earth was melting into the irresistible happiness and Joy of Love that now filled her. The Fire surrounded her with thick fortress-like walls, protecting her from the lustful paws of the darkness. And she gave herself completely to his power. To dissolve in him and flow together, flaring up as a single tongue of Flame — this was her only wish. And the Fire met her wishes — after all, the beloved one's wish is the Law for those who *love*...

The Gods made an abrupt Rotation of the Wheel, letting loose a bursting wall of Fire aimed straight at the Earth. That was a New Round of Time, which people termed *Armageddon*... The Earth had entered into a Mystic Marriage with the Fire, having been betrothed to him ever since those ancient Times when the Gods had just touched the Wheel of Life in order to make the First Rotation... The Earth was glowing in the Fire of Love.

STANZA XI
THE FIRE OF LOVE

101. A throng of angels was whirling 'round, blessing the souls that were soaring towards the Light. The celebration, it seemed, would last forever. Nobody had a desire for war, nobody was anxious to sow the seeds of death, nobody wanted to return to the past. The world was advancing into the Future, where Immortality awaited it. The focus of the Fires clearly pointed to a *goal* that served as the starting-point for those proceeding throughout Eternity along the innumerable pathways of Creation.

102. Man awoke, beholding his new look, which shone with the purple radiance of the Fires. The glare of the battle of Space reflected on him, vividly testifying that he himself had been forcibly drawn into the struggle. The strife of the new Fires with the moribund chaotic whirlwinds and currents of evil were flaring up directly beside Man. Peering into his eyes, the bright tongues of Flame queried: *Will you continue along the path of the darkness or will you join the ranks of the Warriors of the Light?* No one could stand apart, since everything was enveloped by Flame.

103. Many did not see the Fire, for he was invisible. Many did not even feel the intensity of his scorching, for he was Holy. Many

simply did not believe in his existence, unwilling to open their eyes to the true state of things. But Life herself put everybody in place, drawing a strict line between the Light and the darkness. People, without knowing it, already bore the Seal of Death or Immortality on their forehead. They no longer belonged to themselves, as they were now subject to the governing Laws of the Universe. Rubbish was being swept away into the Eighth Sphere allotted to it, so that the feet of Pilgrims on the Path to Evolution would no more be wounded by thorns. Everyone had a specific destiny awaiting them, and all were willingly or unwillingly advancing towards it.

104. The joy of flight awaited those who, arrayed in a fiery suit of armour, took the Sword of All-Triumphant Love in their hands and sided with the Light. The Legion of Love was advancing, and no one was capable of withstanding it, for nothing in the world could equal the mighty, transformative Power of Love.

Love — she was Shield and Armour, Sword and the Rose of the World. Love — she was the Only Law, entitled to subordinate all existing norms and rules to herself. Love — she is always right, because she comes from the Heart that blazes with the Fire of Divine Wisdom. Love waits... She waits for everyone, patiently loyal to all who come to her. She prepares everyone a generous gift, and one who comes to her receives one's own little touch of warmth, a treasure that cannot be gauged by any measure. Love cannot be betrayed; she does not brook treachery, nor is she ever fickle towards those whom she loves. She is fiercely obedient to her own unwritten Law — to *love*; and her Love is eternal.

105. The immortal currents have spread themselves over the Earth, as though covering her with two winged hands, and holding every cell of her earthly body in a warm embrace. Everything is immersed in Love. There is not even the slightest chink the darkness can use to squeeze in her wicked and icy coldness. The roots of evil have been cut off and can no longer grow in the soil now enveloped by the Flame of Love.

Like a mighty hurricane, the giant clot of darkness still advances, attempting to strike its roots deep into human minds. The tree of evil must feed on the effluents of odious thoughts, but their numbers are growing less and less. The tree is withering for lack of nourishment. Therefore, every man from whom can be extracted at least one drop of venom is important, for this is precisely the food craved by the tree of evil. And the slightest drop can poison all that surrounds it. It would, then, unfurl every leaf from which the poisonous current could seep into the world. That tree was indeed grown by dark sorcerers, who fashioned its crown from twisted rattlesnakes; and its leaves were their forked tongues, dripping venom. The tree of evil was to absorb all the good and change it into evil, poisoning the world with its venomous effluent of anger and hatred...

Love had deprived the tree of its roots. She had charred the long poisonous tongues of the darkness and tamed the Ruler of the whole Empire of Evil. He was taken into custody. Deprived of their lord and master, the servants of gloom pressed on alone, attempting to get through to the soil that had nurtured them. But the charred roots were even more sharply scorched by the sizzling soil. Evil understood that his last resort could be only a man — a human being.

106. Sultry midday. The Sun released a new sheaf of rays, which spilled instantly into the regions of Space surrounding the Earth. The Warriors of Love inhaled these currents deeply, thus magnifying their Light-bearing Force. They were helping people save themselves — under the Shield of Love — from the beast that had gone mad with fury, and who, as a tangled ball of venomous snakes, was rushing through space in search of bloodstained victims. Only the Seal of Love on one's forehead could prevent the beast from thrusting its lethal stinger into a Man.

Man had to *love* to save himself. He was loved by the whole world, and was therefore obliged to give back to the world in kind. With new foresight, Man now realized that the darkness would cast him out, after sucking out all blood and bile, for she herself was doomed. He could not give her a chance to take root in himself, and was thus endeavouring to maintain his thoughts in the Light. The

STANZA XI: THE FIRE OF LOVE

smallest vile or unkind thought would at once attract the darkness, ravenous for the slightest crumb. Accustomed to devouring lavish food, she was starving. Her insatiable belly had grown immeasurably bloated by the effluents of humanity's worthless spiteful thoughts. Now humanity was refusing to feed the monster which it had reared by its own hands. The mind was aglow with thoughts of the Light, and the food it offered could not be digested by the darkness. She singed her gaping jaws, losing her appetite... Finally, Humanity brewed the precise mixture it needed — henceforth, it was nourished by the Light.

107. Time in all its glory wisely placed Fires at intervals around the Earth, allowing none of the Lighthouses lit by the Gods to be extinguished. Each one maintained a steady flame, and all the spiteful attempts to blow it out, made it flare up even more strongly. In all her efforts to extinguish it, the darkness was only rekindling the Flame, thereby serving the cause of the Light. The realization that darkness had actually been serving Light drove the Lord of the Gloom into a fitful rage. He was alone. His servants went mad. They kept chasing the Beacons, trying to lure them over to their side, little knowing that, obsessed by their pursuit, they — the servants of gloom — themselves ended up pursuing the pathway of Light.

Bewitching with his array of dazzling colours, the Fire welcomed everyone who had set themselves upon the Light-bearing Path. Scintillating rays of Divine Love were now piercing through, banishing the stifling, musty spirit of anger. It was easy and pleasant to rest in the rays of merciful, all-forgiving Love. The darkness was melting as she lost her cold alienation. Rejected by everybody and desperate for warmth, the darkness was allured and attracted by the Light. Standing at the edge of the fatal abyss, she was offered the Light of Salvation. And she was avidly absorbing it, dissolving her blackness in the radiant colours of the warm Solar Day.

108. Enthroned in the Fiery-White Core of the blazing Sun, Love reigned supreme. Meanwhile, the Earth was preparing a throne for her in her Heart. She was endeavouring with all her might to fill her

own Heart with the Fire and to love as powerfully and purely as did the Fire. Love herself had been waiting for that moment, directing all her tenderest currents into the flaming womb of Earth.

109. Love is everywhere; Love is in everything. When she comes to one place, she does not leave another. She is capable of being at one and the same time in every drop of the boundless Ocean of Eternity and in every earthly speck of dust. She never abandons anybody, unless she is chased out by a pitiless hand. And whenever she — though exiled, insulted, and abased — is called upon once again, she will return and gladly shine in her rightful place, not blaming anyone for anything. All she knows is that she was called! Even if obliged to take a loving step backwards yesterday, Love will take two steps forward tomorrow, and man will enter into the Kingdom of Light, nevermore again to lose it in his Heart.

110. The Fire of Love. The Gods knew what that was. They were full of that Love which was still incomprehensible to earthly beings. And the Gods aspired to share her, generously pouring the Flame of the Crowned Spirit into living Hearts. But Humanity had just begun to study the Alphabet of Fires for the first time, hardly touching upon those shining above. Just a handful of individuals who had absorbed the needed Knowledge, managed to break free of earthly bonds and move forward on the path to Love. So the Gods turned their attention to them — to all who thirsted to fathom the new currents of the Universe.

The Gods strove to produce their own image and likeness and, with that purpose in view, they began stretching out new networks, along which a marvellous, scintillating Love-Current began to flow straight from the Hearts of those who were rotating the Wheel of Love.

STANZA XII
THE BIRTH OF GODS

111. A new whirlwind burst into the Hearts of those who were walking in the vanguard of Humanity, at its front lines. They accepted the current. They began to feel themselves responsible not only for the world as a whole, but for every human being in particular. They turned their attention to the people, first of all to those who were lagging behind. The darkness was still making her influence felt in the back rows, and ignorance reigned among people who still bore the fearfully weighty load of earthly deeds. These specimens of the New Man came to share the burdens of affliction and to save victims from the clutching hands of the darkness. The First became the Last, having made a commitment not to retreat until the last became the First.

112. As it grew ever harder to obtain new provisions of malice — either as food or as thought — the darkness aimed her most aggressive blows at the Beacons, who were shielding the stragglers with their own bodies. They had successfully blocked the channel by which evil could still gulp down several dainty morsels, thickly saturated with blood. The darkness attacked the Light, trying to break through to the victims, but the Beacons were adamant and refused to yield to the greedy pretensions of evil. The world was under the protection of the Light, vigilantly defending its own children and sheltering them with the impenetrable shield of Love.

113. Eternal hymns to the Gods could be heard resounding from the Hearts that were advancing towards the Light. The world around them was gradually revealing itself with new illumination, dissolving the thick grey shroud that had previously cloaked them in gloom. It was as if the Heart were expanding the boundaries of its domains, increasing its capacity to bear the Light. Some people were finally purified through and through; these now resembled fiery spheres, not unlike the Sun. Their Fiery-White Cores radiated never-ending currents of Love into the world, spreading them day and night into every nook and cranny, literally transfiguring the entire world. Those who had successfully transfigured themselves now served the planet as a whole, augmenting her aura of pure, radiant Light. The darkness kept growing smaller and smaller. Only a mass of inventiveness and insidiousness could save her now as she vainly tried to find a secret hiding place where she could escape the burning rays of Hearts afire with Love.

114. The Word of Heaven carried the Law within itself. For the very first time it was actually honoured; for the first time, it was recognized and fulfilled. The Law of Love applied to everyone. It presided over all other laws and constituted their Fiery-White Core. It nourished all the others with its currents, and it alone was able to bring all the norms and rules of Life into harmony with each other. This Law of laws ruled the world, and there was none more just anywhere in the whole Universe.

115. The Solar disc began to lose the density of the tightly knit strands of Fire. He was undergoing a process of renewal. Bearing the new inflow of waves of Divine Love, the Gods transformed the visible, denser forms into invisible, more delicate ones. The Sun, it seemed, was taking on the quality of transparency. Embracing a state of absolute calm and weightlessness, he observed how the Earth was changing shape. She was also becoming more rarefied, while those who only a short while ago had been creeping and

STANZA XII: THE BIRTH OF GODS

crawling on her, without the strength to lift themselves or even stretch their limbs, were now moving freely across her surface, their feet barely touching the ground. The dense, petrified bodies had come through the Period designated by Evolution, growing ever lighter in weight. They were gliding like Gods who had all at once found themselves on the Earth for the first time. After all, the Sons of God were Gods themselves, just as the Son of Man was also a Man...

A Mystery was unfolding throughout the Universe. Only the Gods knew what their Transfiguring Power of Love would do for the world. And that was perfect, for people wholly trusted their Hearts to their Saviours, and filled these Hearts with unspeakable Love for them.

116. The Word of Silence was the chief means of communication. As people's sensitivities became more refined, coarse speech gradually wore out its appeal, and finally lost significance altogether. People began to speak the language of the Heart — the language of Love. It did not need lengthy explanations, since it was simple and immediately understandable. People had nothing to explain or to prove; everything in the world was pure and crystal clear. In this special state, people no longer had any overwhelming desire to speak, and their lips stayed closed for ages, as they were no longer needed. All the motives and aspirations of the soul could be expressed through the eyes. And the Heart-Sun affirmed the Truths of the Spirit, enveloping all with the caressing current of Divinely Pure Love. Love did not know words and never needed them, for she could speak only with the Voice of the Great Silence. And people welcomed that speech with understanding.

117. The Gift of the Gods — the Warmth of Love. The Gift of the Heart — a tribute to Divine Love. The world was aglow. In the Fire there were born Gods. They descended to the Earth to receive the Fiery Baptism of the Spirit. The Warmth of Love embraced the planet, giving her a marked resemblance to the Fiery-White Core of the Sun. Like a blazing star she shone in the vault of heaven, now

as a celestial luminary, generously endowing emerging Life with the Light of Love...

There, far away, dust condensed in the darkness, whirlwinds mingled with currents, and a small planet took shape, capable of supporting Life... And amid the multidiversity of shapes and forms, a single Note of Love would hold sovereign sway. The Earth would endeavour to put into it all the gentle Light of Soul, so that this newborn speck would never know misfortune or affliction, would never experience the tenacious paws of the suffocating darkness. Let the Light hold sway thereon for evermore! Perhaps some day it would even become a star and, full of the Fires of gratitude, would remain near the Earth to adorn the Firmament with a new little star. Then they would help conceive and give rise to another planet, and then another... And these planets would beautify, like a resplendent cluster, the Infinite Ocean of Eternity. The Gods would proudly look upon the bright Fires of the new, enchanting constellation, blessing with their Divine Vision this Highest Labour — the Labour of Love...

118. The colours of day returned to the Earth, imbuing it with the Light of Illumination. Man knew his Future, for he had acquired Divine Insight. And this Future he would have to create by his own hands. The Gods were waiting for Man to take more purposeful steps in their direction. And people were taking those steps. No longer did they stop to fall into a long and uninterrupted heavy sleep. The Future belonged to them, and they were creating it in the rhythm of every instant of Life.

119. The Great Light of Love illumined Hearts. Shining like thousands of Suns, they began to dazzle the gaze of the All-Seeing Eye of the Sun. Now he was closing his eyelids to them, folding his fiery spirals which he had previously opened outward. It seemed as though the Star were exhaling and then imploding...

Inhaling and Exhaling — this was the regular rhythm of Life in the Universe. The Sun was collapsing in order to take a deep Inhaling of the Divine Fires of Immortality. This was his Period, as designated by the Gods who were rotating the Wheel, to take in his next Inhaling in accord with the Rhythm of the Universe. After absorbing billions of particles of the most varied forms of Fire, he would then have to make an Exhaling in order to disperse these particles throughout the regions of the Solar System assigned to them.

People no longer spoke of the end of the world, since they now knew that it has no end; they spoke only of the New Beginning... And they were preparing to enter the New World, joining the Sun in a powerful Inhaling. Perchance it would be so deep that for a period of time it would immerse them in a dream-like state... But they would, of course, be awakened by the Gods, who did not need or even know what we call *rest*. And the Gods would lead them to new triumphs heretofore unfathomable — even by the infinitely expanded human consciousness. But the Hearts were enlightened, for the Gods had already revealed to them the sacred Mystery of Life.

120. A New Day. A New Period for Life. The Gods opened wide the doors into the New Stellar World. There was no evil there, though there may well have been a degree of imperfection — an excellent battlefield for the achievement of further victories. For Gods also aim at self-perfection, polishing their sparkling, diamond-like Facets of Spirit. They must indeed be purer in order to radiate more brightly that miraculous magical Light which is followed by their creations — the Gods of the Earth, created from mortal human bodies... The facets of self-perfection are endless. And people must not lose their faith in the Might of the Gods, as well as those who will follow them, taking them for their Guiding Star. And everyone standing higher on the Great Ladder of Light will be perceived as a God by those at a lower level... And the First shall descend and stand on the lowest rung to raise up the stragglers. Thus will it be forever, until the last become the First... All are Gods...

Was not that precisely what the Gods were after — the Gods who were rotating unceasingly the Wheel of Eternity? And was it not they who periodically descended to the Earth to help the last become the First?... There were Seven of them; they had come to the Earth at different times, and people ever since have remembered their Earthly

Names... Today, no longer do those who once covered their own evil deeds by their Sacred Names of Light go forth to kill one another. Now is the Period to fulfil the Law the Gods foreordained — to love one another as devotedly and purely as only they — the Sons of the Only Begotten God, whose Name is *Mystery* — can love.

"To love... love and love!" — is heard in every rotation of the unceasingly turning Wheel. To love until the "end of Time," which actually will not have an end, if you truly love. Love is free, Love is immortal, and she lives inside of you — a Man of the Earth, moulded from the dust... Die in the body and be resurrected in the spirit, for the Immortal cannot die. Keep on ascending the Great Ladder of Light and stand up by the Wheel, replacing the God who has grown weary without any rest. Perchance He, too, needs to catch His breath and make an Inhaling and an Exhaling, though this time beyond the boundaries of the Solar System. The Wheel of Eternity is in your hands, O Immortal Creator of the Earth, who has perceived the Sacred Note of Love bestowed by the Gods! Now go forth and illuminate the Path of Salvation for the suffering world, weaving it from the bright and tenderly Loving Currents of the Heart, and bring it closer to the feet of the last... Let them be the First, and replace you at the Wheel of Life!

Thus has it been ordained by the Stanzas of Love, granted by the Gods, who are now rotating the Wheel of Eternity.

OM TAT SAT

EPILOGUE

The intersection of Three Times gives rise to a single Octave, expressing the essence of the Melody of Life. Seven basic notes — seven colours of the rainbow, plus five intermediate tones — enable you to now hear and feel with the Heart the Great Mystery of Love. It sounds ever more distinctly in the world, penetrating all the spheres of Being and Non-Being.

The mission of our planet — being transpierced by the Rays of Love-Wisdom — is to bring humanity forth in all its strength and glory, and to rise like a radiantly shining star in the Firmament of Eternity.

We are all being born anew, casting off our outward human skins. Humanity, born in the fires of Cosmic Love-Wisdom, is — *immortal*. And blessed be the stellar tribe that is shaping with human hands and feet its predestined Future; for you — people of the Earth — are the greatest spirits, already prepared to stand tomorrow upon the highest rung — a rung which only yesterday was occupied by the All-Loving Gods!

Zinovia Dushkova

GLOSSARY

Compiled by

Alexander Gerasimchuk

GLOSSARY

Adept	Fiery Baptism	Number
Agape	Fiery-White Core	Om Tat Sat
Agni	Fire	Only Begotten Son of God
Akasha	Flower	Periods
Alertness	Form	Poison
All-Seeing Eye	God	Polarity
Armageddon	Gods	Prayer
Aroma	Golden Fleece	Quest
Art	Gorgon	Race
Ashram	Great Lord of Shambhala	Ray
Atlantis	Hatred	Rhythm
Aura	Heart	Round
Balance	Heaven	Ruler of the Evil Empire
Beauty	Human Hands and Feet	Sacrifice
Blood	Idea	Seal
Book	Ignorance	Seed
Book of Maitreya Buddha	Illumination	Senzar
Book of the Golden Precepts	Immortality	Shambhala
Brain	Implosion	Small Planet
Brotherhood	Initiate	Solar System
Call	Instinct	Sound
Choice	Intuition	Space
Colour	Joy	Spirit
Condemnation	Kalachakra	Star
Consciousness	Karma	Suffering
Cosmic Right	Keys	Sun
Cross	Knowledge	Thought
Darkness	Labour	Threads
Death	Ladder of Light	Time
Destiny	Laws of the Universe	Titans
Distant Worlds	Lemuria	Tower of Chung
Doubt	Life	Treachery
Dzyan	Light	Tree of Evil
Earth	Lords of Destiny	Truth
Eighth Sphere	Love	Universe
Elixir of Life	Magic	Voice of the Great Silence
Esoteric	Mahatma	Volcano
Eternity	Man	Warmth
Evolution	Masters of Wisdom	Water
Exoteric	Matter	Wheel
Faith	Mind	Will
Faith, Hope, and Love	Mystery	Wisdom
Falsehood	Name	Word
Fear	Negation	Worlds

ADEPT — one who has attained true knowledge and mastered the Laws of Spirit and Matter, reaching the stages of Initiation and thus becoming a Master of Esoteric Philosophy.

AGAPE (*Greek*, "Love") — spiritual, selfless, sacrificial, unconditional Divine Love, which serves as a model for humanity. In the Bible it is the highest of the four types of Love. It is Love which is both of God and from God, whose very nature is Love itself. Jesus Christ showed humanity this type of Love for the first time on the Earth.

AGNI[1] (*Sanskrit*, "Fire") — the Fire, the God of Fire. He is the oldest and the most revered of Gods in India. It should be noted that *Agnus Dei* (*Latin*, "Lamb of God") of Christianity — i.e., Christ — is represented by symbols identical with the God Agni of Hinduism.

Agni is one of the three great deities: Agni, Vayu, and Surya, and also all three at once, being the threefold aspect of Fire; in the sky as the Sun; in the air as Lightning; on the Earth as ordinary Fire. Agni was part of the ancient Vedic Trimurti (*Sanskrit*, "three faces" or "threefold form" — i.e., the Trinity) before Vishnu was given a place of honour and before Brahma and Shiva were manifested.

In ancient times, Agni was considered the source of all beings and powers: Agni is manifested in all that exists; he is inseparable from life and there is no life without Agni. It is the very substance of the invisible God's divine essence, ever-present in every atom of His creation, which the Rosicrucians call the *Celestial Fire*. All space is filled with this Fire. All energies and elements originate from the one Primary Energy — the Fire. Each manifestation of spirit and matter is but the manifestation of this same primary energy of Agni.

The circle in the symbol represents endless Time in Eternity, signifying the Divine Unity, from which all proceeds and to which all returns. God can be thought of as a kind of "Circle," the centre of which is everywhere and the circumference nowhere. Thus, for all peoples, the Circle has been the symbol of the Unknown — "Boundless Space," the abstract vesture of an ever-present abstraction — the Incognizable Deity. The symbol of Spirit and Immortality has always

---

[1] As in the symbol on the cover of this book.

GLOSSARY

been depicted as a circle; hence a serpent biting its tail represents the Circle of Wisdom in Infinity.

AKASHA (*Sanskrit*, "Sky") — Primeval Matter, also known as *Materia Matrix*; the refined, supersensible spiritual essence which pervades all space; primary cosmic substance. In fact, it constitutes Universal Space, which inherently includes the eternal Ideation of the Universe in its ever-changing aspects on the planes of matter and objectivity.

The Scrolls of Akasha, or the Akasha Chronicles, are a particular manifestation of the limitless and indestructible memory of Nature, which stores information about all events and manifestations of the Cosmos — man, planet, system, or anything else.

ALERTNESS — the quality of discernment, which is acquired by the heart as a result of labour and experience throughout many lives. The eye of the heart can see, hear, and feel a lot, for the heart lives in the Higher Spheres, while the brain and its five senses live only in the physical world.

Alertness (or vigilance) helps man discern reality and Truth. For all that is called *earthly life* is a grand illusion, and its temptations serve as a test for detecting and separating the real from the unreal, the true from the false, the eternal from the temporal, the immortal from the perishable, the useful from the harmful. Everything on the Earth is but an instrument to gain experiential knowledge from earthly life that one can take further into one's life in the Ethereal Spheres. And this knowledge, which is invisible, imperceptible, and intangible, appears to be more real and palpable than houses, clothes, or money. The more knowledge of the heart is accumulated and the purer it is, the easier it is to discern the true nature of people and things. Of course, one must go through many trials before one can rely on the accuracy of one's keen perceptions. But life is the best school of all.

Restraint in thoughts, words, movements, and emotions accumulates a fiery force within. The more it accumulates, the more certainly will it offer unmistakable recognition. But, at the same time, alertness is also the condition for the conscious accumulation of the fiery energy crystallized in the physical body. For the quality of wise discernment saves man from excessive expenditures of energy, and acts as a means of self-protection. After all, each and every mistake in recognition leads to consequences — their duration and significance depending on the gravity of the mistake.

The vigilant eye of the heart is able to penetrate deep inside the human soul and see the true essence, which man typically hides behind an external mask. Unfortunately, the ability to discern the manifestations of the Light from those of the darkness is possessed by only a few, otherwise there would be far less monstrous delusion and blindness in the world. Because of the lack of heartfelt alertness, the true Messengers of Heaven are rarely recognized by people in time.

ALL-SEEING EYE — the so-called "Third Eye," which is closely related to the centre of the heart, enabling one to see all things spiritually without limits, irrespective of Time and Space. In Ancient Egypt, it was the symbol of the solar God Ra. According to ancient beliefs, it is the property of all Gods.

The All-Seeing Eye is also the symbol of the Akasha Chronicles, that is, the space which registers everything occurring in the Universe.

ARMAGEDDON — in the broadest sense, a trial, or test, which gives the right to advance to a new level of development or into a New World. As Evolution is endless, Armageddon began in the very first days of the creation of the planet Earth.

In its traditional meaning, Armageddon is the Final Battle between the Forces of the Light and the darkness, as proclaimed in ancient prophecies.

After Lucifer's defeat in his war with the Sons of Light in the age of Atlantis, as well as in our present times, the forces of the darkness realized they would never triumph over the Light and, sooner or later, they would be annihilated by the fiery energies approaching the Earth. Therefore, Lucifer, who had no access to the Higher Worlds, decided to blow up the planet, since that alone would allow him to remain in its atmosphere for some time and so prolong his life. The catastrophe

GLOSSARY

could happen in 1899, 1949, 1954, 1977, or 1999. In this case, the Brotherhood of the Great Teachers, together with the best Earth-dwellers, would move to Venus and Jupiter; the majority would wait billions of years for the formation of a new planet in order to continue their evolution, while the worst of them would end up on Saturn. But the Earth was saved from destruction through the incredible efforts of all Forces of the Light in the Solar System.

The liberation of the Earth from the dictatorship of Lucifer began at the end of the 19th century and the beginning of the 20th century on the Subtle Plane; soon afterwards the battle shifted onto the physical plane in the form of the First World War, 1914–1918. At the end of 1931, on the Subtle Plane, a new phase of the struggle for humanity's freedom and immortality began. The calculations unearthed in the Great Pyramid of Giza indicated the significance of 1936 — this was the start of the personal fight between the Great Lord of Shambhala and the Lord of the Darkness, the celestial battle of Archangel Michael and his angels with the Dragon as proclaimed in the Bible.[2] Eventually, the decisive battle of Forces of the Light and the darkness shifted from the Subtle Plane to the physical one, which gave rise to the Second World War, 1939–1945.

The Final Battle ended with the triumph of the Forces of the Light on 17 October 1949, when the Great Lord banished Lucifer to Saturn. However, this did not end Armageddon, for the servants of the Ruler of the Darkness still remain on the Earth, only now the main field of battle lies in the invisible realm of human hearts.

AROMA — one of the aspects of Sound, inherent in every phenomenon and process. Scent is comprised of the smallest particles of matter, radiated by auras and dispersed into the surrounding atmosphere as the result of the combination of the elements forming matter. The Light, its colours and aromas are closely related among themselves. Each sound and colour in the spectrum is associated with its own special aroma. The energies of the Light and the darkness have their own distinctive scent: the former is fragrant; the latter has a fetid stench.

---

[2] See Rev. 12:7–10.

Every condition and process in the human body gives off emanations, accompanied by corresponding scents, colours, and expulsion of gas. Thus, every individual has a particular scent, along with each of their emotions, feelings, and even thoughts. Pure spirits are fragrant, but those immersed in vice stink. Hence one can determine the spiritual condition of man by his scent. The intensity of a scent indicates the tenacity of the corresponding good or evil principle. As man improves, the aroma he exudes becomes more refined and fragrant. The purification of his thoughts, feelings, and nutrition is reflected in the quality of the scents he emits.

Evil deeds, thoughts, and feelings do not disappear into space, but leave fetid crystalline accumulations in the body. The brown gas produced by the darkness, which blankets many regions of the planet, also gives off the stench of decay.

In the Subtle World, scents are especially significant, for they serve as food for subtle bodies. Every sphere differs from another by its smells. Man in his subtle body is drawn to the sphere that matches his own scent: the fragrance of the Higher Spheres or the stench of the lowest layers.

Every High Spirit has their own fragrance, which is close to the aroma of the flower through which they were incarnated in the Human Kingdom or a species of which they patronize in the Plant Kingdom. When a High Spirit approaches a man in their subtle body, one can physically sense the aroma of the corresponding flower. However, this fragrance is perceived not by the nose but by the heart.

Aromas can help cure. Even the mental evocation of positive scents in conjunction with optimistic thoughts can have a restorative effect.

ART — the highest form of creativity accessible to humanity on the Earth, which paves the path to their highest purpose in the Cosmos. Through art, Beauty comes into life — along with, of course, the Light.

Jesus Christ said to people: "Ye are Gods"[3] — this is the goal of human evolution, though not its limit, for the process of self-perfection is endless. Man's destiny is to become a god and the creator of new worlds and forms of life. Man has been given power over all

---

[3] John 10:34.

GLOSSARY

flesh, i.e., over all kinds of matter and energy in the Cosmos; these in fact are concentrated in him. And art is the means of the mastering, educating, and developing this creative force of human consciousness. It awakens in man his dormant and hidden powers, accustoming him to the Fire — the primary energy of the Cosmos, without which no work of art can be created. It is precisely in the preparation of the human spirit for the possibility of cosmic creativeness that lies the great significance of art on the Earth. And the opportunities for cosmic creativity are boundless.

The arts serve to train and intensify the faculties of hearing, sight, and rhythm, along with a sensitivity to beauty — in short, all human abilities, which help in daily life as well. After all, the creativity of man is manifest everywhere: in each word, thought, action, or deed. Creativity moulds human energies into a particular form. Everyone creates their own environment through their own unique energies. Even the inner world of man is but the natural outcome of his creative work and efforts. Of course, these worlds differ from each other, for creativity may be either light or dark, though the latter cannot be considered a favourable phenomenon. Creativity requires the ability to bring compatible elements together and combine them in harmony, for the foundation of true art is Beauty. And nothing in the world but art can teach this marvellous process of creation.

ASHRAM (*Sanskrit*, "hermitage") — a sacred abode, temple, or monastery, where Teachers and their disciples are to be found.

ATLANTIS — Plato's name for the continent whereon the Fourth Race of humanity developed. Extending from the North to the South, it was located in an area now covered by the waters of the Atlantic Ocean.

Numerous islands rose from the depths to form this continent, beginning some five million years ago. At the same time, the Great Teachers started gathering and resettling on one of the central islands the best representatives of the Third Race from the continent of Lemuria, whose time was drawing to a close.

The first Atlanteans were almost three-and-a-half metres tall, later decreasing in height to approximately two-and-a-half metres. The peak of Atlantis' flourishing coincided with the Toltec period, when, after long internecine wars, tribes united into a federation headed by an emperor. The capital was the City of Golden Gates, situated in the Eastern part of Atlantis.

The Great Teachers living among the people had imparted to the Atlanteans an abundance of mystic knowledge, enabling them to achieve success in many spheres of life — they were able to manage the most powerful energies; they knew the mysteries of Nature and could breed new species of plants and animals; they could come up with the most complex technologies, including the science of aeronautics; in addition, they made direct contact with the Distant Worlds.

The decline of Atlantis began with the fall of Lucifer, who had been one of humanity's trusted Instructors. People began to use mystic knowledge not for the good of all but for glorifying themselves, accumulating riches, inventing deadly weapons, waging war, practising black magic, and so on. Those who warned of the inevitable disaster resulting from the actions of the Atlanteans faced a death penalty. This frightful moral decline, along with the humiliation of women and other perversions, led to the Atlanteans consciously repeating the sin of primitive man, the progenitor of the primary apes; the sexual intercourse between some Atlanteans and primary apes produced man-like monkeys.

The violation of Cosmic Laws on such an unprecedented scale, along with the use of black magic by the Atlanteans against the Sons of Light, brought destructive elemental forces into play. These gradually destroyed Atlantis and ushered in the Ice Age, covering whole regions of the planet with ice.

The main continent was destroyed by water a few millions years ago, leaving a number of large and small islands, among which were Ruta and Daitya. The isle of Ruta sank almost 850,000 years ago, and Daitya submerged nearly 270,000 years ago, leaving a smaller island known as Poseidonis, which itself sank below the sea in 9564 BCE.

Prior to these disasters, the Sons of Light resettled the best and most spiritual inhabitants of Atlantis to Egypt, transferring there

GLOSSARY

the entire mystic heritage of the Atlanteans. The Masters themselves moved to Shambhala, which was also an island at the time. They have been helping humanity secretly ever since, without revealing themselves.

Today, Atlantis is slowly rising and will be the continent for the development of the Sixth and Seventh Races of humanity.

AURA — the electro-magnetic radiation of all the accumulated energies of a living organism, especially the heart, retaining its dominant colour, sound, and scent. All bodies and objects of the manifest world are surrounded by an aura.

The human aura is kind of a passport which quickly identifies the individual's essence and destiny. In the future, a person's aura will determine their suitability to hold important positions in every domain of life. Every thought, emotion, feeling, or act leaves an impress on their aura in the form of radiations, which, in turn, magnetically attract elements from space that correspond with their tonality. The more powerful the fiery energy in a man, the stronger the influence of his aura over his whole environment. Throughout his life, a man suffuses everything he touches with the radiations of his aura, brightening or darkening the objects around him. Besides, everyone perceives the world through the prism of their aura, as though they were looking through glasses. Hence, through an aura of light, one sees only the Light, while a dark aura offers glimpses mostly of the darkness.

Nevertheless, the aura of a newborn child is colourless, as a rule, until the age of seven, when the first gleam of consciousness imbues it with the colours corresponding to the accumulations of previous lives.

The margin of aura should be enclosed by a protective net, woven together from the sediments of the most refined fiery energies for defence against extraneous intrusions and influences. But spirits devoid of spirituality do not have such a guard; therefore, they often fall victim to the impact of other people's auras, especially of those possessing a powerful aura of black fire; they also succumb to the indoctrinations of various evil entities from the Subtle Plane. This, of course, affects human health most of all. Remember that more spiritually-minded people have a protective net in the form of fiery ruby sparks. However, dark entities are always attempting to break through, for even the slightest rupture opens the way to control over one's being. The aura of powerful spirits generates a ray, which imbues thoughts — or anything else — with its colour and energy. When a thought like this is aimed in a specific direction, it has the appearance of a real ray in space, equipped with tremendous power.

A planet, too, possesses an aura, along with a protecting net. The aura of the Earth accumulates all the energies produced by the activity and free will of humanity. At the beginning of its existence, the aura of the Earth was golden, but by the mid-20th century it had turned ash-grey with clouds of brown gas and black holes in its protective net. By the end of the last century, the Hierarchy of Light and its earthly colleagues managed to restore the net. But the state of the planet's aura still depends upon humanity collectively and every living being in particular.

BALANCE — grand harmony; the foundation of Being and the existence of everything that is, was, and will be.

Cosmic Balance (or Equilibrium) is a condition underlying the existence of the manifest world, since opposing powers hold it in balance. All visible and invisible worlds, planets and solar systems are held in balance among themselves by their rays and energies. Any disturbance of this cosmic harmony results in the destruction of visible worlds. At the same time, Chaos is the complete destruction of harmony. Hence, there is a Law of Balance ruling the Universe. Even the Cosmic Periods are determined by it. For example, if the strongest star sends its fiery rays to a populated planet before the appointed time, their energy will incinerate the planet and annihilate its humanity.

In like manner, human life is based on the Law of Balance, which presupposes a unification of principles, equal in terms of energy but opposite in force. Once this unification occurs, the process of attraction ceases, restoring the equilibrium. In other words, all earthly desires and emotions are energies, seeking contact and completion. Therefore, the desires and aspirations of man, sooner or later, somewhere and

GLOSSARY

somehow, will attract the object of their desire through a combination of different energies. The more man cherishes his directed energies, the more he is attracted towards the corresponding objects or spheres where such phenomena — or energies — exist. This is especially apparent, for example, in human emotions: a man may one day feel exceeding joy, yet the next day grieve with a similar show of fervour. He may either remain at this neutral point of balance or produce new energies, which will require his desires to be fulfilled if an equilibrium is to be established.

Balance itself is a neutral state that neither attracts nor is attracted; it is a neutralization of the duality which arises when consciousness establishes its authority over both poles of the manifestation of one and the same thing. The conscious extinguishing of directed energy means the establishment of the equilibrium of this energy. When man extinguishes his earthly energies, the sphere of the Earth loses its magnetic power and he is released from the power of terrestrial illusions. But the maintaining of balance is within one's powers only when the human spirit consolidates its power over the lower bodies, when the heart subjugates the mind, when every feeling and deed becomes not personal, but transpersonal. Otherwise, man will only waver between the negative and the positive.

It must be noted that *equilibrium* and *indifference* are completely different states of mind. *Indifference* is associated with apathy, inertness, weakness, and the extinguishing of fires, while *equilibrium* is a calm and unemotional attitude towards everything concerning one's personal self.

Balance (or equilibrium) is a mighty force, for any energy aimed at a man in this state meets absolutely no reaction and bounces back on its progenitor. A balanced consciousness is like a sphere with a surface smooth as glass, allowing nothing to cling to it. It is indeed the establishing of such a balance that Jesus Christ envisaged in His command to "resist not evil,"[4] as well as in His words: "the prince of this world cometh, and hath nothing in me."[5]

---

[4] Matt. 5:39.

[5] John 14:30.

In ancient teachings, balance is called the *Middle Path*, or the *Golden Path*, by which man gains mastery over fiery energies and crystal of his heart grows rapidly. The man who has attained equilibrium — the most difficult quality of all to achieve — attracts the attention of the Great Lord of Shambhala Himself.

BEAUTY — the basis of the expression of the Light through harmony, as well as through the concordant combination of all the elements comprising the structure of the form in which it is manifested. This requires a knowledge of the laws of harmony, measure, and number. The mystery of light, colour, and sound inherent in such a phenomenon produces a powerful magnetic attraction and exerts an influence over man's consciousness. This explains the great impact on human consciousness produced by Nature, beautiful books, or masterpieces of art. For example, one may notice the manifestation of such concordance in the blossoming of a rose.

The quality of harmony and beauty may be equally expressed by a human soul. If *ugliness* — another word for *darkness* — is the progenitor of the basest fires and uncleansed elements, then the Beauty of thoughts, words, feelings, and deeds lays the foundation for the crystals of fiery energy in a human body. Wars, diseases, fanaticism, mediocrity, ignorance, etc. do not correspond to the concept of *Beauty*. Fashion and Beauty are not always concordant, for fashion is all too often the expression of vanity and ugliness. In the Higher and Distant Worlds, Beauty is the basis for the construction of one's entire life. Therefore, in order to enter the Higher Spheres, one should learn to affirm Beauty in everything already on the Earth — from the infinitesimal to the infinite.

Beauty is the foundation of the New World, underlying life in all its forms. Indeed, the Era of the Heart can also be called the *Era of Beauty*, for the heart is the crown of Beauty in any creation. Everything will be marked with the seal of Beauty, especially man — but not so much outwardly as inwardly. Internal Beauty will eventually find itself manifest in an external appearance — after all, sheer physical beauty, not spiritualized by the beauty of spirit, is not true Beauty. Even health is simply a form of internal beauty — an outward expression of balance or harmony.

Note that it is the realization of Beauty which will ultimately save the world.

BLOOD — a borderline condition of matter between the gross and subtle planes, a conductor of vital energy. All living things have blood, even a stone — its form is just different, invisible. The subject of blood has completely escaped humanity's research to date, because of their refusal to accept the existence of the Subtle Plane and their insistence on viewing the heart only as a physical, muscular organ.

In fact, the number of blood groups by far exceeds four. The medicine of the future will classify 24 groups, associated with stellar rays and the signs of the zodiac. Scientists have already discovered that water preserves information about surrounding events and things. Blood, in turn, captures information about people's past lives and develops a structure for their future incarnations. Blood is a carrier of both terrestrial and ethereal energies, uniting in itself the earthly Karma with the Cosmic Karma of Love. One's Karma is fully imprinted with one's blood formula. For example, if a man aspires to the Light, this changes his formula.

There are abodes of the black brotherhood, whose task is to ruin this world, and so they are engaged in making various combinations of destructive currents. Wherever they are, blood is inevitably shed and wars are waged. Evil sorcerers, the darkness, are fed and strengthened by evaporations — or emanations — of blood. To this end they attempt to gain a foothold at some point. While sorcerers of inferior rank need conflicts, irritations, quarrels, etc., the more powerful ones feed on the emanations of blood shed in tragedies on a grand scale. And so, they do everything to ensure that there are people empowered as the sorcerers' reflections on the terrestrial plane, making them foment wars, supplying the darkness with a harvest of blood-soaked dew. Disembodied entities that live in the lower near-Earth spheres of the Subtle Plane can also instigate conflicts, since the evaporations of blood are their only bread. Crystallized bloodstained emanations, spilt out into these near-Earth spheres as a result of numerous wars, may remain there for centuries or even millennia, especially if from time to time they are multiplied through additional layers of new destructive processes.

In the places which have seen the greatest outpouring of the Light and positive energy capable of changing the entire world — such as India, Israel, Russia, Syria, Ukraine, etc. — the darkness, often acting from within, has been attempting to erase this energy from the soil by means of bloodshed, creating nuclei of constant conflicts on religious, political, or any other grounds under the guise of "good intentions." These emanations of blood very quickly change the formula of energy at the level of the physical sphere — thus transforming it into a destructive energy that spreads itself throughout the world. In addition, such bundles of blood energy can be used by extra-terrestrial technocratic civilizations to create a kind of biorobot.

Bloodshed affects Nature too. Thus, ever since the time of Atlantis, when people wanted to subdue the power of stones and establish magical authority over the whole world, when deadly wars were started and blood was shed for the sake of earthly treasures, they — the representatives of the Mineral Kingdom — have been saturated with emanations of blood which disrupted the energy code of their evolution. They moved into the Plant Kingdom, creating poisonous lethal species. And this was followed by their transition into the Animal Kingdom in the form of aggressive animals, aimed at bringing death to the higher Kingdom of Humanity. All the Kingdoms are interrelated with each other, and humanity, it turns out, itself created the deadly classes of Nature. In addition, some representatives of the Mineral Kingdom, owing to the fact that people had used them for evil, declared war on the Kingdom of Humanity. Ores have been melted and forged into bullets, and bullets kill people. The Kingdom of Minerals uses people's hands, and people go off to kill each other — hence the ores are winning this war. Not only that, but people die in accidents even more than in wars. Therefore, humanity has yet to establish peace, but many people, through their open hearts, have already made friends and protectors out of the representatives of the

GLOSSARY

Mineral Kingdom. For example, many cases are known of drivers falling asleep at the wheel, but their cars somehow stopped, saving them from accidents.

Any spilt blood — of either man or animal — attracts a host of lower spirits who are drawn to any form of decay, thus cementing the near-Earth space with negativity. These lower spirits influence the human mind and body, bringing consequences in the form of illnesses. For this reason, meat of any kind can engender all sorts of diseases. The "tradition" of eating dead bodies has been imposed on humanity by evil workers of black magic since the days of Atlantis, as it is one of the factors depriving man of Immortality and separating the Earth from the Higher Spheres. Thus, someone who increases the burden on their Karma through eating corpses shows a criminal attitude, not only towards the animal world and their own bodies — both physical and subtle — but also towards the whole planet and region of surrounding space.

BOOK — like any creation, a particular type of crystallized fiery energy. The author of any work is responsible to the entire Universe, in accord with Cosmic Laws. Each creation of human hands requires the contribution of one's own energy, which manifests either destructive or constructive properties. Therefore, some books serve the Light while others serve the darkness.

The importance of books in the life of contemporary humanity is tremendous, because the process of reading is something deeper and more mysterious than is commonly thought, being only partly physical in nature. Creativity without fire is impossible, and a writer uses it to create on the subtle, invisible plane. So, it is on the Subtle Plane that the author creates actual, real forms, unseen by physical eyes, but clearly visible to a clairvoyant. All of them are invisible, they are not on the pages of a book, but with the help of letters and symbols, the reader calls these images to life, thereby exerting an influence on their consciousness. The more powerful and fiery the thought crystallized in the book, the stronger its impact. Hence books play a significant role as fiery stimulants. Consequently, the power of books consists in their fieriness while the benefit they bring is in their closeness or consonance with Cosmic Laws. Reading brings certain centres of consciousness into a state of tension — or luminosity — of varying degrees, depending on the nature of the fires with which it is imbued. If bright fires are crystallized in a book, they evoke similar fires in a man; if it contains dark fires, then dark fires are generated in a man. Thus, each book contains either goodness or poison within its pages, resulting in appropriate consequences for the reader, even for their physical body.

People cannot help but feel this mighty influence on their consciousness, and that is why some Scriptures are considered sacred, for they are capable of kindling sacred fires not only within man, but also in the space around him. Hence the Initiates, being aware of this capability, have deliberately put sacred books for three or seven years in certain places where the threat of danger lurks — for example, a crust fracture — in order to prevent a cataclysm in the future. A book with crystallized bright fires, even one not in popular demand among the general public, still suffuses the world with beneficial and healing radiations which serve to neutralize negative vibrations.

All the books of the Teachings of Light, both ancient and modern, that have been given and written in the Rays of the Great Teachers, have a special fiery power, for they were created according to the Universal Laws of Harmony and Consonance. As a rule, the Teachers impart their Teachings in the language of the country needing them at a particular time-period, since each period has its special assignment and each nation is obliged to fulfil its own designated task. But at the same time, the Teaching does not lose its global significance, because every truth is universal. Note that sounds are arranged in a certain word order to obtain the required vibrations or rhythm. Consequently, in order to truly appreciate any Teaching of Light, one must read it in its original tongue, since translations, as a rule, tend to lose the accompanying melody and might even distort the truth. Each record has its own special and unique rhythm, suffusing every line with a vital flame. Indeed, their impact on consciousness is powerful: it is literally ignited by them, nourishing the spirit with fire.

GLOSSARY

The reading of the Teachings of Light is, in essence, a fiery process. It is as though sparks and fire are constantly flashing around the reader on the invisible plane — and these may later turn into a permanent and evenly burning flame.

BOOK OF MAITREYA BUDDHA — the Secret Book that Helena Blavatsky was to use along with the *Book of Dzyan* for the creation of *The Secret Doctrine*, as evidenced by her letters.[6] It is a volume of the *Book of Fiery Destinies*, or the Book of Life, composed by the Supreme Spirit — Maitreya — who comes into the world to elevate humanity to the next level of development. Excerpts from this Fiery Autobiography, translated from the Senzar language, were to comprise Volume V of *The Secret Doctrine*.

BOOK OF THE GOLDEN PRECEPTS — contains around ninety short treatises, essentially constituting a code of rules which the Initiates must follow. In 1889, Helena Blavatsky published three excerpts from this work in a book entitled *The Voice of the Silence*, which was later endorsed by the 9th Panchen Lama and the 14th Dalai Lama.

BRAIN — the earthly mouthpiece of the heart, given only for one incarnation. The brain has not been sufficiently explored, even though it is more involved in human life than the heart. Only about 10% of its potential is accessible to people at the moment. However, it will not be long — in the near future, in fact — before man makes use of the rest of his hidden capabilities.

The brain is a physical apparatus for thinking, and it is necessary for the Earth, being closely related to the external senses. One can actually think without the brain and its mediation. Even memory is not connected with the brain and one cannot always retrieve from its archives even something that they most certainly contain. The death of the physical body not only does not stop the process of thinking, but on the contrary, intensifies it, making it lighter and more flexible.

---

[6] See *The Letters of H. P. Blavatsky to A. P. Sinnett*, comp. Trevor Baker (Pasadena, CA: Theosophical University Press, 1973), p. 195.

In the Subtle World and higher, man lives without a brain, although he still sees, hears, feels, and thinks.

The brain emits a particular kind of electromagnetic waves, which, like radio waves, can be transmitted over a distance and received not only by another brain, but also by supersensitive devices. Thoughts themselves flow over the brain. Clairvoyants can see a halo or radiance surrounding the head of someone engaged in complex mental activity. There is a network of invisible luminous thought-bearing channels — one that is superimposed on the grey substance in certain patterns, forming convolutions. It is known that lines on one's palm mirror a map of the brain's convolutions. Hence, as one's thoughts shape one's destiny, this destiny is imprinted on the grey substance of the brain in the form of convolutions, which are in turn reflected on one's palms. Hence, an expert in palmistry is able to read people's destinies which they themselves have created — in their past lives as well as their present ones.

The brain is currently limited by its five senses as well as by its terrestrial dual world or earthly illusion. Consequently, it finds it a challenge comprehending anything that goes beyond this frame of reference. The fact is, it is difficult to make sense of two completely opposite statements at once, and so, as a rule, only one of them is accepted while the other one is denied. The heart, on the other hand, is able to perceive anything inaccessible to the brain. While the path of the brain is long, convoluted, and horizontal, the path of the heart, by contrast, is short, straight, and vertical.

Now, like everything else on the Earth, the brain is in the process of transformation, and in the future its grey matter will take on an emerald-ruby hue. It will keep on developing and being refined as long as human speech exists, until people learn to understand the language of the Silence spoken by the heart. In the meantime, the brain is designed to serve as the mouthpiece for the heart. Precisely, the brain represents a registry of the subtle energies coming through the heart, expressing its thoughts and feelings in verbal form. The heart and the brain must act in mutual accord and harmony, complementing each other, and so expand consciousness. But this so rarely happens that

GLOSSARY

the brain, because of its excessive activity, is only occasionally able to register the flashes of the heart we often call *intuition* or *conscience*.

BROTHERHOOD — the Community of the Seven Messengers of the Distant Worlds and their disciples, who have lived side by side with humanity on the Earth for millions of years, developing the human mind and heart.

The previous Solar System was tasked with giving people knowledge and developing their intelligence. The present System is aimed at bringing people closer to Love, and the focus of Love is the Heart. Therefore, the Great Lords have divided themselves into two Brotherhoods — the Western and the Eastern.

The Western Brotherhood — also known as the Brotherhood of Luxor or the Thebes Sanctuary, located in Egypt — was to provide knowledge, as well as to develop and expand people's consciousness, with emphasis on the mental body, the mind, the human intellect, in order to help to take a step towards the heart. All the knowledge accumulated in the past and present Solar Systems, resides exclusively in Egypt.

The Eastern Brotherhood — Shambhala or the Himalayan Brotherhood — was to develop the intuition of the heart, always bearing Love and serving the highest energies. In other words, the West is the mind, and the East is the heart. We learn from ancient traditions that the Masters left the West for the East. Many people, in fact, left the Sanctuary in Egypt to go to the East. This happens approximately once every two thousand years.

At the end of the 19th century, before the start of Armageddon, all the Secret Schools and Ashrams of the Western Brotherhood were closed and moved to the Himalayas. All the Great Teachers who had worked in the world — holding Initiations and imparting knowledge — were also summoned to the Stronghold of Light in the Himalayas. Humanity was abandoned for a hundred years, but knowledge was still given through their disciples. However, there was no longer any direct contact between the Masters and the vast majority of people.

The Theban Sanctuary is now re-opening and once again starting to serve Love. While previously it was working through the Ray of Knowledge, now these two Sanctuaries — the Eastern and the Western — are uniting and interpenetrating their Rays, imparting a single Ray of Love-Wisdom. Similarly, all the Great Lords who had been saturating humanity as much as possible with knowledge are now beginning to serve Love. Thus a Great Synthesis is being born, and the two Greatest Schools are merging into one, affirming a single path for the whole world: the ascent to the steps of Wisdom through the illumination of the human heart.

CALL — the energy set in motion by the magnet of the heart, which is aimed into space to attract consonant elements by its magnetic force.

The call and the response constitute a law of magnetic attraction and harmony. It is received with accordance and complete correspondence — i.e., the response of space will correspond exactly with the call. A good call will meet with a good response, while an evil one will be answered in kind with equal force. Since in the Cosmos the free will of man is something sacred, whatever help is provided must come in response to the call of the heart alone. Similarly, while all of space is permeated with the Call to the Light by the Heart of the Cosmos, it is still up to each person's will to respond to it.

For example, it is by the Call of the Great Heart of the Cosmos that new Races are formed, through the gathering together of concordant spirits. Thus the First Call for the assembling of the Sixth Race rang out in 1920. In 1997, 77 years later, a Second Call resounded, heralding the start of the gathering of the Seventh Race. And now a spatial Call is sounding all over the planet, summoning everyone to stand up under the Banner of the Lord Maitreya. Those who can give a resonant answer to the call are drawn into the circle of attraction of the Light, and they consciously embark on a course of infinite ascent.

CHOICE — the inalienable right of every creature endowed with the Highest Reason. The conditions of choice are determined by stars and karmic predestination. Choice depends on the will; and in turn defines the cause that brings irrevocable consequences — for which one has to bear responsibility.

The Hierarchy of Light holds sacred the human freedom of choice, and never dictates its own will: man is free to choose the path he wants, even if it leads to destruction. Whereas the forces of the darkness are by no means above violating this sacred Cosmic Law.

Each cycle of Evolution presupposes the making of a Final Choice, also known as the Last Judgement: to move forward or backward. In the Fifth Race of humanity, the time of the Great Choice began on 19 July 1999 when all of humanity was divided into four general groups: 1) those who have made their choice in favour of the Light and are under the guidance of Supreme Forces; 2) those who are in the process of finishing their battle for choosing the Light; 3) those who openly identify themselves with the dark forces that work against Evolution; 4) totally indifferent, or "lukewarm" beings.

The Final Choice of the Fifth Race will end on 19 July 2017, when everyone in their spirit will choose either the Light or the darkness.

COLOUR — fire produced by Sound. Colour is an aspect of the existence of the material world in all phases of its manifestation. Each atom possesses a spectrum of a particular colour, so it is impossible to separate matter from its colour expression. A spectral analysis of colour allows one to determine the presence of specific substance. Every phenomenon, object, and process is accompanied by its own colour.

The spectrum of colour is septenary, based on the number 7: there are seven colours of the rainbow, which interpenetrate each other. Each colour should also be examined in terms of the sevenfold composition of tones. Every colour corresponds to a particular sound, making seven dominant notes. Thus, colour may evoke sound, while sound in turn may evoke colour, manifesting a certain quality of Light.

All living things react to all colours. The importance and influence of different colour vibrations on man and surrounding space is significant, since each colour emits an invisible and inaudible sound. Every creature and object has its own dominant colour. Many instances of incompatibility between people stem from the colour disharmony of their auras. One's dominant shade of colour can be discovered in the eyes, but only a careful observer is able to notice it. It is most discernible in the early morning or immediately after awakening from sleep. Thus, almost all people belonging to the Fifth Race have shades of red or yellow as their dominant colours, but also one can find shades of blue or green.

Now is the start of a New Era, which is dominated by the Seventh Ray — the Violet Ray of Transfiguration. This is the manifestation of the First Ray of Will and Power, which cannot be revealed in its pure form in the present Solar System, but will be in the next one. Violet is the colour of spirituality, purification, advancement towards renewal and a New Round. Hence this colour will make itself manifest over time and prevail in Nature. Indeed, even today, many people around the world have noticed — but do not understand why — that the leaves of their plants' are green on one side and violet on the other.

CONDEMNATION — a destructive force which uses the dual, chiaroscuro nature of man to evoke the darkness and evil. From this nature it always awakens and intensifies precisely what a man is accused of. So, whoever takes the stone of condemnation and throws it at another man becomes a servant of the darkness.

Indeed, through condemnation, especially when it is unjustified, even a decent person might turn bad. When a man does an evil deed, and people start to blame him, they only strengthen his dark features and make them worse, provoking him to commit an even greater evil. At the same time, they who condemn take the blame of the guilty one partly upon themselves, thereby submerging themselves in the layer of the lower vibrations; and if the condemned one should happen to have a superior fiery essence, the stones are simply bounced back. A secret condemnation is no less harmful than one uttered aloud, and condemnations uttered behind one's back are just as damaging, for thought knows no barriers or distances. It is far better to react to a wrong with Love, mentally concentrating on the individual's positive characteristics, however slight they may be. For inside every man exists both the Light and the darkness: it is what we summon into being that is all-important.

GLOSSARY

The understanding that everyone shares the same fiery energy, albeit manifested in tremendous variety and uniqueness, engenders respect for others' fires and eliminates any justification for condemnation of others. Nevertheless, it is essential to see, know, and understand man and what man is motivated by. For every spirit advancing towards the Light must be capable of discerning white from black, the Light from the darkness. However, discernment and condemnation are two completely different things, as different as truth and falsehood. To see and know everything without condemning is a quality of a High Spirit. Similarly, recognizing the wrongness of a fault is by no means the same thing as condemning the individual at fault. Discussion, an impartial analysis of misdeeds or shortcomings, and indicating how to avoid them in the future — may serve for good.

The Law of Karma will wisely reward everyone according to what they deserve.

CONSCIOUSNESS — in essence, this designates the accumulated fiery energy around the Seed of the Spirit during all one's lives within a particular Grand Cycle of Evolution, or Fiery-White Core. However, consciousness, expressing the essence of the spirit, has no form, but is clothed in this essence in accord with the current stage of its development. The more developed and broader one's consciousness, the more refined and flawless its forms. Thus, through consciousness, the human spirit gives shape to all of its coverings: from the fiery body to the physical body.

All forms of life — animal, vegetable, and mineral — are endowed with consciousness. Furthermore, all machines, mechanisms, and other creations by human hands fashioned from elements of the Mineral Kingdom, are similarly endued with a supplementary degree of consciousness. Evolution has bestowed on man a gift of self-consciousness, elevating him to a higher level in relation to the other Kingdoms of Nature. The following step must be the *continuity of consciousness* in all the Worlds, which is the acquisition of true Immortality.

The focus of consciousness is flexible, being directed by the will, and can be concentrated either in the brain or in the heart.

CONSCIOUSNESS — COSMIC RIGHT

Nevertheless, a man with an ordinary consciousness identifies it with his physical, mortal coverings. But the goal of evolution is to transfer the consciousness to the heart, to the Seed of the Spirit, thereby attaining not only immortality but also omnipotence. The accumulations around the Seed, which determine consciousness, are subject to change, while the fire of the Seed is constant, being directly united with that Divine Principle which engendered it. In this way, man may become a conscious bearer of unfathomable depth, hidden within himself. Man is the potential Absolute, the eternal and immutable First Principle of future Universes within Infinite Eternity. That is why the Bible says: "Ye are Gods; and all of you are children of the Most High."[7]

The awareness of any phenomenon is a step towards its realization and mastery. But this awareness depends on the comprehension of the phenomenon by the heart, for the heart embraces and feels its essence long before the brain understands it.

COSMIC RIGHT — determines the inherent place of every creature on the Ladder of Hierarchy, taking account of the astrochemical combination of rays and the position of the stars, and endows them with appropriate powers. Consequently, man is, first and foremost, the holder of this Right. The Cosmic Right has several aspects of manifestation:

1. Each Seed of the Spirit, or Monad, is engendered under a particular star, having its own Father, and thus may lay claim to His "inheritance" in the form of, for example, Secret Knowledge. This aspect depends upon the awareness and understanding of the significance of this right. It is inseparable from the ability to attract and use the spatial Fire with the help of the heart's magnetism.

2. Each Monad belongs to one of the elements, which bestows a preferential right to the mastery of a certain element.

3. By virtue of his long, persistent, and conscious endeavours, a man may deserve more, reaping the fruits of his own labour and achievements. The quality of immutability is bestowed on the fiery strivings of such a spirit, as well as on his right to receive according

---

[7] Ps. 82:6.

to his strength, harmoniousness, and level of aspirations. In other words, this right is earned by dint of the spirit — as the verdict of the Law of Cause and Effect.

Even in ordinary life, one may observe how the Cosmic Right is fulfilled, guiding circumstances towards the realization of something that seems impossible and against logic. For example, sometimes people come to power unexpectedly and by virtue of circumstances beyond their comprehension.

Knowledge is the inalienable right of humanity, and the freedom of learning is part of evolution. Therefore, Truth is given according to the level of consciousness of all humanity, not by a wish or a request, but by virtue of the Cosmic Right.

It bestows the right to true leadership over inferior beings on the Ladder of Evolution. Thus, the authority of Hierarchy, based on the primacy of the spirit and knowledge, is a natural power, with no doubt as to its legitimacy or authority in the Cosmos, regulating human life on the planet Earth.

CROSS — the most ancient cosmic symbol: the vertical line symbolizes spirit while the horizontal one symbolizes matter, which together create all that exists.

Christ said: "If any man will come after me, let him deny himself, and take up his cross, and follow me."[8] The cross is Karma. One who is unwilling to accept the cross cannot follow, but to take it means expressing humility before the karmic discharge of old debts, the conscious extirpation of vices, and the unconditional acceptance of probations. The higher the human spirit, the heavier the burden it accepts, but the cross is lifted by the spirit and therefore it cannot destroy man by its weight. However, as the time of release draws nearer, the burden becomes more and more unbearable — but it is an illusion, amplified by the darkness, and one has to pass through this without deviating from the path. In this way, after a symbolic crucifixion on the cross, when a man overcomes the desires of his baser bodies, atoning for his karmic sins, a resurrection occurs — the fiery transmutation

---

[8] Matt. 16:24.

of the lower nature and its unification with the spirit, or the Heavenly Father. This fiery renewal breaks the vicious circle of Karma.

The Fiery Cross is the symbol of the *swastika* (*Sanskrit*, "well-being"), whose motion is caused by the presence of opposite poles. Everyone has their own rhythm associated with the rotation of the cross. Initially, man must establish himself as an individual; for the first forty-two years of his life, the rotation of his cross is directed inwards; he absorbs everything that is outside by way of knowledge and information. When the balance is reached, then the cross must be reset to an outward rotation — to return. The individuality, the Karma of Love, begins its task of giving to the world all the treasures that the man has gathered in his Chalice for many lives. In this way we may observe the simultaneous rotation of the two crosses: one — inside, the other — outside. And when these two crosses unite in harmonious movement, the symbol of balance appears — the swastika, or the sign of the Fiery Cross of Life, or the "Seal of the Heart," which marks the High Spirits.

DARKNESS — the absence of the Light; unspiritualized matter, in a state of Chaos. Among humanity at large, there are certain individuals who bear in their structure these currents of chaos, destruction, and evil.

The darkness has its own hierarchy, and although its head was isolated long ago and is now exiled to Saturn, it is still quite strong. In contrast to Shambhala, located high in the mountains, the black brotherhood established its stronghold at the lowest point, burrowing into subterranean layers closer to the earthly core, in order to gain strength from its fire. One should not underestimate the hierophants of evil, because they know many secrets of Nature, especially the ones relating to the mortal quaternary of human bodies. However, the domain of the Supreme Triad and spirituality is inaccessible to them.

The servants of the darkness now act under the guise of "bearers of light." A great many hold key positions in the organizations intended to bear the Light and undermine them from within. Therefore, one may often notice how representatives of some organizations condemn those of others, despite the fact that the ideas of the Light are one.

GLOSSARY

They manipulate the sources coming from the Light, cleverly selecting quotes to defame some other light source. And the human mind, being unable to comprehend the multifold facets of the same Truth, blindly falls into this trap, not realizing that man himself is becoming a servant of the darkness. That is why it is so important to listen to one's heart, which is incapable of falling into the snares prepared for the mind. But with rare exceptions, such organizations are headed by leaders who truly serve the Light and humanity. Moreover, the black brotherhood has set up their own "world government," which attempts to destructively influence the policies of earthly leaders, especially of those countries having the most points of Light.

The hierophants of the darkness use the Signs and Symbols of the Light. But in doing so they destroy themselves, for these signs are bearers of the Fiery Force, which is impossible to apply in a harmful manner. Thus, one may remember the example of the swastika, when those who used this solar symbol of Life for evil ended up only punishing themselves.

The Light and the darkness are the two poles of the gross world. Both are magnetic and fill space with their fires, attracting the related elements that are inherent in the soul of every man. And man has the right of free choice between the phenomena of both poles. However, one should bear in mind that the darkness is temporary, for it acts contrary to the Laws of Evolution, while the Light is eternal.

DEATH — a birth into a new life — a life richer with opportunities and beauty than earthly existence. One's entire human life on the Earth, from the very first days, should be viewed as a preparation for life in the Higher Worlds, for man is a sower here and a reaper there.

For good, spiritual people, the transition into the Subtle World is facilitated by the Higher Spirits, who take care of them and help them to adapt. Similar attention is shown them during the final minutes before the transition, when their consciousness is being prepared for the impending change. It is not wise to mourn over the deceased, for no one departs before the Karma-appointed date, and who knows where they are better off — on the Earth or in the Higher World. Premature death is also determined by the Law of Cause and Effect.

In this case, the man remains in the near-Earth layers for as many years as he had left as a dweller of the Earth — if he is a good person, he just falls asleep for this period of time. Suicide is one of the most serious crimes, with terrible consequences for the future evolution of the spirit.

It has been said, and truly, that "sleep is similar to death." And if death be the transition of man from the world of causes to the world of effects, then the state of sleep may be regarded as a stay in the world of effects on a miniature scale; these effects may serve as a basis for judging the causes underlying the effects over the course of the preceding day. In this frame of reference, a dream can be viewed as a test and examination of one's daytime thoughts, and the affirmation of one's thoughts just before going to sleep is particularly important. Man may judge the depth and sincerity of daily decisions by his dreams. For example, if a man drives out an impure thought during the day, but it returns at night, then he has not yet been completely liberated from it. This enables man to carry out a strict self-examination of his true nature and prepare himself for the life in the Subtle World.

In the scriptures of the Initiates, earthly lives are called the *dreams of the Earth*. Man awakes from them after death, for death is a liberation from the illusions of the Earth. This is followed by the illusions of the Subtle and Mental Worlds. Only the Fiery World is real, for the first three are transient and temporary, albeit very long. That is why all the Teachings of Light urge people to free themselves from terrestrial illusions, negative feelings, thoughts, habits, and passions, for it will be too late to do this in the Higher Worlds.

Death as such does not exist, since everything flows from one form into another. If man has been so bad and wicked during his lives that all his bright fires are extinguished, then comes the so-called "death of the spirit." But even this is not death within the context of Infinity, because once the Divine Seed leaves this man, it begins its evolution from scratch, under completely new conditions. And the Seed is allowed as many chances as necessary for the man it has endowed with life to start following the path of the Light. Of course, this might take billions of years.

Nevertheless, the scenario in which man grows old and dies is a violation of Cosmic Laws, resulting from Lucifer's desire to separate the Earth and its inhabitants from the Higher Worlds. Hence death symbolizes involution, whereas life is the emblem of evolution.

DESTINY — the course of life, conditional upon one's free will, Karma, and the stars. Everyone's fate is actually in their own hands. But whatever be the personal destiny of a particular individual, one thing is certain: their entire future is decided through attachment to one of the poles — either the Light or the darkness. There is no middle ground, for everyone has to educe the potential of either positive or negative qualities within themselves.

It is the polarity that permits the phenomenon of transmutation, for it is impossible to transform something that is not revealed on the poles. Even a negative potential enables one to express it positively to an equivalent degree. Those who are in the middle are not suitable for evolution, because they have nothing to show. Jesus Christ said: "I know thy works, that thou art neither cold nor hot: I would thou wert cold or hot. So then because thou art lukewarm, and neither cold nor hot, I will spue thee out of my mouth."[9] That is why, the Teacher would rather deal with a thief or a harlot than a lukewarm follower, for the former's potential can be transformed into its positive opposite, while the latter, try as he might, will not succeed in achieving anything. Certainly, the fate of those who consciously remain on the side of the darkness is, to say the least, unenviable. But even more tragic is the destiny of those who convert the bright qualities of spirit into dark ones, for the higher they climb, the harder they fall.

DISTANT WORLDS — the other planets in our Solar System, such as Venus, Jupiter, Uranus, and Pluto, as well as other star systems, for example, the constellations of Canis Major, Orion, Coma Berenices, and the Pleiades.

All planets and stars in the Universe are home to living beings, but they have varying degrees of tenuity in their matter structures.

---

[9] Rev. 3:15–16.

Therefore, people cannot see them either with the naked eye or with their telescopic devices, which are as yet far from perfect.

The Seven Great Teachers of Humanity, together with 144,000 High Spirits, who "follow the Lamb whithersoever He goeth,"[10] came to the Earth from the Distant Worlds to help humanity, most of them nearly eighteen million years ago. Gradually, they will leave the Earth, and their places will be taken by the Spirits, who have passed through their evolution on the Earth and attained the degree of Masters.

DOUBT — the progeny of the dark influences, aimed at leading man away from his evolutionary path. Doubt extinguishes fires in man and opens the way for other evils, such as ignorance, negation, fear, and treachery, to come in.

Doubt is not to be confused with *alertness*. The former comes from the brain and the thoughts it has generated, having a distinct personal and selfish colouring, while the latter is the voice of the heart, trying to warn about danger.

DZYAN (*Tibetan*) — Secret Wisdom, Knowledge.

EARTH — the youngest planet in the Solar System, called the *Cradle of Gods* by the Masters. It is a living conscious being, governed by Cosmic Laws. In the esoteric tradition, it is believed that the Mother and Father of the Earth is the Sun, whose feminine aspect is represented by Venus and masculine aspect by Mars.

The Earth is the successor to the Moon, which gave to the planet all its vital force, and life from the Moon migrated to the Earth, clothing itself in new vestures. As a rule, a planet that yields its life-force to another planet becomes its satellite until a New Round of Evolution begins. The Moon significantly affects the Earth and maintains its balance.

Like everything else in the Solar System, the Earth has a septenary structure. Thus it has seven bodies, or globes, or spheres, which concentrically interlace with one another, comprising a Planetary Chain. These globes are the invisible spheres of the Subtle, Mental,

---

[10] Rev. 14:4.

GLOSSARY

and Fiery Worlds which surround the Earth. Each of these seven spheres represents a particular plane of consciousness or existence. It should be understood that the Planetary Chain is not comprised of the individual planets of the Solar System, but of different levels of the same planet.

Physical humanity lives on the most material globe, representing the Physical World. Souls, leaving this dense world, migrate to the higher spheres of the Earth — the Subtle, Mental, and more distant Fiery Planes. And then, in being incarnated on the Earth, the soul traces a reverse path — from the Fiery World to the Subtle, and finally to the Physical — thus passing through all seven globes of the Earth's Planetary Chain. In the Higher Worlds — that is, the Highest Spheres of the Earth, as well as on other, more advanced planets — there is no evil as such, though there is imperfection, or chiaroscuro.

The more material the world, the more of a binary nature it manifests. Thus, in the period of its greatest density — which had begun eighteen million years ago and peaked in the time of Atlantis — the Earth experienced its days of maximum confrontation between opposites: the Light and the darkness, Good and evil — which significantly worsened its condition.

And so in attempting to separate the Earth from the Distant Worlds, the forces of the darkness under Lucifer obscured the atmosphere around the planet in the Subtle Plane so that the rays from the Sun and other stars, sent to help humanity, could not penetrate. This contributed to parts of the planet being covered with ice. Its melting in the present age is a sign of the Era of Fire, where there is no place for any suggestion of cold. It means that the Earth is gradually being released from this "heritage" of Atlantis and that its atmosphere is being purified. However, people are not yet accustomed to the new stellar rays, having been deprived of them for centuries. Therefore, it is only the willingness and desire of humanity to assimilate these new energies that can completely destroy this heavy dirty-grey atmosphere, which is suffocating the entire planet from the viewpoint of the Subtle Plane.

The Earth must exist for the Seven Rounds of Evolution — the stages of its development and progress. During the first three Rounds, it takes shape and solidifies; through the Fourth (current) Round, it establishes itself and hardens, possessing the highest degree of materiality; and over the last three Rounds, it gradually rarefies, ending up as a star.

Such conditions as now exist on the Earth facilitate the quickest evolution of all its forms. It serves as an excellent launching platform for the spirit, providing the firmest possible foothold. So unique are the conditions of the Earth that it is studied by more than three thousand civilizations; indeed, the Earth is the epicentre where representatives come together from a variety of different planets, each of which brings their own ideas into the world.

EIGHTH SPHERE — a special channel connecting the Earth and Saturn, designed to take care of the outflow of human masses not suitable for evolution. These are the most vicious and hopelessly fallen people, who by and by will be decomposed into their primordial elements and begin their process of evolution anew on Saturn, under the extremely difficult conditions of this two-dimensional world.

ELIXIR OF LIFE — a miraculous potion, consisting of life-giving emanations from flowers and plants, forming a special combination of Light, Colour, and Sound. In combination with the crystallized fiery energy of the human heart, this Elixir is able to impart Immortality. For example, one of the ingredients is *strophanthus*, which strengthens the heart.

Studies by alchemists tell us that if man drinks it before he finds the Philosopher's Stone, the Elixir of Life will become for him the elixir of death. The Philosopher's Stone is a Solar Stone in the heart which constitutes its Fiery-White Core. And the quest for it — that is, accumulation of fiery energy and growth of the heart crystal, can be undertaken only while one remains in the dense conditions encountered during one's many lives on the Earth. Whereas, in the Higher Worlds, man reaps the effects of his earthly life. Therefore, it

GLOSSARY

is important to listen for the guidance of the vigilant heart in order to make the right choices in life and not be deluded by earthly illusions, which only lead to the priceless treasure going to waste. Thus, if the man has dissipated his heart crystal by the time he draws near to death, then the Elixir will have no effect on him and might even result in unforeseen consequences. But if he has lived a spiritual life, devoted his labours to the Light, and accumulated the crystal of a particular energy constant, then he may continue to exist in the same body for as long as it meets his need. This is why, as a rule, the Elixir of Life is given only to those who serve the good of the Evolution.

Many of the Great Teachers possessed this Elixir of Immortality. The first to experience it in the conditions of the earthly existence was the Lord Rákóczi, known as the Count of Saint-Germain, who was responsible for the testing of new formulas. Hence He has gone down in history as a most mysterious character, appearing in different centuries, remaining ever young.

The Cosmic Law of Expediency does not currently permit the wide application of the Elixir among the masses of people or its production on an industrial scale. In the future, when the multitude of destructive souls disappears, the Great Teachers will impart the formula of the Elixir of Life to the best scientists on the planet.

The Elixir of Immortality is also given at the level of the currents crystallized in the books of the Light. The perception of such books by the heart facilitates the accumulation of the Fiery-White Core. Additionally, each Teaching of Light, provided that the commandments given there are fulfilled, leads to a process of fiery purification and hence to the growth of the heart crystal as well. And the higher the level of development of spirituality, the broader will be the consciousness allowing man to consciously exist in all his seven bodies and in all the Worlds accessible to him. This is how true Immortality is achieved.

It should be borne in mind that the Currents of Immortality now pouring forth over the Earth affect only those who have already found their own Philosopher's Stone. Otherwise, they either simply will not work, or will result in unexpected alchemical reactions.

ESOTERIC (*Greek,* "inner") — hidden, secret; intended solely for Initiates with the aim of avoiding use by untrained people that might result in destructive consequences.

ETERNITY — an aspect of Infinity, the source and ultimate destination of all phenomena in the manifested world; that is, the place of existence of all that was, is, and will be. Eternity and Infinity are where the life of the Spirit is visible, creating ever new forms of life from eternal Matter, but by spiral ascent, wherein one can develop and perfect one's self endlessly.

Each atom, along with its energies, originates from the fathomless depths of Eternal Infinity. They constitute forms of life, forever flowing from one shape to another with every new cycle. After each phenomenon comes one more advanced, and so on forever throughout a never-ending chain of cause and effect. But everything is linked with everything else by countless connecting threads, for they are all One.

From the One Incognizable Divine Principle in Infinite Eternity, numerous Universes unfold, each with its own Mission and Cosmic Laws. Here, in turn, the Supreme Spirits, who were once human beings, create worlds that enable every spirit to evolve and multiply their might without limit, in accordance with prevailing Laws. Each world provides a limitless field for the manifestation of the spirits' creative power, from its very early stages to the creation of planets, stars, and whole star systems. And all the worlds differ from one another in their unique diversity of forms. Of course, there are worlds that are similar to each other, but no two are exactly the same. There are worlds where human spirits have attained such a degree of might and power that they may be legitimately called Gods. There are even higher worlds than that. But there are also antiworlds, or worlds of Chaos, which are not made manifest in spirit.

As above, so below; as here, so there; as now, so then; and vice versa. In this way, observing the evolution of the planet Earth, one can understand by analogy the evolution of the entire Universe in Eternity, too.

GLOSSARY

EVOLUTION — a cosmic necessity, which consists in eternal and endless development, self-perfection, and advancement into Infinity of all that is made manifest in the world, according to Cosmic Laws.

The uninterrupted Chain of Evolution can be symbolically pictured as a spiral, arranged loop by loop. With the point of exit at their base, a number of rings begin growing in a spiral formation, expanding indefinitely. Then they start to narrow and return to their initial position, where they experience a brand new beginning — and this is only one small link of a Great Chain. Each new round of the spiral presupposes a repetition of the loops already traversed before ascending a step higher into Infinity.

Evolution cannot be stopped. Even that which appeared unable to evolve according to the Laws of the Universe, disintegrates into a primordial state in order to have a chance to ascend again and again the rungs of Evolution from the very beginning. After all, a step backwards sometimes gives an opportunity to gain a firmer foothold, from which one can push off and strive towards reaching the intended goal at a speed many times faster than before.

EXOTERIC (*Greek*, "outer") — public; intended for the masses.

FAITH — a foretaste of knowledge; the knowledge of the heart, inaccessible through earthly feelings, but accessible through the spirit. Faith is the actual motive force of life, for one must first believe in the possibility of something before starting to realize it in life. Hence the greatest deeds, achievements, discoveries, and inventions have all been realized through faith.

Faith is the fiery energy of the heart, manifested in action. Therefore, faith and confidence are two exceedingly mighty magnets, with the power to attract the elements necessary for the realization of a right desire. Hence, unwavering faith — in the face of everything and against all odds — underlies the success of any worthy undertaking. By contrast, a mere intellectual faith, without the energy of the heart, is unsteady and thence fruitless.

Faith can also be the spirit's reminiscences of what was predestined for the world as far back as the beginning of the Grand Cycle of Evolution. In other words, it is the spirit's knowledge of what is beyond all doubt, and must absolutely be asserted; it might also be termed a *realization of the future*, of that which inevitably must be. Such knowledge is consciously discernible by the High Spirits; hence their firm and unconditional faith in humanity.

FAITH, HOPE, AND LOVE — the Three Persons of Sophia, the Spirit of Wisdom, Love, and Truth, the Greatest Spirit of the Feminine Principle not of earthly evolution, who has Her personifications in many religions of the world: Isis, Ishtar, Lakshmi, Tara, Athena, Mary, the Mother of the World, and so on.

Sophia veiled Her Face from humanity after the Atlanteans humiliated Woman and the Cult of the Spirit. Hence, in ancient times, only the Initiates possessed any part of the secret knowledge of Sophia — the Power and Wisdom of God. From them, fragments of this knowledge ended up in the hands of the Gnostics. However, despite the fact that Sophia forbade any mention of Her until the Time should come — and there is no information about Her in Christian canonical texts — Her Name invisibly descended and abode in the hearts of the very best people. Thus the most beautiful temples and icons were dedicated to Sophia, especially in Eastern Europe.

Christ and Sophia are One, like Spirit and Soul, constituting the head of the Hierarchy of Light of the Solar System. Sophia sent Christ forth at the time of the First Advent and stayed beside Him. And She alone is able to give life to Him who descends into the world during the Second Advent. And although this Spirit cannot become incarnate as a human being on the Earth in Her full strength, She sends Her Rays to accompany Her Daughters — who can justly be considered incarnations of Sophia — on the thorny path of service to humanity. For example, Sophia conducted the most important Initiations as the Eternally Young Virgin-Mother in Atlantis and as Isis in Egypt. That is why She is called the *Revealer of Mysteries* in the gnostic texts.

Two thousand years ago, Christ, having sown the first seeds of Divine Love on the Earth, left His Soul on probation, so that She might continue to sustain these shoots of Love. All that time, Sophia was to remain concealed in the body of an earthly woman, undying on

GLOSSARY

the plane of Her subtle bodies. Thus, Pistis, Elpis, and Agape (*Greek*, "Faith, Hope, and Love") periodically replaced each other, never abandoning this world. One Hypostasis departs only when the following one is born, and Her subtle bodies flow into the womb of the woman who is the bearer of the next Hypostasis. In this way Sophia and Her Rays have continuously manifested themselves on the Earth for two thousand years.

In their physical bodies, each time traversing the difficult and thorny path of self-sacrifice for the good of humanity, Faith, Hope, and Love carry out the highest Cosmic Tasks that often remain beyond the sight and knowledge of the masses. Sophia, being a reflection of Christ, must traverse His Path, and therefore Her Hypostases, too, are crucified morally and physically. Therefore, they have frequently perished at the hands of the same killers.

Faith passed through the religions that the Messengers of Light gave to humanity. Faith alone could accustom people who had long lost the ability to see and hear the Higher Worlds to thinking about their existence and connection with them. These religions soon experienced distortion of their teachings. Messengers were exterminated, but they were replaced by others. And so Faith has never faded in human hearts.

Hope went hand in hand with knowledge. The Wisdom of Sophia descends to humanity through scientific discoveries imparted to scientists by the Messengers of Wisdom. Many of them were burnt at the stake for their discoveries, which were misunderstood, but were subsequently incarnated anew in order that these discoveries might be embraced by following generations.

The most difficult path towards humanity was experienced by the Third Hypostasis of Sophia — that is, Love. Every manifestation of sacrificial Love was trampled upon by people right from the start. But until all Three Persons were established in the world, the Mother of the World — Sophia — was unable to descend to the Earth. It is through Love alone that the synthetic Ray of Sophia may be made manifest, uniting within herself all the Rays of Faith, Hope, and Love.

FALSEHOOD — the instrument of the darkness, which causes ugliness and destruction.

FALSEHOOD — FEAR

Thoughts and words are energies. When thought corresponds to its expression in words, the energy of action is doubled. When thought and words are diametrically opposed, one type of energy clashes with the other in an attempt at mutual annihilation. In space, such dissonance engenders a chaos of tossing energies, strengthening the forces of the darkness and destruction. For man, falsehood becomes a painful blow that tries to tear his essence to pieces. In this way, falsehood extinguishes the life-giving fires in his body, and this in turn may lead to bouts of illness. Therefore, it is more beneficial and practical to tell the truth or to simply keep quiet. We are not talking here about inadvertent mistakes — anyone can make a mistake. It is the conscious and deliberate distortion of reality that is especially harmful, above all for the liar.

FEAR — an obscurer of consciousness, which paralyses man's will and saps his strength, thereby attracting exactly those things that he is afraid of. A human heart in a state of fear loses its radiations and envelops itself in an ashen-grey mist, which extinguishes the fires within; at the same time, the aura, being devoid of vibrations, seems to congeal.

Fear is, first of all, a *thought*, which in turn influences human consciousness. Therefore, it is possible to eliminate it by another, *fearless* thought. If the thought of fear enters the human aura, its energy essence attempts to stay there as long as possible. And this means vibrating and receiving sustenance through causing anxiety about anything — just so as to maintain perpetual motion within itself. That is why fear has many faces and why its guises are so diverse and deceptive. Just one tiny hint of fear begins to pull in other fear-vibrating hints from space. In this way the originating thought flows from one form into another, turning man into its slave. Each black flash of fear only serves to reinforce the darkness. So, one can only imagine how much "sustenance" is supplied to the dark hierarchy, for example, by the single viewing of a horror movie in a cinema.

Alertness and caution are not fear, but the exact opposite: the protecting of one's self from the influence of the fear-thoughts the darkness uses to saturate space.

FIERY BAPTISM — the spiritual transfiguration and fiery transmutation of humanity and the planet under the influence of the Fire which comes from the Cosmos. In other words, this is the contact of the human body and all living things with new fiery energies — their assimilation or destruction of unprepared bodies. All ancient Teachings have forewarned us of the inevitable Age of Fire.

In the period from 1924 to 1955, Helena Roerich, who carried on Helena Blavatsky's Mission, voluntarily and consciously agreed to undergo a kind of individual Fiery Baptism under the supervision of the Great Teachers; this was termed the *Fiery Experience*. Under ordinary terrestrial conditions, this is an excruciating and agonizing process, accompanied by extreme and persistent pains in the physical body. But the Mother of Agni Yoga, as the Masters of the Ancient Wisdom call her, had drained this cup to the dregs, thus helping them find the ways to alleviate the sufferings of the world when the time comes for all humanity to undergo the Fiery Baptism.

There are several main stages of the Fiery Baptism which are inextricably linked to the Advent on the Earth of the Supreme Spirit, the Messiah, known to all nations but under different Names: Christ, Maitreya, Mahdi, Kalki Avatar, Saoshyant, and so on. He is the Fire, who administers the Fiery Baptism. The Periods of His Coming, and therefore of the Fiery Baptism, have always been cloaked in strictest secrecy and could not be disclosed prematurely. That is why all sacred scriptures have veiled these Periods in some manner. According to many prophecies, right at the end of the Kali Yuga (*Sanskrit*, "Black Age"), Maitreya was to be incarnated in Shambhala. Thus, in the Puranas, the period of the Kali Yuga is calculated in gigantic numbers, the true meaning of which is known solely to the Initiates. Helena Blavatsky, too, was unable to disclose the dates of the manifestation of the Kalki Avatar, and therefore used the same figures.

However, in the first half of the 20th century, the correct calculations of the end date of the Black Age began to spread among the population of India — the year 1942, which Mahatma M. also confirmed to Helena Roerich. At precisely the same time, the process of the Fiery Transfiguration of the world commenced and He, having passed through all the planets of the Solar System, was born at level of the Supreme Triad, or at the level of the Fiery World in Shambhala for the first time on the Earth, since until that time He could only manifest Himself at the level of the Quaternary of His Bodies. Thus, the Great Lord of Shambhala, Morya, and Maitreya — are One and the same Supreme Spirit, who is the Solar Hierarch, known as Sanat Kumara (*Sanskrit*, "Eternal Youth").

Moreover, on 1 August 1943, the predicted Cosmic Event occurred, namely a rare combination of stars and planets at the time of the solar eclipse, indicated in the Vishnu Purana: "When the Sun and Moon, and the lunar asterism Tishya, and the planet Jupiter, are in one mansion, the Krita [Golden] Age shall return."[11] This event was widely celebrated in India, Tibet, and Mongolia; solemn services were held in all Buddhist temples. In 1949 the Great Lord of Shambhala, now for the first time in possession of all of His Fiery Might, entered the final battle to defeat Lucifer and his dark army.

From that moment began the preparation for the Advent of the King of Shambhala into the world for the final overthrow of the darkness. The whole world is awaiting the coming of the Messiah, and each people gives Him a very dear and beautiful Name, often unaware that these Names belong to One and the same Supreme Spirit. But, as always, the specific Periods could not be revealed prematurely. Nevertheless, correct hints and even exact dates were predicted by the greatest prophets, but people misunderstood them.

For example, in 1568 there was published the complete collection of the predictions of Nostradamus, who was an Initiate and knew how to safeguard the most sacred knowledge. Hence no one is able to understand his indications without the key; moreover, they bear the imprint of the Dark Ages. So, his famous quatrain 72 of Century X says: "The year 1999, seventh month, from the sky will come a Great King of Terror." It should be understood that for humanity, which by then had lapsed into the darkness of ignorance, the Messiah, who was to put an end to the Black Age, represented a direct threat.

---

[11] *Vishnu Purana*, Book IV, Chapter XXIV, transl. Horace Hayman Wilson.

Another great prophet, Edgar Cayce, predicted the exact year of the Advent of the Messiah, when commenting on the mathematical and astronomical calculations that had been found in the Great Pyramid of Giza: "the entrance of the Messiah in this period — 1998" (30 June 1932);[12] "a Liberator of the world ... must enter again at that period, or in 1998" (29 July 1932).[13]

The Lord Morya in Book II of *Agni Yoga, Leaves of Morya's Garden: Illumination*, first published in 1925, says: "So, I shall gather under the Banner of the Spirit 1,000,000,000 — this will be the sign of My army. Calculate when this manifestation will be fulfilled and the seven banners will be affirmed!"[14] It is known that the cyphers or zeros are used as a veil to conceal the real numbers. And in this case, esoterically, three zeros signify nine. That is, the year 1999 was indicated by the Lord M.

At the same time, Helena Roerich, not being empowered to speak openly, gave repeated warnings to her correspondents. For example: "There is time as yet, for the last Cosmic Period will strike in a few decades, but our century will not be able to see its end." (23 June 1934);[15] "In the Gospel of Matthew, Chapter 24, Verses 27–39, the Advent and Judgement Day awaiting our planet are described rather precisely, but you will have time to grow old before this day, although partial catastrophes may occur earlier." (12 April 1935);[16] "The decisive hour of the Judgement Day is not far off, and many children will live until this *day*. That is why the Teaching of the Lord M. is given so urgently

---

[12] Edgar Cayce, *The Complete Edgar Cayce Readings* (Virginia Beach, VA: A.R.E. Press, 2006), CD-ROM, Reading №5748–5.

[13] Ibid. Reading №294–151.

[14] *Uchenie Zhivoi Etiki* [Teaching of Living Ethics], vol. 2 (Minsk: Zvezdy Gor, 2007), p. 11.

[15] Helena Roerich, *Pis'ma Eleny Rerikh: 1932–1955* [Letters of Helena Roerich] (Novosibirsk: Viko, 1993), p. 36.

[16] Roerich, *Pis'ma Eleny Rerikh: 1929–1939*, vol. 1 (Minsk: Zvezdy Gor, 2009), p. 474.

and so many extraordinary signs are being poured forth upon the Earth, but people are blind and deaf!" (11 October 1935).[17]

On 15 September 1989 many people in Salsk, Russia, observed an unexplained phenomenon known as the *Salsk Celestial Code*. On that day, huge squares appeared in the sky. At first, the squares were empty, but soon mathematical signs, question marks, and numbers began to appear inside the geometric shapes, as though someone were drawing them in the sky. After transforming the signs into numbers and the numbers into the Glagolitic alphabet (in which each letter has its own number, just like the old Hebrew), researchers deciphered the following message: "To Rus, Russians. Jesus Christ, the Son of God, alias God, will save you on 19 July 1999. (signature) His Mother."[18]

And so the Great Period of 1998–1999 was marked by the further descent of Maitreya into Shambhala, from the Fiery World into the Subtle World of the Earth. In 1998, the Sacrament of the descent of the Spirit of the Messiah into the aura of His Mother took place in the Tower of Chung in Shambhala. This was followed a year later by the beginning of the Great Fiery Baptism of the planet and humanity on 19 July 1999, as well as the Final Choice. The total solar eclipse of 11 August 1999 coincided with a planetary alignment. The planets arranged in the shape of a Grand Cross — the sign of the Son of Man in the sky. It is precisely this Cosmic Event, proclaiming the Advent of Christ, that is described in the Bible: "Immediately after the tribulation of those days shall the sun be darkened, and the moon shall not give her light, and the stars shall fall from heaven, and the powers of the heavens shall be shaken. And then shall appear the sign of the Son of Man in heaven: and then shall all the tribes of the earth mourn, and they shall see the Son of Man coming in the clouds of heaven with power and great glory."[19]

---

[17] Roerich, *Pis'ma Eleny Rerikh: 1929–1939*, vol. 2, p. 44.

[18] The message was deciphered by Alexei Priima and Mikhail Gaponov. More detailed explanations can be found in Chapter 4 in Alexei Priima's book *19 iiulia 1999: Konets Sveta?* [19 July 1999: The End of the World?] (Moscow: Tatianin Den, 1993).

[19] Matt. 24:29–30.

Since then, the inflow of the Cosmic Fire has intensified constantly every day, being accompanied by an anomalous increase or decrease in temperature. The new Fires of Transfiguration may have a destructive impact on physical bodies, causing extreme pains and other health problems, along with natural disasters such as earthquakes, floods, downpours, avalanches, and tornadoes. In addition, these energies, if not accepted, may cause revolutions and epidemics. If man's material organism is not able to accept the Fire, his body dies, but in his next incarnation he will be born in a body with a different formula. All this happens because human hearts are unable to assimilate the new currents, as people have not yet learnt to fulfil the Prime Commandment given by all Teachers in different periods of history — to *love*.

That is why humanity's spiritual decline, heartlessness, and inability to perceive the fiery energies of the Cosmos have threatened everyone with devastating cataclysms that could cause partial catastrophes — as happened with the continents of Lemuria and Atlantis — or completely destroy the planet. Edgar Cayce predicted this future for humanity by the end of the 20th century — a future people created with their own hands. But after the triumph over Lucifer, who did his utmost to implement this scenario, the entire Hierarchy of Light — together with enlightened people all over the world who had made their choice in favour of Good — managed to save the planet from destruction. And humanity has survived this period, completely unaware of their narrow escape.

The Mystery of the birth of the Highest Spirits on the Earth, especially the Messiah, has always been devoutly guarded by the White Brotherhood, just like the Periods. But now some part of it may be revealed. Each Saviour of the World is born in the Ray which dominates in a particular territorial space and period of time. This Ray projects onto the corresponding energy centre of the Mother and in this way brings about an Immaculate Conception and Birth, as recorded in the legends of almost all the Saviours proclaimed by various religions and beliefs. For example, Buddha appeared from the side of His Mother — this is the solar plexus, the third energy centre; the Immaculate Conception of Christ is the second centre, which is associated with the fifth. Humanity is now in the Fourth Round, which means that the fourth centre — the heart — should experience the greatest development. Consequently, the Conception and Birth of the Supreme Spirit must come through the heart. This is a higher level, called the *Third Fire*, which is typical for the most developed planets. If one projects this onto earthly conditions, then one can imagine that two people, thanks to their Fire of Love, create a Third Fire at the level of the heart, within the membrane of which, just as in an amniotic egg, a luminous creature is born. He may be borne for a long time by this pair, germinating in the heart of his mother for seven, nine, or even twelve years. And then, if this spirit feels compelled, he may be born on the physical plane, but his body will have a completely different material structure from that of Earth-dwellers. If not, he will go higher, and his parents will be able to see their baby in the Subtle World, where he will appear as an Angel or Archangel.

The Advent on the Earth of the Greatest Spirit of the Solar System comes about in like manner. Nevertheless, it should be borne in mind that His Coming proceeds in strict accordance with Cosmic Laws, taking billions of causes into consideration. No matter what the planet, He can be incarnated solely upon the call of its residents. By this time, the answer is being weighed on the Cosmic Scales as to whether people are waiting for Him: "yes" or "no." It is the same on the Earth: if "yes" outweighs "no," then He will be born in the flesh, and people will be able to behold Him with their own physical eyes. If humanity says "no," then the eyes of the heart alone will be capable of seeing Him. And, after fulfilling His invisible Mission, He will depart again, but higher this time, tracing a gigantic circle. In the Plan of Evolution it is foreordained that the Messiah must come in the flesh, being visible physically. But He cannot violate the Cosmic Laws. This Earth belongs to the Kingdom of Humanity, and it is the people's prerogative whether to invite Him into their house or not. Moreover, two thousand years ago people deprived Him of His physical flesh. By their own will, they signed the death-sentence: they had no use for God in a human body.

According to the Cosmic Laws, the Messiah has the right to be born in the Heart, descending only as far as the fourth level, which,

GLOSSARY

from the perspective of the Cosmos, is the Physical World of the Earth, but at the same time it does not cause discomfort to people who are not waiting for Him. Under the Law of Expediency, the absence of a response from the heart supposes the *Advent* to take place in the Spirit, the *birth* on the level of the Centre of the Heart and the manifestation of the *Androgynous Fires*, which proceed from heart to heart. The hearts alone are able to perceive the Fire of Immortality, in other words — the Fire of Eternal Youth, which Sanat Kumara brings. It is clear that if He were born in a physical body, it would be a struggle and a waste of Fires and Energies, which is inadmissible according to the Laws of the Universe. Suffice it to recall how people derided Helena Blavatsky and the Mahatmas — the Lords of Shambhala — when they, for the first time in the history of present humanity, revealed themselves to the public at large in the second half of the 19th century. The Messiah comes not to take away the sins of humanity just so that people might deride Him, call Him the Antichrist, and crucify Him again. The main goal — is to advance the Chain of Fiery Evolution. His Advent from the Supreme Divine Worlds transmits the mightiest current of the Fire, which gives an impetus for the Ascent up the Ladder of Evolution to all the Worlds — i.e., those located not only within the Solar System, but also beyond its boundaries.

The Periods of the Advent in the Physical World were obscurely indicated in *The Teaching of the Heart*, first published in 1998-2000: "The day and hour of the Advent of the Messiah is appointed in strict accordance with all available data, weighed on the Cosmic Scales. Questions of Universal importance are not solved through any earthly measurements. Our Fiery Calendar is different from yours, for all the combinations of invisible stellar currents are marked on it, along with visible ones. The Tiger, indicated on the clock face, moved the hand of the Clock towards the Dragon, although the Movement of the Earthly Clock had been adjusted in accord with the beat of the Cosmic Clock at the hour when the Cock crowed, heralding the awakening for the Earth."[20]

---

[20] *Uchenie Serdtsa* [Teaching of the Heart], vol. 3 (Moscow: Zvezda Vostoka, 2004), p. 373.

FIERY BAPTISM

The Calendar of Shambhala is known as the Calendar of the Kalachakra. According to it, 1998 is the year of the Tiger and the year of the Cock is 2005. Moreover, each year of the 60-year cycle of the Kalachakra Calendar is related to a corresponding minute on the clock face. Hence 2005 is the 19th year — the Sacred Number of the New World, known as far back as Ancient Egypt.

So, humanity foreknew neither the day nor the hour when on 19 July 2005, Sanat Kumara descended from Shambhala. His first colossal Impulse of the Most Powerful Fire occurred in the area of the sacred Mount Kailash, and lasted for 24 days: the currents of the Great Masculine Principle dominated for twelve days and then the currents of the Great Feminine Principle for the remaining twelve days. Not being androgynous, but binary, the world is able to absorb either one or the other pole, but not both at the same time. Everyone who was at that time in the area, noticed that even the grass was charred in the Himalayas. The forces of Nature were manifest in all their might: on one and the same day one could feel the strongest heat of the sun, followed by the most powerful cold, snow, and hail. This was how the gigantic energy waves expressed themselves — the waves which accompanied the descent of the Teacher of Teachers from Shambhala into the Dense World of the Earth. But all this happened at the level of the Heart, since it is not expedient for Him to be incarnated at a lower level.

In addition to the abovementioned reasons, the division into Masculine and Feminine Principles is also inappropriate now. If He were incarnated as a man — this would not be right, because the Epoch of Woman is coming. If He were embodied in a woman — the imbalance would be in the direction of the Feminine Principle, since today there are many men with evident female characteristics. In other words, this would tilt the balance of the matrix structures in the fabric of the manifest Physical World. Therefore, the lowest point of His descent is the Chalice, the heart of His Mother, Sophia, wherein He will be borne for a period of twelve years. It is shown symbolically on the miraculous icon of 1878 known as *The Inexhaustible Chalice*. Thus, Maitreya, as was foretold in the prophecies, has already been

GLOSSARY

ruling invisibly visible, performing the Fiery Baptism of humanity on the Earth.

In 2012, the Earth was enveloped by a most powerful incandescence of Fires coming from the surrounding constellations and Sirius, whose apogee occurred on 19 July. At the level of the heart's centre, the Chalice, the matrix structures, and people's subtle bodies, a new formula of the Light and of the New World was manifested. At the same time, the formula of the former world has lost its significance — that is, a symbolic "end of the (old) world" took place. The end of 2012 revealed the basic energy framework that will crystallize over the next three years and by the end of 2015 a new pattern will emerge. This will be "another" Earth at the level of energy resonance, which later on must result in an even greater unification of humanity and countries — at the geographical level as well.

For a period of twelve years ending in 2017, Sanat Kumara, visible only to the colleagues of Shambhala who have passed the high levels of Initiation, is transpiercing the entire planet with currents of Eternal Youth and Immortality through His Mother — along with the embodiment of twelve Apostles, each of whom bears their own Colour and Tone (with sharps and flats). But one of them carries the White Colour. And after that, as described above, on 19 July 2017, He will be born in the Subtle World as a Planetary Spirit.

Certainly, if the call of the hearts of Earth-dwellers is sufficiently strong that "yes" outweighs "no" on the Cosmic Scales and they are ready to accept a Fire of even greater incandescence, He will be able to manifest Himself in a "physical" body in the earthly world as well. This may happen at any time after the Final Choice, as soon as human hearts are ready. From the perspective of Cosmic Justice, humanity must return the Son to Mary at the age where She had lost Him because of the sentence pronounced by Earth-dwellers. Then His body will be visible to the "physical eyes" of those who are pure in heart, but this will be the densified subtle body, the "Glorious Body," composed of the matter in which Jesus Christ was resurrected and seen by His disciples.

It is interesting to note that the Messiah's Heavenly Nativity in 2017 was symbolically depicted in sacred texts long ago:

FIERY BAPTISM

"Maitreya, the best of men, will then leave the Tushita heavens, and go for his last rebirth into the womb of that woman. For ten whole months she will carry about his radiant body.... He, supreme among men, will emerge from her right side, as the sun shines forth when it has prevailed over a bank of clouds."[21]

"And there appeared a great wonder in heaven; a woman clothed with the sun, and the moon under her feet, and upon her head a crown of twelve stars. And she being with child cried, travailing in birth, and pained to be delivered."[22]

These citations should be understood with the help of an astrological key. In 2017, there will be a unique alignment of the celestial bodies: the Moon, Jupiter, Mercury, Mars, Venus, and Regulus; the Moon will be "under the feet" of the constellation of Virgo, "clothed with" the Sun, and the nine stars of Leo together with three planets (Mercury, Mars, and Venus) will form the "crown of twelve stars." Since ancient times, the planet Jupiter, the King of Planets, has been a planetary symbol of the Messiah, while Regulus, the King of Stars, is His stellar symbol. Thus, symbolically, the King of Kings will descend from the "Tushita heavens" through the aligned planets into the "womb" of Virgo, being represented as Jupiter, which will enter her "womb" for 42 weeks, or almost ten months. Similar findings indicating the significance of the year 2017 have also been discovered in the geometrical construction of the Great Pyramids in Egypt.[23]

However, as mentioned before, whether the Messiah will manifest Himself in the Physical World or not depends upon every single person and the collective will of the people of the Earth, since stars never force something to happen against human will, but merely create the necessary conditions. That is why it is absolutely impossible to say when exactly He will appear: in the coming years, decades, or

---

[21] *Maitreyavyakarana*, transl. Edward Conze.

[22] Rev. 12:1–2.

[23] More detailed research on these matters can be found in Chapter 12 of *The Coming Epiphany* by William Frederick, and Chapter 16 in *Signs of the End* by Daniel Matson. Do bear in mind that, in any case, no "end of the world" is coming.

GLOSSARY

centuries. But those who are really waiting for Him must be prepared, "for in such an hour as ye think not the Son of Man cometh."[24]

So, blessed are they who do not sleep, but watch; blessed are they who have preserved the purity of their souls; for, owing to the Fiery Baptism accomplished by the Solar Hierarch, their human structure will change over the next few decades. And in the subsequent generation, the children of those born after 2012 will give life to human beings who possess Immortality. Also, this process will enable all people currently living to reach the Higher Spheres when departing into the Subtle World, for the more they assimilate the Fires now pouring forth upon the Earth, the higher they will be able to rise in the Ethereal World. From now on, more and more people will have new abilities, and some of them will even succeed in conquering Time and Space and other mysteries of the Universe. And thus will the New Humanity summoned by Maitreya come into its own.

FIERY-WHITE CORE — a crystal situated in the heart of a living being: man, planet, star, etc. It is the crystallized Fire which has been accumulating for centuries. It could be called a *Solar Stone*, for it fills surrounding space with the flaming rays it emits.

The crystals of the fiery energy are deposited by using the life-currents it emits — either bright or dark. An equal amount of the light poured forth externally by the heart is crystallized in the form of deposits. Thus, the crystallized Fire of Light grows like a pearl, accumulating over long millennia through doing pure deeds for the good of the world and a selfless and spiritual devotion to Love. Besides, the crystal grows under the influence of external Fires. Negative energies, on the other hand, form, as it were, a black lump of coal in the heart without any inherent immunity from destruction, though capable of destroying its possessor.

The energy potential of the crystal is measured by the coefficient of *Argo* (*Greek*, "shining," "bright"). Everyone has their own number, accompanied by either a plus or a minus sign. This numerical value is expressed in energy units, being permanent as of the time of one's

---

[24] Matt. 24:44.

birth. It may stay unchanged for many incarnations, until it is removed from the point of death by some sort of good deed. For example, a good deed for the benefit of humanity increases the already accumulated value by a certain degree. After death the crystal remains on the Earth, but the man who has cultivated it, carries it away in his breast in the form of a blazing bundle of Fire. In his new incarnation, a man will embody this crystal once again in the dense form, and it will have an energy value equal to that of its previous life. In other words, this priceless treasure can be wasted, multiplied, or left as is.

The Argo coefficient of an ordinary man can vary within the range of one energy unit, slightly deflecting upwards or downwards. Once somebody has reached three units, they begin to attract the attention of the Great Teachers and come under their observation. Human beings with seven units are very rare — they work closely with the Hierarchy and may become Initiates. Someone who has attained nine units, as a rule, is already an Adept, though still living in a human body. By comparison, the Teacher of Teachers has twelve units.

In Tibet, these crystals are called *Ringsel* (*Tibetan*, "treasure"), which relates not only to the formations in the human heart, but also to the depositions of two glands in the brain: the pineal and the pituitary. After the cremation of a high lama, his closest disciples immediately begin to search for the Ringsel in the ashes, which is all that remains intact and undamaged. This crystal looks like a small seed of amber, unusually solid and beautiful. The bigger it is, the better, for a Master's disciples judge his level of spirituality by its size. Such sacred relics have been gathered, and now, with the blessing of His Holiness the 14th Dalai Lama, are presented on *Maitreya Heart Shrine Relic* exhibitions all over the world. Moreover, it is also known that the heart of Joan of Arc was not burnt in the flames, since it was filled with the crystallized and indestructible Fire.

FIRE — the supreme primary energy of the subtlest vibrations, which is the foundation of the entire Universe. The Fire, when manifesting itself, engenders Spirit and Matter — the Fire of Love, clothed in the matter of Thought — that compose the Triad of Light, Colour, and Sound, the source of all that exists.

GLOSSARY

The Fire is the main element and energy of the Cosmos — all the chemical elements and energies, known and unknown, are simply modifications of the Fire that saturates all of space. Electricity is spatial Fire. Every manifestation of matter and spirit is merely the expression of Fire. As the primary energy, it breathes life — and therefore consciousness — into everything. Thus, the Fire lies at the basis of each and every creature, every form of life. That is why all the Teachings speak of the Unity of All, the One Principle, from which the Universe arose. In ancient times, from the very beginning of the conscious evolution of humanity, the Cult of Fire was above all.

Everything is endowed with the quality of fire, for the manifestation of any object is preceded by a thought that creates a particular matrix, which already bears the element of the fiery property in its fundamental principle. In like manner, all human actions, processes, feelings, and thoughts are connected with the Fire. Indeed it would be impossible for them to exist without its participation.

The gradation of the Fire is infinitely diverse, ranging from the lowest forms of expression — e.g., visible flame on the physical plane — to the invisible Light of the Highest Layers. One type of flame may be divided into hundreds of subtypes. Within the flame one can notice a strict geometrical construction. The number, colour, and sound absorbed into the form are the inalienable characteristics of the Fire. They who succeed in comprehending the sevenfold nature of the Flame will find that the Fire is multifaceted and, when analysing any given spectrum, will be able to discover the number that comprises 144,000 types in the gamut of the fiery radiations. But this is just the starting-point for characterizing the conditions for the creation of Life on the Earth.

There are creative bright Fires and destructive dark ones. And so the appropriate type of Fire is applied to each phenomenon. Being magnetic, it attracts other consonant and related Fires from space. For instance, a lit candle evokes spatial Fire to a manifestation on the physical plane. If the candle goes out, the invisible Fire that has been attracted still remains out there in space. And so the Fire summoned from space with good intentions will continue to bring bliss, even after its physical extinction. In the same way, every flash of Fire in man — in other words, his thought, feeling, action, and so on — attracts corresponding Fires from space (which contains all Fires, both bright and dark). All surrounding spheres are ablaze with Fires, aspiring to contact anyone who is in accord with them. Dark fires — or negative phenomena — are extremely tempting and infectious.

Habit is a collector, accumulator, and crystallizer of Fires kindred to it in the human body. Occasional flashes are of little significance, since only deeply ingrained qualities are important, for their magnetism has a constant effect. Therefore man's destiny and his ability to influence others are determined by the magnetism of his Fires or auric radiations resulting from the corresponding crystalline deposits in his body.

Bright Fires prevail over dark ones, for the scope of lower, black fires is limited by the borders of their manifestation, while Bright Fires are boundless. For each dark fire there is a corresponding bright one which subordinates it. Control over one's thoughts, words, actions is the first step towards mastering the fiery power hidden in man.

The elements of Earth, Water, Air, and Fire are controlled from the top downwards. Fire governs everything; Air is superior to Water and Earth; and Water is over Earth. Spatial Fire moves the masses of air and water, warming both them and the Earth, winds cause waves to rise, while winds and waters destroy and bring into motion the masses of the most inert dense matter, i.e., Earth. As a creature of the Fire, a man treading his spiritual path can consciously preserve the Fire in his body in the form of a crystal. After accumulating a sufficient number of energy units, he can use this power to govern the elements of Earth, Water, and Air which are subordinate to it. Hence a man who has mastered the spatial Fire literally becomes omnipotent.

FLOWER — the concentration of spatial fiery energies in an earthly form. Crystals of vital energy are precipitated, as it were, in the creation of floral pollen. One can say that the Heaven settles down on the Earth in flowers, which form the only living link between the Heaven

GLOSSARY

and the Earth. Flowers transmute cosmic energy and purify space. If it were not for them, the Earth would be devoid of half its vitality.

The form of a flower has an ethereal origin. Its refinement, colour, and fragrance testify to the subtlety of the energies concealed within it. The flowers of the Earth, however lovely their beauty and variety, are merely weak and imperfect reflections of the indescribable beauty of the flowers of the Fiery World. Fiery flowers are in constant motion, living their own lives. They are resplendent with a tremendous variety of extraordinarily beautiful and diverse flaming colours, tones, and shades, exuding ethereally marvellous aromas.

The energy centres of man, especially the solar plexus, are nourished by the emanations of flowers. Hence one's favourite flower often has a special significance, since the spirit can express itself more strongly in the presence of a certain plant.

Flowers make the best medicine, but healing comes only from the emanations of natural flowers, not those that have been cut or picked.

FORM — the means by which the spirit attains self-knowledge. The purpose of life is to know the world and one's self, and this is possible solely through the forms in which these are manifested. Hence the spirit is continuously creating new forms from eternal matter, clothing itself therein for a gradual accumulation of life experiences and the expansion of consciousness, thanks to whatever environment it is made manifest in. As soon as certain qualities and properties of the spirit are developed, it discards its outward form and shifts into another.

The consciousness that clings to its external form dooms itself to death along with this form. But the consciousness that aspires to the spirit and concentrates thereon, continues its life without further dependence on the life of outer coverings, and so attains true Immortality.

There are the worlds of these manifested forms, including those available to humanity, but there are also the Worlds of Eternal Light, devoid of forms — these are the worlds of creative principles and energies. Creative energies have no forms, but still they are material, for they consist of varieties of Primeval Matter.

GOD — the Divine, Unchangeable, Invariable, and Infinite Principle; the eternally Unknowable Cause of All that exists; omnipresent, all-pervading, visible and invisible spiritual Nature, which exists everywhere, in which everything lives, moves, and has its being; the Absolute, including the potential of all things as well as all universal manifestations. Upon being made manifest, out of its Absolute Oneness God becomes the Absolute of infinite differentiation and its consequences — relativity and opposites. God has no gender and cannot be imagined as a human being. In the Holy Scriptures, God is Fire, God is Love — the one primeval energy that conceives the worlds.

In the case when this word does not refer to the above, in ancient Teachings it has always meant the collectivity of the working and intelligent Forces in Nature. Thus, the world is ruled by the Creative Forces of the Cosmos, together constituting the limitless Hierarchy of Light, known as Jacob's Ladder in the Bible.

However, the Great Unknown was, is, and always will be hidden from the eyes of those who live in the manifested world. The Primal Cause, the Absolute, has been and will be unknowable — forever and ever.

GODS — the Spirits of the Higher Spheres and Distant Worlds. In Tibet, such a Spirit is called by the ancient word *Lha* (*Tibetan*, "Spirit," "God"), which covers the entire series of celestial Hierarchies. Every Supreme Concept of the Cosmos is personified in a High Spirit, who takes a human form as well. That is why every ancient religion has a pantheon of Gods, each of whom, being an embodiment of a certain Idea, represents a particular Force of Nature.

The Sons of God, the Sons of Light, the Sons of Heaven, the Sons of Fire, the Sons of Reason, the Archangels, the Regents of Planets, the Masters of Wisdom, the Bodhisattvas (*Sanskrit*, "Enlightenment Beings"), the Dhyan Chohans (*Sanskrit*, "Lords of Light"), the Rishis (*Sanskrit*, "Sages of Insight"), the Kumaras (*Sanskrit*, "Youths"), and so on — these are High Spirits, who, like the Avatars, assumed a human

GLOSSARY

appearance to raise the consciousness of humanity and accelerate its development. The Seven Great Spirits have taken care of the planet Earth and its humanity. Again and again, they were incarnated as the greatest founders of kingdoms, religions, sciences, and philosophies in order to help people unite with their Divine Nature. And so they have left deep traces in every domain of life and in every land.

For example, among their incarnations on the Earth are: Akbar the Great, Anaxagoras, Apollonius of Tyana, Confucius, the Count of Saint-Germain, Francis of Assisi, Gautama Buddha, Giordano Bruno, Hermes Trismegistus, Jakob Böhme, Jesus Christ, John the Apostle, Joseph, Joshua, King Arthur, Krishna, Lao-Tzu, Mahatma Koot Hoomi, Mahatma Morya, Melchizedek, Menes, Moses, Muhammad, Numa Pompilius, Origen, Orpheus, Paul the Apostle, Pericles, Plato, Pythagoras, Rama, Ramesses the Great, Sergius of Radonezh, Solomon, Thomas à Kempis, Thutmose III, Tsongkhapa, Tutankhamun, Zoroaster, and many others.

All the Gods have their Spouses, who in the Higher Worlds are united, and one does not exist without the other. But, since the Masculine Principle must express itself in the visible aspect of life and the Feminine Principle in the invisible, the Female Deities were revered as the most sacred and secret in all ancient religions. It is they — who have been incarnated on the Earth as mothers, sisters, daughters, and wives — through self-sacrifice, heroism, and continuous giving, inspired the Sons of Light and the peoples of the Earth, as well as humanity as a whole. Similarly, the entire Hierarchy of Light devoutly honours the Mother of the World — the Great Spirit of the Feminine Principle, who was manifested in earthly reflection as Isis, Ishtar, Lakshmi, Tara, Athena, Mary, Sophia, etc.

GOLDEN FLEECE — the golden wool of a ram in Greek mythology, which symbolizes supreme spiritual values.

The quest for the Golden Fleece is the search for spiritual enlightenment and the Higher Truth; it is the acquisition of Immortality and an attempt to achieve something that seems impossible and unattainable. In order to win it, one must overcome the dark side of one's nature.

GORGON (*Greek*, "terrible") — in Greek mythology, a female monster with serpents instead of hair, whose glance had the power to turn every living thing into stone. There were three Gorgon sisters: Stheno (*Greek*, "The Mighty"), Euryale (*Greek*, "The Far Springer"), and Medusa (*Greek*, "The Protectress"). Medusa, being the only mortal among the three monstrous sisters, was defeated by Perseus.

Underlying every myth there is some kind of basis in historical fact. The inhabitants of Atlantis could harness and control the forces of Nature, including the spirits of the elements of Earth, Water, Air, and Fire — such as genies, elves, undines, dwarfs, etc. Similarly, the High Initiates of Egypt built the pyramids at Giza, and King Solomon constructed the Temple with this kind of knowledge and the help of genies.

The black-magic sorcerers of Atlantis created mechanical creatures, which were "animated" by what are called *elementals*[25] and *elementaries*,[26] using their secret knowledge. These unique biorobots were endowed with various abilities. For example, they could speak and warn their master about some impending danger, or perform tasks assigned by the master. Subject only to the will of their producer, they were able to operate on different planes of matter, visible and invisible. And so warlocks sent whole armies of such monsters against the Sons of Light, incapable of being stopped by ordinary people. However, a man with a pure heart, imbued with the Power of Love, could annihilate an entire army of these visible and invisible monsters.

GREAT LORD OF SHAMBHALA — the Solar Hierarch at the head of the Hierarchy of Light of the Solar System; the Creator, Preserver, and Transfigurer of the Solar System; the Teacher of Teachers, Lord of the World, Lord of Civilization, Lord of the White Flame, Holder of the Wheel of the Law, the "Ancient of Days" in the

---

[25] *Elementals* are the spirits of the elements of Earth, Water, Air, and Fire.

[26] *Elementaries* are the disembodied souls of evil people, unsuitable for Evolution, who have lost their immortality.

GLOSSARY

Bible, Sanat Kumara in the Puranas. He is the Mover of the evolution of humanity, the Earth, and everything that exists in the Solar System.

Many times has He incarnated Himself among Earth-dwellers under different Names, amid different peoples and races in various eras of the planet's history. But His essence has forever remained unchanged, and His goal is always the same: to uplift humanity to the next stage of the spirit. Whatever earthly garments He donned could not hide His Light, and those unable to withstand His mighty empyreal fires reacted furiously, with persecutions, torturings, and killings. The long-suffering Lord, the "Great Sacrifice," bore the burden of the Earth on His shoulders.

The Solar Hierarch is the Head of Shambhala and reigns together with the Seven Kumaras — the Great Teachers, or the Masters of Wisdom, who personify the Seven Rays. Each era must be permeated with the energies of a particular Ray, in whose Light the next stage of planetary evolution develops. And so for each period of time He designates one of the Mahatmas as the Ruler of Shambhala, who bears the titles of Maha-Chohan (*Sanskrit*, "Great Lord"), Rigden (*Tibetan*, "Holder of the Lineage"), and Kalki (*Sanskrit*, "Destroyer of Ignorance"). And right now it is a special time called the *Era of the Heart*, which is to bring about a Synthesis of all Seven Rays.

In 1924, Mahatma Serapis was replaced by Mahatma Morya in this responsible position. The Master of Helena Blavatsky and Helena Roerich became the Great Lord of Shambhala, changing His Name to Maitreya, for each era requires an affirmation of the power of a particular Name. If the calculations were made correctly from the ancient texts, He is the 25th King of Shambhala — Rigden Dragpo Khorlocan (*Tibetan*, "Wielder of the Iron Wheel"), also known as Kalki Rudra Chakrin (*Sanskrit*, "Forceful Wheel Holder") — under whose reign, according to legends, the Great Battle of Armageddon was to be fought between the forces of Good — the Warriors of Shambhala — and the forces of evil. The Master M. is the Bearer of all Rays, who brings the Synthesis of all the energies given to the world throughout the history of human civilization. He is the highest among the Seven Kumaras (or Gods), who, coming from the Distant

Worlds, were responsible for the evolution of the planet Earth. In other words, the Lord Morya and the Solar Hierarch constitute the One Individuality, made manifest in both earthly and Heavenly forms.

In the Puranas and other sacred texts it is stated that it is from Shambhala, the City of Gods, that the Kalki Avatar would come forth to establish the Golden Age on the Earth. The present Great King of Shambhala is the Messiah promised by all world religions: Christ of Christianity, Maitreya of Buddhism, Mahdi of Islam, Kalki of Hinduism, the Messiah of Judaism, Saoshyant of Zoroastrianism, Li Hong of Taoism, and so on.

In 1924, while participating in the Central Asiatic Expedition, Helena Roerich heard a prediction which she later published in her book *Cryptograms of the East*: "One, two, three, I see three books of the Advent of Maitreya. The first is written in the West, the second is written in the East, the third is written in the North."[27] Later, in 1929, the Master M. told her in §7 of *Hierarchy*, *Agni Yoga*, that the Lord of Shambhala reveals three Doctrines to humanity.[28] So, according to these prophecies, before the Advent of the Lord of Shambhala in the world, His Three Doctrines must be revealed to humanity: in the West, in the East, and in the North.

A similar prophecy is contained in the lost manuscript of Nostradamus, known as *Vaticinia Nostradami* (*Latin*, "Prophecies of Nostradamus"), which consists of mysterious watercolour images. It was accidentally rediscovered in 1994. However, as with other coded messages of the Initiates, no one has succeeded in interpreting them correctly.

One of those pictures depicts a King with a book in his hands. At the top is a golden veil surrounded by an empty scroll; to the right hangs a lock, and over the veil is Dharmachakra (*Sanskrit*, "Wheel of Law"). In Buddhism, the Wheel of Law is the main emblem of Chakravartin (*Sanskrit*, "One who turns the Wheel") — an ideal

---

[27] Helena Roerich, *Kriptogrammy Vostoka* [Cryptograms of the East] (Moscow: Amrita, 2011), p. 66.

[28] *Uchenie Zhivoi Etiki* [Teaching of Living Ethics], vol. 7, p. 15.

GLOSSARY

Universal Monarch who rules ethically and benevolently over the whole world. He is most often incarnated as an Avatar, who is to lead humanity out of its earthly misery into Paradise. The Lord is holding an open book — His Doctrine or Law. Since Teachings have never appeared by themselves, the Doctrine of the Lord must be recorded as well. Therefore, depicted underneath are three women who are united by a scroll: they are destined to rewrite the Lord's Teaching on the scroll and to open the lock on the curtain of mystery. So these three disciples were summoned by the King of Shambhala to remove the veil of ignorance from the eyes of the world.

The Three Teachings were to unite many countries of the world with Shambhala by a single fiery thread. Thus, Mahatma Koot Hoomi wrote in the autumn 1881: "Notwithstanding that the time is not quite ripe to let you entirely into the secret, and that you are hardly yet prepared to understand the great Mystery, even if told of it, . . . I am empowered to allow you a glimpse behind the veil. . . . [Helena Blavatsky was] sent out alone into the world to gradually prepare the way for others. After nearly a century of fruitless search, our chiefs had to avail themselves of the only opportunity to send out a European *body* upon European soil — to serve as a connecting link between that country and our own. You do not understand? Of course not." [29]

It is known that *The Secret Doctrine* was written by Madame Blavatsky between 1884 and 1888 in Western European countries such as Germany, Belgium, and the United Kingdom. And she left a message to humanity that "in century the twentieth, some disciple more informed, and far better fitted, may be sent by the Masters of Wisdom." [30]

This disciple was Helena Roerich, who continued on the path of service to humanity. In 1920 she began recording the first book of *Agni Yoga* right where *The Secret Doctrine* was completed — in London, Great Britain. Roerich further outlined her own energy circle — first

---

[29] *The Mahatma Letters to A. P. Sinnett*, comp. Trevor Baker (Pasadena, CA: Theosophical University Press, 1992), p. 203.

[30] Helena Blavatsky, *The Secret Doctrine*, vol. 1 (London: Theosophical Publishing Company, 1888), p. xxxviii.

visiting Western lands — the UK, the USA, and European nations — and then the countries of the East: Mongolia, Tibet, and India, where the major part of the Second Doctrine of the Great Lord of Shambhala was written from 1924 to 1947.

And a year before her passing, Helena Roerich wrote to one of her colleagues about the next disciple who would continue her labour: "It is also necessary to pass on the foundations of the Fiery Experience. Many people at the end of our century will come to it, and one of the Sisters of the Brotherhood will be my successor, and she will carry out Agni Yoga under new and, possibly, improved conditions."[31] (10 October 1954)

Furthermore, in Helena Roerich's diaries, from which she compiled her published works, it is clearly indicated that the two books concerning the Advent of Maitreya *have been* written in the West and in the East, while the third book *will be* written in the North. This prophecy — with the same distinction — also appears in Nicholas Roerich's *Heart of Asia*.[32] Indeed, the future appearance of the new Teaching of the White Brotherhood in the North was foreseen not only by the Roerichs.

Edgar Cayce, for one, predicted that new religious ideas would come from Russia: "For changes are coming, this may be sure — an evolution, or revolution in the ideas of religious thought. The basis of it for the world will eventually come out of Russia; not communism, no! But rather that which is the basis of the same, as the Christ taught — His kind of communism!" (29 November 1932);[33] "Out of Russia, you see, there may come that which may be the basis of a more worldwide religious thought or trend." (25 August 1933);[34] "In Russia there comes the hope of the world, not as that sometimes termed of the

---

[31] Helena Roerich, *Pis'ma* [Letters], vol. 9 (Moscow: Mezhdunarodnyi tsentr Rerikhov, 2009), p. 468.

[32] See Nicholas Roerich, *Heart of Asia* (Rochester, VT: Inner Traditions, 1990), p. 97.

[33] Cayce, *The Complete Edgar Cayce Readings*, Reading № 452–6.

[34] Ibid. Reading №3976–12.

GLOSSARY

Communistic, of the Bolshevistic; no. But freedom, freedom! That each man will live for his fellow man!" (22 June 1944).[35]

Then, in 1978, the famous Bulgarian clairvoyant, healer, and prophetess Vanga[36] said that the New Teaching of the White Brotherhood would appear in Russia in 1998: "The New Teaching will come from Russia. That country will be the first to be purged. The White Brotherhood will spread across Russia and from there its Teaching will begin its march throughout the world. This will happen in twenty years — it will not happen earlier. In twenty years, you will reap the first rich harvest."[37]

So, in 1995, Zinovia Dushkova began to record the Third Doctrine of the Lord Maitreya, *The Teaching of the Heart*, where Helena Roerich completed *Agni Yoga* — in Kullu Valley, India. From there, over a three-year period the fiery thread of the One Teaching was extended to Egypt, Israel, and Japan, but the main part of the work was written in the North, in Russia, outlining a new energy round. And the first volume of *The Teaching of the Heart* was published, just as predicted by Vanga, in 1998 — one year before the beginning of the Great Fiery Baptism.

Thus the three cycles, the three Doctrines of the Great Lord, as was prophesied, have been written in the West, in the East, and in the North, connecting with Shambhala by the unified thread of energy and geography. They have paved the way from intellectual knowledge to the wisdom of the heart.

It should be mentioned that it is not by chance that all three recorders of these Teachings hail from Slavic lands. According to many

---

[35] Ibid. Reading №3976–29.

[36] Vanga (1911–1996) — full name: Vangelia Pandeva Dimitrova (also known as Vangelia Gushterova and Baba Vanga) — a blind Bulgarian, Macedonian-born peasant known for her clairvoyant powers. In the countries of the former USSR she is as famous for her prophecies as Edgar Cayce in America. It is said that 80% of her predictions have already come true. Please note that on the Internet there are many false and negative predictions about the future mistakenly attributed to Vanga.

[37] Zheni Kostadinova, *Vanga* (Moscow: AST, 1998), pp. 71–72.

prophecies and predictions in both the West and the East, the Slavs, by virtue of their astrological association with the Sign of Aquarius and the New Age, are destined to play a key role in the evolution of humanity on the Earth through creating a new spiritual pattern of life for the whole world. Therefore, all the blows the darkness can muster are vehemently directed at the Slavic lands in order to prevent this from happening.

HATRED — the most destructive force known to man, which ignites the black fire, depositing corresponding sediments in the human body. It is as magnetic as love, only the fires it draws from space to man are wholly black.

Any form of hatred is a dangerous black flash capable of inflaming a dark fire. For example, self-loathing is destructive. It is virtually impossible to notice how the black fire of hatred spreads from self-haters to people around them. Often some clergymen urge their parishioners to detest sin, considering this as "service to the light." But, in fact, it is actually service to the darkness, for when each cell of the body is filled with black poison, it infects not only the hater but the whole world. And so the haters bring themselves closer to falling prey to some kind of illness. Further, religious ignorance urges churchgoers to hate Satan — the Fallen Angel Lucifer. However, this spirit came to the Earth as an act of self-sacrifice, leaving his beautiful world to help humanity. He was unable to withstand the test, perhaps being infected with pride by Earth-dwellers. After all, he could not possibly have led humanity to spiritual doom if people and their collective will had not given their consent. And now, in sending him thoughts of hatred, people darken their own souls most of all. Therefore, it is far wiser to treat him with compassion.

Even though on the Earth one can utterly avoid meeting with the object of one's hatred, in the Subtle World hatred will draw the hater to the very individual whom they hate and will hold them in proximity until the energy of hatred completely exhausts itself. It is extremely hard and painful to release one's self from the accumulations of black fires there, because in the Subtle World all human desires and aspirations are intensified a hundredfold. Moreover, if a person does not

GLOSSARY

rid themselves of hatred of another here, then in their next life they will definitely meet each other again, and may even be incarnated into the same family. Karma claims its own, and so only through overcoming one's self in other people is it possible to free one's self from them. The karmic ties of either hatred or love are stronger by far than any other emotion.

Hence forgiving one's enemies, along with Love and Compassion towards all creation, has a purely practical significance, for dark feelings can turn into fetters, not only in this world but also in the Higher Realm.

HEART — the most important organ in man; the centre of spiritual consciousness. It is a mover, producer, and collector of fiery might. The heart is the concentration of the energies of Fire always pulsating in man, on the tonality of which his state of being completely depends.

The structure of the heart is sevenfold: each of man's seven bodies has its own heart — the physical, the subtle, and so on — the highest of which is the Fiery Heart. During a person's life on the Earth, they are united with their physical heart. The heart is the focal point in all human bodies — from the densest organism to the Supreme Triad. The whole experience of previous lives, all abilities and knowledge — inaccessible to the brain, which lives only one life — are concentrated in the spiritual Fiery Heart, called the *Chalice*. The heart remains a man's inalienable property throughout all his incarnations, since only its physical covering is mortal, while its fiery essence is immortal.

The heart thinks, just like the brain, only in its own way. The logic of the heart works through fiery channels, sometimes with no time being required — the heart just knows, without a tedious and tortuous process of reflection. The words of the heart always harbour extreme simplicity, along with profoundness, wisdom, and selflessness. The voice of conscience is the voice of the heart, which sounds especially clear when all else is silent. The heart owns an energy which is not subordinate to the brain. For example, thoughts sent by the brain are brief and ineffective, and immediately self-exhausting; whereas thoughts from the heart know no obstacles, distances, or time.

Many mysteries are hidden in the heart, and these will be revealed by the science of the future. A scientist who knows the secret of numbers, in comparing mystic knowledge with the knowledge of science, will make significant discoveries in the domain of cardiology. For example, blood flows through the greater circulation in 22 seconds on average and through the lesser circulation in 5–6 seconds. Matching the numbers that indicate Rounds and Races, one can trace signs of a person's racial identity in the operation of the heart.

The heart is designed to love, for Love is the mission of the heart. One who loves attracts and assimilates the highest vibrations through the heart. But not everyone is capable of accepting the Fire, since not everyone's flesh can endure the Divine Currents. The Fire transmutes that which is able to evolve while that which cannot evolve is destroyed. Therefore, cardiovascular diseases are more prevalent than others, especially in our age, for the Era of Fire, which has already begun, is the Era of the Heart.

HEAVEN — in the spiritual sense, the Fiery World, or the Higher Spheres which surround the planet Earth.

HUMAN HANDS AND FEET — the formula, or law, associated with the achievement of any steps on the Ladder of Evolution through one's own efforts.

The Teachers of Humanity give people as much as they need, as much as they can understand, and as much as Cosmic Laws permit. When people aspire to attain Truth, the Teachers help and guide them, pointing out the right direction and giving advice. But in order to reach their goal of self-perfection, to achieve or master something, each individual must work on their own. For this reason, in any Teaching of Light there are no formulas or pat answers to questions, but only hints at them — since everyone must harness their own creative abilities and endeavour to understand them through their own efforts.

Consequently, it is absolutely wrong to assume that the Supreme Spirit comes to the Earth to take upon Himself all the sins of humanity and end up being mercilessly crucified. One cannot follow the path on another's shoulders. In any case, humanity is obliged to pay all its debts. Even the Supreme Spirit has the right to redeem only 50% of all karmic debts, for everyone must learn from their own mistakes.

The "human hands and feet" formula is also referred to as the Signs of Christ. According to the Eastern tradition, when Jesus Christ was in Leh, India, He said there: "With human hands and feet shall we achieve!" — and drew the formula on sand in the form of signs. Nicholas Roerich depicted this episode in his painting *Signs of Christ* (1924).

IDEA — the true essence of thought, unexpressed in form; forethought. Thus, at first, an idea appears in consciousness, which clads itself in the matter of thought and develops into an image that then acquires material form (visible or invisible) and is embodied in life.

According to Cosmic Laws, which also exist beyond forms (but are manifested in Primordial Matter), all phenomena unexpressed in forms subordinate whatever is clad in forms — according to the degree of rarefaction of the matter-covering, the physical degree being the lowest. Hence Plato was right in stating that "Ideas rule the world." Ideas as such, unlike thoughts, are always invisible, even in the Higher Worlds.

The Great Teachers saturate space with the most advanced ideas. The birth of an idea calls forth the particles of consonant elements which act as a magnet, creating a field of attraction around it. So, an invisible search for allies apparently occurs among people who are willing to turn this idea into reality by using human hands and feet. The border between two ages, as is happening right now, is marked by the largest penetration of new ideas into the depths of space in order to awaken dormant consciousness. And they enter the consciousness of many people, dividing humanity into two camps: those who follow them and those who counteract them. If one's consciousness is ready, it accepts the new ideas without difficulty. Those who follow evolution develop them — from different points of view — all over the world. But no barriers or restrictions can keep them from spreading to all hearts and minds. Thus, ideas are borne through the air, compelling everyone to make a firm decision as to what they support: whether they are for peace or war, for freedom or slavery, for remaining in the old world or entering the New World, and so on.

The published Teachings of Light represent the thoughts expressed in words and gathered together in printed books. Many sections of the Secret Teachings are not published at all; they are contained in the manuscripts stored in Shambhala and other Abodes of Light. But the major part of these is sealed in the archives of space, or Akasha, which is inaccessible to ordinary people. However, the Great Teachers have permeated space with the thoughts that are in tune with the evolutionary stage reached by humanity to date. In this way, they share with the world what every sensitive spirit may perceive from the spheres surrounding the Earth. Even in cases where the Teaching is not published, its ideas still fill space, as if borne through the air. They reach many hearts and, in different parts of the world, people begin to speak and express the same thoughts and espouse the same formulas, although they have never had contact with this Teaching on the physical plane. As they bring the light of sincerity into the world around them, they begin to facilitate the unification of humanity into a single family. In this way they prepare the ground for the future transformation of each individual's consciousness, as well as their whole life.

Ideas never die, but live in space, although they may be forgotten by people. But as time goes by, they once again spark interest among human minds and, as they increase in strength, they are embodied in life, even after thousands of years. And the ideas which express indisputable truths are immortal, only changing their form of manifestation simultaneously with the evolution of consciousness.

Naturally, progressive ideas are seldom accepted immediately. They generally require a period of time to take root in the consciousness of the masses. But as the majority of people become accustomed to them, accepting them as their own thoughts, ideas begin to rule the world not theoretically but practically.

IGNORANCE — lack of knowledge; conscious resistance to knowledge and learning; the inability to understand and admit the diversity of Truth.

GLOSSARY

Ignorance is the source of all humanity's misfortunes. By manufacturing illusions, it compels people to value whatever is utterly worthless. They waste their lives chasing after despicable things, disregarding what is indeed important — *self-knowledge*, which leads towards genuine reality.

As a rule, ignorant people are unable to perceive the relativity of all the knowledge accessible to their mind at their present stage of evolutionary development. They are unable to understand that there are no limits for perceiving the world and its laws. Thus, the darkness of ignorance becomes a basis for negation and denial.

The New Era for humanity will start with the dispelling of ignorance and learning the Cosmic Laws, which give paramount importance to spiritual life.

ILLUMINATION — a new level of consciousness based on the accumulated knowledge in the heart as well as on formulas existing in space.

Sometimes a flash of illumination suddenly dawns upon man. This is not accidental, rather a result of the accumulated knowledge of previous lives. Similarly, space is permeated by Rays which illuminate every consciousness having aspirations towards Truth.

IMMORTALITY — a quality natural to those creatures of the Earth whose structure includes an immortal eternal principle — the Divine Spark known as a *Monad* (*Greek*, "unity") which is eternally reincarnated, taking on various forms. In its true meaning, immortality is the absolute clarity of consciousness that permits a continuous self-realization in various bodies and Worlds. Another aspect of immortality consists in a life above the self, when man devotes himself to society, a people, humanity as a whole, or the planet. In rejecting his mortal personality, man joins the planetary flow of cosmic life that enables him to discover his Higher Spirit and Immortal Individuality.

In the Universe there are technocratic civilizations with broken monads, which are devoid of immortal principles. Their representatives live a mere 600–700 years. Then their matter decomposes and, without the ability to be reincarnated, they simply cease to exist.

These civilizations look for the opportunity to advance to the plane of Immortality. Therefore, knowing that humanity possesses this quality, they study the planet Earth, including man, in order to find a way to transform their material component and to communicate this information to their worlds.

Death on the physical plane is an unnatural phenomenon which violates the Cosmic Laws. This is a result of the delay of human evolution due to the activity of Lucifer, who wanted to limit Earth-dwellers solely to the dense world. As an infant grows into a youngster, an adult, and an elderly person, the human body, too, should develop into a higher form, and not die.

It is known that the entire cell structure of body completely renews itself every seven years. Not a single atom of the previous structure remains. It turns out that the human body has a continuous stream of matter flowing through it. However, a person still grows old, because the cells of their body lie dormant, deprived of their full vitality. After a certain time their fieriness fades away, despite the constant renewal of atoms. Not only that, but a person fills their body with the emanations of decomposition in the form of impure food, along with base thoughts, emotions, desires, and deeds. In other words, man extinguishes his fires of vitality by his own hands. Consequently, man's control of all his thoughts, feelings, and actions together with the proper diet — ought to strengthen the fieriness of each cell and raise the level of their vibrations, thereby increasing man's power over his body. Hence the body of a saint is not susceptible to decay for, given its fieriness, it is formed from another type of matter entirely. And yet, even though they can alter the properties of matter, saints die. The mystery consists in the fact that atoms take whatever form or image is shaped by the spirit. If one creates, say, the fiery formula of an eternally young physical body and, through a moral lifestyle, succeeds in preventing the usual extinction of the body's fieriness, the combinations of atoms in the cells do not follow the common path, but that which is outlined by the fiery formula of spirit. However, in man's structure of the Supreme Triad, this formula for the physical body is absent.

GLOSSARY

Therefore, in order not only to help intensify the fieriness of terrestrial organisms but also to change the structure and formula of human bodies, the Currents of Eternal Youth have been pouring out upon the Earth since 2005. On 19 July 2012, humanity was given the currents containing the Formulas of Immortality, which were to enter into the heart of everyone, and everyone was to make the choice whether to accept the new formula or not. As a result of this alchemical process, children born after the year 2012, as well as those who are growing up at present — assimilating the Fires of Immortality and who also possess a sufficient level of fiery accumulations — these will give life to a generation with entirely different formulas. Hence the New Man will have another structure formed over a period of twenty-four to forty-two years, where the ageing process will be replaced by a process of fiery regeneration at the cellular level. And at a certain point in time man will consciously make his way into the Higher Worlds, not through dying on the physical plane but through adapting his body to new conditions by his own will. The Great Teachers can do this and, especially in the 19th century, there were many eyewitnesses confirming the fact that the Mahatmas did not age for hundreds of years, looking the same as they had looked in their prime of life.

IMPLOSION — a period of rest, or collapse of life within a planet, system, galaxy, or the Universe, referred to as *Pralaya* (*Sanskrit*, "dissolution"), or the "Night of Brahma." It is equivalent in duration to the period of activity involved in the manifestation of life — *Manvantara* (*Sanskrit*, "Age of a Manu") or the "Day of Brahma."

When the Solar System reaches perfection in this cycle of its evolutionary development, implosion will take place. And whatever has been achieved by that time — all forms and types of matter — will serve as the foundation for the genesis of a New Solar System. Immersion in a sleep-like state occurs under the supervision of High Spirits. Then, after a certain period of time, they awaken life anew, but on a higher level. The same will happen with the Earth.

INITIATE — one who has been entitled to acquire the Secret Knowledge of the Cosmos and man. Each new stage of Initiation reveals ever new mysteries and imparts new abilities.

Initiation ceremonies — or Mysteries — took place in Ancient Sanctuaries such as the Pyramids of Egypt, the Temples of Greece and India, and so on. Secret Sanctuaries with halls for Initiations were built in places of powerful energy, mostly in the mountains. Mountains are the source of the strongest energy because their summits are covered with snow, which, like a natural lens, serves to receive the currents of other constellations and planets. Similarly, representatives of other worlds who study the Earth have their bases in the mountains, too.

The procedure of Initiation is a mystical penetration to a higher level of perception and comprehension of the mystery of Being, thanks to the acceptance of higher-order currents and the ability to use them effectively. It is the transition from life to a temporary death by means of a magic dream, which in turn allows a candidate to experience a disembodied Spirit and Soul in the subjective world. Each Initiation requires moral purity, strength of spirit, and an aspiration towards Truth.

For example, Hermes Trismegistus (*Greek*, "Thrice-Greatest") underwent three Initiations, although he is already the Four-time-Greatest, having successfully passed through yet another. His father, Arraim, is a Four-time-Greatest as well. Christ passed through Eight Initiations, and His Second Coming is associated with His Ninth Initiation.

However, not only people and the Great Spirits may go through Initiations, but also realms of Nature, planets, stars, solar systems, etc. Thus, in the present day, humanity as a whole, also the Earth, are undergoing the next level of their Fiery Initiation.

INSTINCT — hidden and unconscious knowledge concealed in fiery energy, which is present everywhere, even in the lower realms of Nature.

At the dawn of his physical evolution, man was for a long time guided by his instincts, even after the acquisition of the Supreme Mind. Many millennia passed before the higher abilities of the mind could develop, thereby creating the true man. If it were not for the Great Teachers of Humanity, people would still today be living as cave dwellers. Their main goal, however, is the development of the heart, for

GLOSSARY

only through it can the human spirit manifest itself and consciously guide man's ascent up the steps of Evolution.

INTUITION — the manifestation of the knowledge possessed by the heart, which comprises the Supreme Mind. This is knowledge confirmed practically — i.e., the consequence of labour and experience, accumulated in the spiritual heart, called the *Chalice*, which is man's invisible property throughout all his lives.

Hence the knowledge of the heart, as a prototype of omniscience, constantly accumulates and grows in every new life. Often man is not aware where he learnt something he had never even thought of. However, it is almost always impossible for man to hear the voice of his heart, as he is too preoccupied with his personality. Selfishness drowns out this soundless voice. Consequently, in order to hear it, man must extinguish the noise of his own egotism and begin to pay attention to the heart — then its voice of Truth will be heard more and more often.

JOY — a special kind of Wisdom. This Joy is perfect, cosmic, and transpersonal, not associated with the illusive earthly world. It is not comparable to anything on the Earth. After experiencing true Joy, it is quite impossible to exchange it for imperfect, fragile, and ephemeral earthly joy. It will never fade away, for it transcends that which either delights or grieves those who are not illumined by the Light of Wisdom.

Joy is inseparable from Light and Love, for it is a special fiery state of the highest order. When the fires of Joy are stable and permanent, it signifies the victory of the spirit over the dismal darkness and the great illusion of existence. It may be called the *elixir of immortality for the heart*, because it is nourished by Joy from the Higher Worlds. It fills all space, and resounds with the most elevated notes, as yet inaccessible on the Earth. Though disharmony and destruction may be the keynotes of the Earth, Joy is the basic form of expression of life in the Higher and Distant Worlds — and in the future it will crown the New Earth as well.

As one of the aspects of harmony, even earthly joy is capable of overcoming fatal diseases. And since earliest times, people have learnt the healing properties of joyous feelings that attract the best vibrations, both earthly and ethereal. And so the sick have often been surrounded by joy to bring about successful healing.

One can learn Cosmic Joy even on the Earth. To do this, one must begin to experience joy — not personal and selfish one over trivial things of life, but joy for others and the very highest things. A consciousness preoccupied with itself alone has no room for Joy. But when people help someone else, it brings them joy — a little spark of Divine Joy, which can then be kindled into a steady Flame. Thus, in expressing joy for the Common Good, one acquires the Joy that constitutes a special Wisdom.

KALACHAKRA (*Sanskrit*, "Wheel of Time") — the Teaching of Fire, brought to humanity of the Third Race by the Great Teachers eighteen million years ago. Combining the knowledge of many domains, it facilitates the mastering of hidden powers and energies contained in man and the Cosmos.

Today the Kalachakra is widely known in Tibet, where it was brought from Shambhala in the 11th century. The esoteric aspect of the Kalachakra has always been imparted directly from Master to disciple. Whereas, the aggregate of written texts comprises a multitude of commentaries intended for the spreading of superficial knowledge and advice, which inevitably serves to distort the true essence of the Teaching. Hence the actual Kalachakra is unknown, being accessible only by a few people who have maintained direct relations with Shambhala.

The Kalachakra Calendar is the Calendar of Shambhala. It is based on a sixty-year cycle, which consists of five smaller cycles of twelve years each. Therefore, when the word *century* is used in the Teachings of the East, one should first of all understand that it comprises not a hundred years, but sixty.

KARMA (*Sanskrit*, "action") — the Cosmic Law of Cause and Effect. Karma neither punishes nor rewards, it is simply a single Universal Law that infallibly guides all other laws, producing certain effects in accordance with corresponding causes. Every word, action, thought, or

GLOSSARY

desire leads to an appropriate effect — and, eventually, to everything in one's surroundings. Nothing happens accidentally. Karma may be not only individual but also collective, embracing whole peoples, continents, planets, and star systems. One cannot change or get rid of it except by eliminating the causes underlying the human actions.

Every man bears the mark of karmic predestination right from birth. And his free will is limited by the frames determined by Karma, which is created by his own human will. However, the placing of obstacles and restrictions in one direction opens opportunities in another. The purpose of Karma is to direct everyone towards the path of evolution. Hence Love is the quickest way of redeeming one's Karma.

The age of 42 years — 24 years for future generations — is considered the age of "cosmic majority." After this period begins the **Karma of Love**, when man is to work with the Cosmos on a spiritual level: for example, helping others by sharing his life experiences or developing some spiritual quality within himself. He, of course, lives on. But it happens that, after the age of 42, some people pass on from a heart attack. This is because before reaching 42 they needed to fulfil a certain programme associated with their former Karma. Once the soul completes its task, it brings about a new incarnation. Or vice versa: a human spirit may realize that its present body will not be able to perform divine tasks and, so as not to waste time, attempts to weave together another body. Thus, as is evident, most people after age 40 begin to take an interest in spiritual practices and ponder their mission in life — this is the Cosmic Karma of Love coming into effect. However, the Karma of Love may touch not only a human life but also the life of humanity as a whole within Races and Rounds.

KEYS — the knowledge necessary for a full understanding of esoteric truths. There are seven keys, each of which has seven sublevels: physiological, symbolical, psychological, metaphysical, astrological, geometrical, and numerological. Different sources use different names for the same keys, so the above list is tentative. In the future there might be as many as twelve keys.

When the reader perceives the symbolism of the words, they will no doubt read the text in a different way. Each word can have an esoteric symbol: e.g., *city* may be translated as "unity," *forest* as "people," *sword* as "order," *arrow* as "thought."

In many sacred texts, lines and paragraphs are marked with numbers — these are keys to their secret meaning. But it should be borne in mind that all seven turns of the numerological key can be applied only to the original text, not a translation. Someone who knows the mystery of numbers may add words and sounds, or the number of words and syllables, or something else, and hence read a completely different text. Whereas in the case of a translation, one can apply only a few sublevels of the numerological knowledge.

Only the Lords of Wisdom possess all seven keys to Cosmic Knowledge, revealing them one after another to their disciples. Therefore, in order to gain a complete understanding of all seven layers of any esoteric Teaching, one must reach the level of the Masters. Until then, one may read any Teaching of Light of any epoch many times and discover more and more new thoughts as consciousness expands.

There is a great deal to be discovered between the lines, and sensitive hearts may freely discern the entire meaning, regardless of whether the reader is in conscious possession of all the keys. Thus, if one's consciousness has broadened to some degree since the last reading of any book of the Teaching, one will again come across something new, while if it has remained on the same level, the next read will yield nothing. Consequently, as one's spirit grows, each new reading of the book will always reveal new findings, at the same time supplying fiery food to the reader's spirit.

KNOWLEDGE — the realization of reality through comprehension of the endless facets of Truth. It is poured forth throughout space, constituting a single unified Treasury, or Ocean of Knowledge, which is constantly being filled by the Great Teachers with thoughts, images, and ideas. This Treasury is open to everyone aspiring towards the Light. So, anyone who finds the path to it by the purity of their vibrations, thoughts, and readiness to serve humanity, begins to draw

GLOSSARY

knowledge therefrom. However, when man transmits this knowledge through the prism of his own consciousness and ray, tinting it with his own colour and tonality of sound — emotionality, astrality, or mentality — this inevitably results in a serious distortion of Truth.

For this reason there is a law, according to which in each century — whether marked by the 60-year Eastern or the 100-year Western cycle — the Great Teachers give from the Treasury of Knowledge to humanity such elements of Truth as may be understood by the minority. Thus the Teachings of Light which appear are recorded by those directly connected with the Masters of Wisdom through a particular Hierarchical Ray, which prevents distortion.

Of course, not everything can be revealed on printed pages, for the Secret Knowledge is conveyed only by word of mouth. Hence all Teachings are basically an outline, or a starting-point, that the reader can further develop in the directions consonant with their spirit. As a rule, the Great Brotherhood selects one or two disciples every century to renew the consciousness of humanity. The physical structure of such an individual must be ready for the tremendous currents of the Fire in order to record the Teaching of Light. And so, those who write down the Great Teachings are either Masters of Wisdom themselves or their disciples who have undergone special training under their supervision, for the Gift of the Teachings absolutely excludes transmission through a medium. There is always someone who works in the Hierarchical Ray — as did Helena Blavatsky and Helena Roerich. Others may connect to this Fiery Current, and the purest of them may receive small luminous books, but never the entire series of books of the Teachings.

Every Teaching is a new facet of Truth, which enhances the former facets with new elements, manifesting itself on a new level of previously obtained knowledge. Nothing new is said, but a new approach to a new understanding of the same immutable Cosmic Laws makes age-old knowledge ever new for the consciousness aspiring towards Infinity. Hence, while each Teaching has its own unique beauty, together they comprise the One Cosmic Knowledge.

Knowledge is useless unless it is applied in life. Experiential knowledge enters the heart, the Chalice; after being imbued by the energy of the heart, it becomes man's invisible and unalienable property for all his subsequent lives. That is why the human heart feels and intuitively knows much more than the brain. Still, no matter how much man knows and understands, all of his knowledge is simply a stepping-stone to a higher knowledge that is even more absolute. There is never an end to knowledge; this is only a necessary step in the direction of Wisdom.

LABOUR — a fiery process that accumulates and enkindles fire in the body; its purpose lies in the mastering of the fiery energies at the disposal of man's will. But labour must be both voluntary and joyful. If a man does not like what he does, this extinguishes his fires. In the Cosmos and Nature, everything labours, for there is no development or progress without labour. The higher the world, the more intensive the labour.

It is none other than joyful and creative labour which enhances the luminosity of the human aura and dispels the surrounding darkness. That is why one may consider labour as a service or a prayer to the Light. Similarly, the heart's prayer to the Light is labour, too. Labour for the good of all is of paramount importance throughout all Worlds. However, *rest* is also important, for overload and excessive tension of the same kind of energy may have detrimental effects on the body. The best way to rest is to exchange one activity for another which requires tension in different fiery centres.

Systematic, intense, inspired, and rhythmic labour makes the fiery crystal in the heart grow and develop. Hence such accumulations of honest perspiration constitute a most valuable treasure for all a person's subsequent lives. By contrast, laziness and idleness offer but a sad future for man.

LADDER OF LIGHT — the Hierarchy known as Jacob's Ladder in the Bible. It is a collective unity of the countless multitudes of Gods and Creators existing in the Universe. They have reached divine status,

GLOSSARY

having passed through human evolution on one of various planets in different solar systems. And now they are themselves the Creators of not only planets but entire stellar worlds and galaxies. They all are subordinate to the One who stands at the head of the Hierarchy. There is a Hierarch on each rung of this Hierarchical Ladder. Thus, the Gods of the Solar System are subject to the Solar Hierarch, who in turn is subordinate to the Hierarch of the Milky Way Galaxy, and so on into Infinity.

The whole Cosmos is governed hierarchically, and the higher governs the lower — this is the basis of evolution. No one is appointed in the Hierarchy of Heaven, but each one's position on the Ladder is the result of individual achievement. In the case of human evolution, the basic principle of ascent is *free will*, which determines one's path of life. This liberty consists in freedom of choice at any given moment, making decisions leading upwards or downwards. In this way, following a Hierarch is the main condition of advancement. But it is always voluntary, because the Sons of Light, in contrast to the servants of the darkness, never violate the Law of Free Will.

At the lowest rung of the Ladder of Light is the Mineral Kingdom, and above them all the other Kingdoms of Nature, including humanity, according to the level of consciousness. For example, at the top of the Hierarchy of the Mineral Kingdom are diamonds; the Plant Kingdom is crowned by roses; elephants, horses, and dogs are at the top of the Animal Kingdom; while the Kingdom of Humanity is headed by the Great Masters of Wisdom. There is nothing in the Universe which does not stand on the Ladder and does not have its Hierarch. The higher the step, the mightier the Hierarch.

LAWS OF THE UNIVERSE — the absolute and immutable Foundations which underlie the Cosmos and the entire Order of the Universe. All creation is subordinate to them; nothing and nobody can evade their influence. Being both restrictive and permissive at the same time, they direct Evolution into a particular channel.

The Cosmic Laws condition the infinite self-perfection of all phenomena, provided they do not violate them. Otherwise, Nature destroys her own forms, sometimes destroying whole worlds and systems in the process. Ignorance of these Laws is no excuse, and so they were inculcated, in one form or another, into every religion and philosophy known today.

The foremost Law of the Universe is the **Law of Divine Love**. It is the basis of everything and all other Laws are subordinate to it. As to the remaining Laws, none of them is more important than the others — they are all equal. They all operate in close correlation with each other, sometimes overlapping in their actions.

There are many Cosmic Laws, but some of them can be specified here:

The Law of Cause and Effect — All creatures endowed with Mind (such as human beings) fall within the scope of this Law of Karma or Justice, which determines retribution for each thought, word, and action.

The Law of Commensurability — "Hitherto shalt thou come, but no further."[38] This refers to the need to keep within limits in everything, everywhere, and always, to give exactly as much as one is able to digest and understand in order not to harm.

The Law of Communicating Vessels — A change in one results in a change in the other — in the interests of establishing a Balance, for all things in the Cosmos are interrelated, exerting an impact on one another.

The Law of the Equality of Principles — As the two poles of the One Divine Principle, the Masculine and Feminine Principles are equivalent, and they in turn create the Universe as Spirit and Matter.

The Law of Expediency — The expenditure of forces and energies should be reasonable and correspond to the benefits bestowed; processes and phenomena which are of no advantage to the Common Good cannot exist in the Universe.

The Law of Free Will — The liberty of spirit lies in the freedom of choice of how to act and think in every case, and one's free will is inviolable.

---

[38] Job 38:11.

GLOSSARY

The Law of Hierarchy — The entire Cosmos is constructed and managed hierarchically: the higher governs the lower. Every manifestation in the world has its own Hierarch, obedience to whom is a fundamental condition for progress.

The Law of Magnetism and Consonance — Like attracts like: magnetic attraction, tuned by will, naturally attracts to itself consonant elements, and everyone receives exactly what their inner essence strives to attain.

The Law of Reincarnation — Every creation of Nature passes through a multitude of lives: Mineral, Vegetable, Animal, Human, and other Kingdoms.

The Law of Rhythm — The whole Universe consists of vibration, based on the repetition of events, movement, or rhythm. All that exists in space evolves through the spiral and cyclic pulsations of life.

The Law of Sacrifice — Underlying the whole Being, this Law ensures the eternal circulation of energies in which one sacrifices itself in the name of the conception, existence, development, or self-perfection of another.

The Law of Unity of All Things — Everything originated from the One Divine Principle, and all forms of the visible and invisible world, from a blade of grass to a star, are united and interrelated, for each contains a particle of this Principle.

LEMURIA — the name commonly used to designate the continent where the Third Race of humanity developed. It covered most of the present-day Pacific and Indian Oceans, stretching along the equator. It included today's Australia, New Zealand, Madagascar, and Easter Island.

Lemuria was the birthplace of physical humanity, since the first Races did not have matter bodies. The ethereal and sexless beings slowly began to take on density and, by the middle of the Third Race, people resembled beast-like giants, up to twenty metres tall. Even though their shapes were similar to animals, these were already human beings, though not yet rational. At the same time, a separation of the sexes of all creation gradually took place, and distinct male and female individuals appeared, along with certain animals of those times, i.e., dinosaurs. Being mindless, many male Lemurians had sexual intercourse with female animals and procreated a vicious breed of monsters — primeval apes. It was from these creatures that some Atlanteans — this time consciously — later engendered all currently existing species of man-like apes.

When humanity was ready to perceive knowledge, the Great Teachers came to the Earth from the Distant Worlds and endowed people with the Supreme Mind. This happened nearly eighteen million years ago.

The Great Teachers lived together with human beings. They cultivated morality in them through their examples, always being by their side as Elder Brothers. There was no need for religions in those days, since the Gods were right there with the people. The Messengers from the Distant Worlds had taught the Lemurians much in the way of science, providing them with the knowledge of highly developed planets. For example, they knew the properties of the Fire and fiery energies; they had knowledge of architecture, construction, mathematics, astronomy, agriculture, etc. Some of the plants — wheat, for instance — do not have wild-growing counterparts on the Earth, as they were the gifts of the Sons of Light from Venus. Likewise, bees and ants were brought from Venus for the edification of people: their diligence, along with their communal and hierarchical system, could serve as an example for humanity.

By the end of the Third Race, the Lemurians had achieved a highly developed civilization. Their physical bodies had become more perfect, and their height had been reduced to between six and seven-and-a-half metres; there was a similar evolution among animals, unusual species of which are still preserved in Australia. The Lemurians had built huge cities, and were impeccable masters of both arts and sciences. Humanity of that time can be compared with the civilization of the 19th century of the current era, but their knowledge of Nature and the Cosmos were far superior. Even so, those days saw the beginning of fierce confrontations between the Forces of the Light and the darkness.

GLOSSARY

When the Cosmic Period came for the next change of Races, the Great Teachers resettled the most spiritual and advanced representatives of Lemuria to new islands, which were soon to form a new Race on the new continent of Atlantis. Lemuria was destroyed by the Fire, that is, by extremely powerful earthquakes, and then submerged into the water about four million years ago.

Evidence of the existence of the Lemurians and their civilization has been preserved in the form of mysterious sculptures on Easter Island. And archæological excavations have also revealed huge skeletons which once belonged to the giants of that time.

LIFE — the affirmation of the varying degrees of Fire, which is the highest form of the Light, as a result of the harmonious implementing in visible form of the Laws of Sound and Colour. Thus, Life and Light are the same in the essence, and Life itself is simply a way of drawing closer to the Light and asserting the Light in one's self. Life lasts forever, flowing from one form to another, and since all life is in continual change, Life as a whole is immortal.

Every living form is animated by a Fiery Seed that is unique in itself and is directly connected with the Cosmic Fire by a seamless thread, just as a solar ray is inseparably linked with the Sun. The Seed evolves through the growth of outer coverings, accumulating crystallized energy around its centre, whose fiery essence remains unchanged. In this way, the Fiery-White Core is constantly forming. Its subtlest energies of Fire are magnetic, gathering different degrees of matter around it, depending on consonance, or likeness. Hence the diversity of forms in both Nature and the Cosmos — nothing is identical.

The Seed's degree of consonance depends on what the will is attuned to. Man, endowed with free will, both consciously and unconsciously attracts external energies and their corresponding matter. The freedom of choice and will determines their reception in accordance with the Cosmic Law of Consonance, which operates in all spheres of life. This means that the variety of each individual's life conditions is defined by the magnetic properties of the energies contained in their aura, the centre of which is the Seed. For example, the accumulated fiery energies weave the fabric of all seven of man's bodies. People's bodies — either healthy or sick — are often simply the effects of the magnetic attraction of the energies concealed in their Seeds. However, consciousness is able to control the selection of particular types of energy out of the infinitely diverse world of energies of every possible kind. Thus, the conscious efforts of the will to attract a certain kind of energy gives man power over his own life.

All earthly life is like a fleeting dream, testing the steadfastness of one's spirit. It is but a preparation for life in the Ethereal World. The severity of a life path full of difficulties and hardships compels the fires of the spirit to flare up ever more brightly. The deprivation of earthly goods and comforts of a carefree existence makes the transition into the Subtle World and the assimilation of its ethereal conditions relatively easy and painless. That is why many Teachings warn us not to become too attached to anything, as then there will be nothing to lose and nothing to grieve over.

LIGHT — the highest form of Fire, being the manifested might of Sound. Everything is from the Light and made of Light. Only the forms, nature, and extent of illumination are as diverse as the world.

Matter consists of tiny particles of luminous electrons that form atoms and, therefore, any combination of atoms is light-bearing too. Consequently, if one abandons the usual limitations of sight, one can imagine that all existing things shine with varying intensity and in different colours. Everything has the potential of the Light, from the Sun to a planet and from an atom to a man. The essence of the evolution of all forms consists in unlocking this potential.

The Light is in each individual man, and everyone absorbs it, for without it even the physical body cannot exist. Even though the "dark ones" deny the Light, they owe their very existence to its gleams, since even the most darkened one must have at least a tiny spark of Light to be visible — otherwise one would be nothing at all.

As the size of an object can be determined by its shadow, even so the grandeur of the Light enveloping the Earth may be discerned through its opposite, the gloom. The very nature of evil's unique forms of expression points to the power of the opposite pole — the Light. It may seem that more and more evil appears in the world every day, but actually it is the other way round. Hence one may notice that lies, deceptions, and other negative things and qualities in human beings and situations are detected today much faster than before. This means that the Light that illuminates and reveals the true essence of all these — to help people's eyes see better — is constantly increasing.

LORDS OF DESTINY — the Spirits of the Universe, known as *Lipikas* (*Sanskrit*, "Scribes") in esoteric philosophy. These Divine Beings are mystically connected with Karma, the Law of Retribution, for they are the Recorders, who impress on invisible tablets a "grand gallery of scenes of eternity" — i.e., a faithful record of every word, act, and even thought of every man on the Earth, and of all that was, is, or ever will be in the manifest Universe. It is the Lords of Karma who project and make objective the ideal plan of the Universe, according to which the God-Creators re-create the Cosmos.

The Lipika Lords direct the evolution of the world, following Cosmic Laws and harmonizing their will with the evolution of the Cosmos. Against the will of the Lords of Karma human will is powerless, for the latter has created the former. To determine the course of human destiny, they use special matter that outlines the basis of the way which man must walk, being bound by karmic necessity.

However, the Lords of Destiny create precisely those conditions for humans, planets, systems, etc. that are necessary for the ascent along the Ladder of Evolution.

LOVE — an energy of supreme intensity, the all-creating power, higher than which there is nothing in the Universe. In other words, Love is the Sacred Fire to which all other fires are subordinate.

Love is the One Law, which crowns all other laws. It creates and transforms all creation in the Universe.

Love is a powerful force, the generator and accumulator of which is the heart. From the bipolar inner world of man, it elicits the elements of Light, good principles, the very best in man. Love conquers everything:

time, space, death, darkness. Thought governed and animated by Love can perform miracles, for the magnetic power of such a thought is great and irresistible.

MAGIC — the universal knowledge about the forces of Nature. It is customary to speak of white and black magic. White Magic is divine magic, devoid of selfishness, lust for power, ambition, or greed, and entirely directed towards the good of the world in general and one's neighbour in particular. Whereas the slightest attempt to use one's extraordinary powers for the gratification and benefit of self turns these powers into sorcery or black magic.

However, in earthly conditions, not only black magic is inadmissible, but also white, for in dense spheres it acquires a tinge of greyness. Any attempt at magical practices on the physical plane evoke low-frequency vibrations, which provoke a reaction with elemental forces. Since man is not able to control the elements, even white magic can result in unpredictable consequences. The real White Magic exists only on the Subtle Planes, where high-frequency vibrations accurately allow for the achievement of the expected result.

The only thing that has the power of a magical influence and can safely be used in earthly conditions is a prayer of the heart, continuously effectual for the good of humanity and the world.

MAHATMA (*Sanskrit*, "Great Soul") — an Adept of the highest order. The term designates exalted beings who, having attained full mastery over their lower natures, are in possession of extraordinary knowledge and power commensurate with the stage they have reached in their spiritual evolution.

MAN — a being destined to *become* the bearer of the highest spiritual principle on the planet Earth, and to *be* a creator. His evolution on the Earth passes through Seven Races, Seven Spheres, and Seven Rounds, incarnating at least 777 times in each Round.

Man develops through the following stages: mineral, plant, animal, man, God-man, and God. Each stage presupposes the attainment of perfection on a particular planet; and each higher level involves the

GLOSSARY

repetition of previous experiences. Thus, humanity had been evolving in the Mineral Kingdom on a planet which no longer exists. Then it passed through the Mineral Kingdom once more, but by now it had reached the Plant Kingdom on another planet, which also disappeared. Subsequently human Monads emigrated to the Moon, where they continued their evolution in the Mineral, Plant, and Animal Kingdoms. On the planet Moon, the wave of life appeared one stage earlier than on the Earth. This means that the current Animal Kingdom of Earthly Evolution was the Plant Kingdom on the Moon. When the Moon completed its life cycle, when all its forms of life reached the highest point in their development within the Seven Rounds, they ascended to the next higher step and thereby to another planet — the Earth. Now, when humanity achieves perfection on the Earth, it will move to a new planet, where there will be new conditions for higher development still — and so on endlessly into Infinity.

Man goes through all the Kingdoms of Nature in turn — not only from the moment of conception as an embryo, but also throughout his lifetime his structure is continually being formed in accordance with these steps. Hence for the first seven years he lives as a mineral; the next seven years, up to age 14, as a plant; further, up to 28, like an animal; then up to 35 as a man; and later, up to 42, as a soul. The number 42 is inherent in the Solar System for the maturation of the sevenfold human structure. In other words, from the perspective of the Cosmos, man attains his age of majority at 42 years.

The evolution of High Spirits, who came to the Earth from the Distant Worlds to help humanity, implies an exception: in order to become human beings, they can avoid the Animal Kingdom through additional incarnations in the Plant Kingdom or pass through this stage in the Kingdom of Birds.

Human structure, as everything in the Solar System, is septenary and consists of seven principles, which go by different names in various philosophies and can also be represented in a traditional tripartite concept:

I. **Spirit.**
   1. *Spirit*, or *Atma* (*Sanskrit*, "Spirit") — the fiery element united with the Absolute.
   2. *Soul*, or *Buddhi* (*Sanskrit*, "Soul") — spirituality, the conductor of Spirit.
   3. *Supreme Mind*, or *Manas* (*Sanskrit*, "Mind") — the principle, which endows man with self-consciousness and responsibility, bringing the Law of Karma into force. Man is the only one among all the Kingdoms of Nature of the Earth endowed with higher consciousness. Therefore, his immortal part, the sixth and seventh principles, is integrated with the Supreme Mind. It brings together in itself the entire accumulated experience of all past lives, in contrast to the intellect, the lower mind, which is renewed in every life.

II. **Soul.**
   4. *The astro-mental body* — expresses physical and mental desires, emotions, and thoughts. It consists of two parts:
      a) *the mental body*, which includes the lower mind, or intellect;
      b) *the subtle body,* or *the higher astral body.*

      The mental body is more perfect and is used for interplanetary flights by the Adepts, while the subtle body can be used for travelling within the limits of the Earth. The astro-mental body is mortal, although it may live for thousands of years.

III. **Body.**
   5. *The etheric double*, or *the lower astral body* — the transmitter of cosmic and solar energy to the physical body during its lifetime, being closely associated with nervous system. A state in which man is insensible to pain — either under narcosis, certain drugs or hypnosis — is achieved by the weakening of the link between the etheric and physical bodies. Containing all the physical features of man, the etheric body constructs man's physical appearance

GLOSSARY

according to the pattern inculcated in him at the moment of conception: hence the physical body, in fact, is the precise double of the etheric one. It disintegrates soon after the death of the human being; some sensitive people see etheric bodies as ghosts in graveyards. Again, mediums use their etheric doubles to demonstrate various phenomena.

6. **The energy covering**, or **vital principle**, called *Prana* (*Sanskrit*, "breath") — consists of various energies intrinsic to the Earth. After the death of the physical body it is discarded and is immediately assimilated by the Earth.

7. **The physical body** — the densest covering for communication with the Physical World.

All the principles mentioned are also sevenfold in their structure. The four lower principles form a *quaternary* — the mortal personality; while the three higher principles comprise a *Triad* — the Immortal Individuality, also known as a *Monad* or the Seed of the Spirit. Hence in the Physical World, all seven coverings are encased in the physical body. After leaving the Dense World, the three lower bodies die, and man lives on in the Subtle World with the remaining four principles in his subtle covering. Further, man casts off his higher astral body as he moves into the Mental World. Finally, he passes into the Fiery World only with the Supreme Triad, which is encased in the fiery body.

It is not correct to conclude that if someone is bad, they will become an animal in their next incarnation. Sometimes it happens that their Highest Principles might abandon them even during their lifetime. Such a person may show no outward difference from others — they might even be highly intellectual — but the person is only an empty shell of a living corpse. The living dead keeps being reincarnated until the complete separation of the Supreme Triad from the lower principles occurs. According to Cosmic Laws, such an individuality begins their evolution all over again, that is, from a mineral, but on a completely different planet with new conditions for life. A striking example of this is Joseph Stalin, whose principles were fractured in the 1930s. Unfortunately, there are many such living corpses on the Earth at the moment.

Man himself constructs the bodies of his seven principles. So, he builds his subtle bodies by his thoughts, feelings, and actions, and his physical body in conjunction with food. He is the creator of his own Karma, which is expressed within set limits. It is possible that a man's essence is not always fully reflected in his physical appearance, for it is sometimes difficult to find suitable parents and a suitable body. In the Higher Worlds, however, he acquires an external appearance which precisely corresponds with who he actually is.

Each of the abovementioned principles, save the physical and etheric bodies, is in fact only an aspect or state of human consciousness, made up of various qualities of the one primary energy of Fire, life, or consciousness. Man is Fire, manifested in constant action. All actions and processes in the body are Fire-derived. Therefore, the control over any one of them involves mastering the Fire.

In the future, the structure of man at the stages of God-man and God will be twelvefold: with seven lower and five higher principles. Now the human body is being refined under the influence of the Cosmic Fire, becoming subtler and more attenuated. Unusual feelings and abilities are gradually beginning to awaken. Also man will reach the maturity of his subtle and physical bodies not by age 42 but by age 24. From 24 to 42 he will then experience the formation of a different structure, which will not include ageing. That is, a New Humanity is being born this very moment. The hundred years of the 21st century are entirely devoted to this.

MASTERS OF WISDOM — the Great Teachers, the Lords of Shambhala, the Sons of the Only Begotten God, the Mahatmas, the Seven Instructors of Humanity, who have taken responsibility for its evolution. Through suffering and sacrifice, they have achieved a high level of development, far surpassing that of ordinary people — and, of course, to human understanding they can be seen as Gods. In the 19th and early 20th centuries, six Mahatmas were incarnated, known under these names: Morya, Koot Hoomi, Saint-Germain, Serapis, Hilarion, and Djual Khool. Now they are no longer in their former bodies, and they have also changed their names; some have gone to other, more advanced planets, leaving worthy earthly successors in their place.

GLOSSARY

The Masters are the Great Guardians of Truth, who implement the Divine Plan. They know when, what, and how much should be given to people, and attentively watch over the course of their evolution. There is so much intense work that the Mahatmas have no time for anything personal. They create new causes that bring about the effects needed for Evolution — thereby helping humanity to liquidate its former Karma. They know in advance the course of consequences, and are able to project them for millennia ahead. And sometimes, when the Teachers foresee the future, they simply know the effects of the causes consciously produced by them. So, they create the future, which is pliant in the hands of their fiery will. The Masters know the course of the stars and their future combinations, and co-ordinate their creative work with the energies of the Cosmos.

One of the most important tasks of the White Brotherhood is the selection and guidance of colleagues and disciples. For a variety of reasons the Teachers cannot enter into direct and close contact with multitudes of people. But they act through their colleagues, disciples, and messengers. When their disciples are incarnated on the Earth with a definite mission, the Masters follow and guide them right from childhood. The karmic relationship of long millennia enables the Instructors to make contact with their disciples without difficulty. In addition to being taught secret sciences, they usually undergo a fiery transmutation that enables them to maintain communication with the Masters. The disciples are constantly on probation, even at the higher levels of development. The most terrible betrayals are also unavoidable in their lives.

Each century the Mahatmas admit into the Abode of Light a maximum of two candidates, with the aim of conveying through them a part of the Secret Knowledge. But this may not always be necessary, for various reasons. The chief consideration is that the messenger's body must be ready to receive the Teaching. The Teachings of Light, of course, never appear spontaneously — there are certain periods allotted to them. In order to record them, the disciples go through many incarnations of preparation and probation, sometimes for thousands of years, and when the time comes, they are warned about the work they are about to undertake. As a rule, preliminary preparation takes place over a period of three years, when the Higher Spirits work with the disciples, getting their bodies in tune.

Contrary to established opinion, the Great Teachers never come into contact with mediums or channellers. Helena Blavatsky had to take the body of a strong medium, which was necessary in view of the tasks assigned to her during her last life on the Earth. She had to work with a large number of people and perform miracles in order to convince them of the existence of the higher Laws of Nature and Supreme Knowledge. Nevertheless, with the help of her Master, she brought this ability of hers under full control. Before revealing *The Secret Doctrine* to humanity, Blavatsky had been undergoing the fiery transmutation of her body for three years under the supervision of her Teacher in one of His Ashrams in Tibet. For those who have endured this process, it is extremely difficult to be out amongst people, and all the more so amongst those adversely disposed against them. This is why Blavatsky had such poor health. The situation was similar with Helena Roerich, but it was even more intense when she received *Agni Yoga*. However, she lived in India almost in solitude, being surrounded by loving people and the pure mountain air — which allowed her to almost completely accomplish the mission of her last earthly incarnation.

Initially, when the Leaders of Humanity came into the world, the continents were divided into seven spheres, wherein each of the Great Lords was giving off their own luminous vibrations. As the rainbow is dispersed into seven colours, so all the Seven Great Teachers represent the Seven Rays, bringing with them the currents consonant with their particular note. By the present time, each of the Seven Masters of Wisdom has educated disciples who have reached a high level of consciousness, and the exact number of the Leaders of Humanity is now 777. Certainly, the Teachers have their own Teachers too, for cognition is limitless.

In essence, the Seven Great Teachers — the Seven Rays — are the components of the One Supreme Lord, who represents the White Ray and personifies the Spiritual Sun. Thus, there is One Individuality,

GLOSSARY

but His partial manifestations enlightened such earthly incarnations as Buddha, Christ, Maitreya, and other Great Teachers.

MATTER — the crystallized spirit, the state of spirit; the Feminine Aspect of the Absolute, or the Primordial Fire; the Universal Soul. Matter is eternal, but the forms created by it are temporary. It consists of fiery particles in constant motion, corresponding to programmed rhythms or vibrations. Since the fire, or the spirit, lies at the foundation of matter, one can say that matter is rational and expresses the Cosmic Laws in its manifestations. The higher and subtler the type of matter, the more luminous it is and the more powerful the manifestations of its reason. However, the essence of this rationality is far above ordinary human understanding.

All that exists in the manifested world is material: Light, sound, colour, smell, feeling, thought, and so on. Beyond matter, nothing visible or invisible exists. In all sorts and forms of matter, there is a striving for evolutionary development. Matter is subject to the laws of number, proportion, and harmony. Matter can be influenced by the will, but only through the corresponding fiery energy. The less dense the matter is, the more susceptible it is to influence.

The gradation of types and states of matter is infinite, stretching into the Highest Spheres of Spirit and Light. Because of the constant evolution of all creation, matter is eternally subject to change, generating ever new types and conditions. In the Solar System, matter can be found in seven states: solid, liquid, gas, and plasma, along with three higher states which are still beyond the comprehension of earthly humanity. Each of these types has its own diverse gradation, as density and all other conditions are different on every planet.

The matter of the Earth is especially dense, but it is a kind of turning point in the Solar System, since on planets inferior to the Earth matter is even denser, whereas on superior planets matter is already harmonized with spirit. That is, on the higher planets matter becomes inseparable from spirit without opposition. Granted, there are imperfections, but there is no serious resistance on the part of the environment, and one need not waste one's strength on an unnecessary struggle between opposites.

MATTER

The four elements — Earth, Water, Air, and Fire — are the forms in which life in matter is expressed. They are reproduced on the planes of existence above the Earth, but modified to the conditions and specifics of each individual plane. For example, in the Subtle World one can see mountains and prairies, seas and rivers, and feel the element of air, but in a changed state. As it becomes transformed and refined, matter undergoes appropriate changes on each plane, all the while increasing its mobility and luminosity.

In Esoteric Teachings, the following types of matter are specified:

Materia Matrix — the equivalent of Akasha, the Primeval Substance, which fills the entire space of the Universe and serves as the material for its construction. This is the Matrix of the Universe, *Mysterium Magnum* (*Latin*, "Great Mystery"), from which all that exists is born by differentiation. It is the primordial conductor and carries the sparks of the spatial Fire, or Cosmic Electricity. And so a ray is created from a multitude of the particles of the Materia Matrix and the entire Solar System is enveloped by this matter, connecting all the planets together. Any thing can be "extracted," or rather created, from the Materia Matrix by the power of thought and will. This is the secret of the materialization of bread or diamonds "out of thin air," as demonstrated by such High Spirits as Jesus Christ and the Count of Saint-Germain.

Materia Lucida (*Latin*, "luminous") — the next stage of the Materia Matrix, pliant and light-bearing matter which the Supreme Worlds consist of and which clothes all cosmic energies (for example, Love and thought). It conceives all existing forms in space, therefore it can justifiably be called the *Matter of Love*. Materia Lucida radiates all shades of tones and colours, and may sometimes be visible to sensitive sight in space as streams or spots of light. It can also be observed around the Sun during a total eclipse — i.e., it comprises its corona. The higher bodies of the Great Teachers are clothed in Materia Lucida, as is man's higher mental body, though to a different degree.

Materia Agidya-Mani (*Senzar*) — the matter used to create the subtle bodies of the Higher Spirits who are to be incarnated on the

GLOSSARY

Earth. It has the property of regeneration and imperishability. Hence the permanence of relics of saints.

Materia Mai-Ga-E[39] (*Senzar*) — the matter forming the body of the Messiah. It is made by the combination of the three abovementioned types of matter. Materia Mai-Ga-E is used in the Empyreal Spheres to prepare the bodies of the Teachers for earthly incarnations. Thus, the physical bodies of Gautama Buddha and Jesus Christ had this matter in their structure. It is woven from the supreme energies and, just as Agidya-Mani, has the quality of immortality, involving transfiguration, refinement, and rarefaction.

The colleagues of Shambhala, in the process of their embodiment on the Earth, consciously subjected themselves to the Fiery Experiment. This enabled the Great Teachers to discover the formula of new matter which, during the Fiery Baptism, allows people to go almost painlessly through the process of transition from dense structures to subtler and more refined ones.

Everything these days is being transformed and renewed, seemingly melting, although it is not yet noticeable to the human eye. However, this qualitatively new matter will be revealed in the near future, bringing with it benefits for humanity as yet unknown.

MIND — the thinking nature of man, referred to in esoteric philosophy as *Manas* (*Sanskrit*, "Mind"). It consists of two components: the lower mind and the Supreme Mind.

The lower mind is part of the mental body of man and is represented by the intellect and the brain. This principle is also present in developed animals. The lower mind is mortal, bestowed only for a single incarnation. With the death of the physical body, man passes into the Subtle World in his astro-mental covering, but it is impossible to take this body further into the Fiery World.

Man was endowed with the Supreme Mind eighteen million years ago. It is this principle that gave man self-consciousness, the feeling of "I am I," which distinguishes man from animal. The Supreme Mind comprises the Supreme Triad of man and is therefore immortal,

---

[39] *Pron.* my-gah-ee.

moving from one incarnation to another in all the Worlds. In the human body, the Supreme Mind is represented by the subtle heart.

In the Physical World, the majority of humanity is subject rather to the lower mind, which expresses its own selfish desires, being concerned solely about the welfare of the transient earthly personality. And as such, it muffles the voice of the Supreme Mind. But when the Supreme Mind subordinates the lower one and the two become a united whole, this facilitates a rapid transformation and ascension up the steps of the Ladder of Evolution.

MYSTERY — the foundation of all Creation, the Causeless Cause of all Existence, which is the Primordial Fire.

In the heart there is a particle of this Fire, which comes from the Mystery at the beginning of time and dissolves in the Mystery at the end of the Grand Cycle. Jesus Christ called it "Father who is in Heaven," at the same time saying: "I am in my Father, and ye in me, and I in you."[40] The greatness of a spirit is determined by the degree of unification with Him, the Father of all, who abides within. It is He who speaks with the Voice of the Silence, when the heart feels the grandeur of Mystery without need for words.

By Mystery is Mystery maintained. The comprehension of mysteries is a long process. Every secret revealed is simply a key to opening another — and so on, endlessly. But within, i.e., in himself, man cognizes the Mystery of unity with the Father and the surrounding world. And at the summit of the highest achievements, where the path of the manifested Grand Cycle of Evolution ends, the path of the fiery union of the spirit with Him, the Primordial Fire, commences.

By Mystery is the World maintained, and one of Mystery's Names is Sophia — who is "all that hath been, and is, and shall be; and [her] veil no mortal has hitherto raised."[41]

NAME — a vibrational key to the spiritual essence of its owner. The importance of names is indicated in the Bible, since true names represent accumulations of spiritual forces. Names include sound,

---

[40] John 14:20.

[41] Inscription on the temple of Isis in Sais, Egypt.

GLOSSARY

light, colour, and numerical elements, and have a specific place on the scale of cosmic life.

As a rule, people get their names from their parents; these names become a part of themselves and play a significant role in their evolution. But people are not aware of the impact of their name on both the nature and the material construction of the body. That is why it is necessary to choose a name which reflects noble qualities that would extend their influence to the children's evolution, rather than a meaningless set of sounds that does more harm than good.

An earthly name places a stamp of limitation on man within time and space. For this reason, people entering a monastery consciously renounce their names to gain freedom from worldly chains. Similarly, during their Initiation, candidates receive new names from the Master as a symbol of their renunciation of the past. These new names become their most sacred possession and should not be "spoken lightly" — i.e., without a specific need. Besides, the Master gives the disciples their names in accordance with the nature of the rays which they will express with time. Hence the secret properties of such a name are profound; they define the course of its owner's evolution and the attachment to a particular range of the Lord's Ray.

In the Book of Life, each Individuality has their own eternal cosmic name, which is in a perpetual process of formation, changing the pace of its vibrations. It contains all the merits and accumulations of its owner. During a true Initiation, this name is conveyed by word of mouth.

The vibrations contained in the Names of the Lords bring into action hidden forces, evoking the flow of fiery vortices. The power of these currents, not being directed for a specific purpose, swirls around like a whirlwind, drawing circles in space. And if whoever has caused this firestorm is not able to control its force, they expose themselves to danger. Therefore, the true Name of the Solar Hierarch is ineffable, being a Mystery, for it cannot be uttered in vain. His Name is the Word — the Sound — which created the Solar System. For example, one of His Names, Maitreya, when pronounced with understanding, even mentally, produces striking whirlwinds of fire in space. And the

Name of the Lord Maitreya, repeated seven times, serves as a powerful shield against dark influences.

NEGATION — conscious ignorance, which does not allow man to aspire beyond generally accepted limits.

Man is the greatest mystery, surrounded on all sides by the visible and invisible mysteries of Nature. But each time a mystery is revealed, even in part, it is always met by furious denial and resistance from humanity in every sphere of life. In this way, negation, being engendered by the darkness, suppresses all the predetermined possibilities of man, thereby considerably slowing his evolution.

All the Teachings of Light take into account the binary nature of human thinking, which is full of contradictions. And many people either deny or accept the points contained in them. But when the Great Teachers, through their messengers, delve into concepts more deeply, blending two opposite principles into one — those who can make no room in their understanding for even one more facet of Truth, immediately begin to negate it violently. However, it is often in opposite and antagonistic phenomena that the different sides of the same issue are perceived.

The Vedas, the Puranas, the Bhagavad-Gita, the *Tao Te Ching*, the Avesta, the Bible, the Quran, *The Secret Doctrine*, *Agni Yoga*, and many others, past and future — are all the Teachings of Light, given to humanity from the One Source for thousands of years. But each of them contains precisely the knowledge which people of different nations needed to learn at the time, taking into consideration a multitude of evolutionary factors. None of them denies the verity of the previous Teachings, but extends and supplements them with the new facets of the One Truth, urging people in their own unique way to purify their hearts and minds. Consequently, the synthesis, or comparative study, of all religions, philosophies, and sciences — uniting into one the pearls of Cosmic Knowledge which have been fragmented and scattered everywhere — is the path towards comprehension of Infinite Truth. And within Infinity, nothing can come to an end.

Negation has a destructive effect on human consciousness, even though its consequences are invisible. Whatever a man denies is excluded from his consciousness, and thus ceases to exist for his consciousness. So, if man denies the immortality of spirit and life in the Higher Worlds, then, when he departs into the Subtle World, he will be deprived of what he denied, i.e., life — he will simply sleep through it. The full power of negation is particularly noticeable in the Subtle World, where everything is created and set in motion by thought. What man believes in, that is, what he affirms, continues to exist in the affirmed forms, while what he denies ceases to exist. For example, if he denies the possibility of flying in the Subtle World, he will not be able to fly, but will continue moving in the same way as he did on the Earth.

Thus, negation simply destroys what is denied without creating anything in return, while affirmation creates a specific form for whatever is affirmed. Therefore, the High Spirits always overlay even obviously incorrect statements with true affirmations.

NUMBER — sound which produces Light and, therefore, certain vibrations. Since numbers represent different frequencies of vibrations, then one who knows the secret of numbers may evoke the Fire through expressing the constant of a sound wave by a combination of figures. Hence the world and life are ruled by numbers, and for this reason they are most sacred; their mystery is revealed only during Supreme Initiations. They who perceive the secret of numbers become Creators, and there are no more mysteries of Nature for them.

Each planet and system has its own Number, Note of Sound, and radiated Colour. Thus the Bible mentions the number 666, known as the Number of the Beast.[42] It has a secret meaning.

The number 6 is the number of the Earth, and therefore of the entire Life created by it. Three sixes symbolize the three lower bodies which the Earth has produced for all its forms. Hence, the most advanced life form of the planet — animal — has the number 666, since it does not have the Supreme Mind, the nature of which belongs to the Higher Worlds, but not to the Earth. In this way, when evolving from animal to man, the lower triad of humanity still carries the

---

[42] See Rev. 13:18.

Number of the Beast, or 666. If added together, 666 yields 18, which in turn is equal to 9 (1+8), and this bears the Spirit of Transfiguration. The number 9 symbolizes the Supreme Mind which transformed the animal into rational man.

Man is destined to become a God, whose number is 999. Therefore, he must cast off his bestial heritage through transforming each of the lower bodies, converting the number 6 into a 9. And so the Divine Triad will be reflected in the lower one, which will acquire a qualitatively new expression.

The number 666 also symbolizes the old era, marked with brutish strife between people, for the beast was dominant in man. But now the time has come for the Divine Number to gradually become dominant in the creature who is advancing a step towards the stage of God-man. Likewise, the Earth must transform its number from 6 into 9 as well.

Only the Fire and the Fiery Baptism are capable of transfiguring, through the heart, the lower to the higher. If man still lives in the lower vibrations and has failed to overcome the beast in himself, he will ascend no higher on the rungs of Evolution. But if, at the hour of final summation when the Great Choice must be made, he has already transformed at least one of the sixes into a 9, his soul has found salvation, preserving the connection with the Empyrean World.

The number of the New World is 19. This sacred number is associated with the manifestation of the Fires of Sirius, of which there is ancient evidence concerning the Initiations conducted in the secret halls of the Egyptian Pyramids. The pyramid system was of great importance, because in ancient times the Theban Sanctuary, located in Luxor, Egypt, worked mainly with humanity. The pyramids were built by the Initiates in such a way so that once a year, on 19 July, Sirius appears in the vertical corridor and illuminates the whole interior chamber of the pyramid where the Initiations occurred. Ancient Egyptians celebrated the New Year on 19 July and, according to legends and myths, their Supreme Gods came from Sirius. Therefore, this star has always been related to the cult of Isis, and 19 July is the day of the God Ra, the Lord of Civilization, the Eternal Youth, named Sanat Kumara, who descended from Sirius and has taken responsibility for

GLOSSARY

earthly humanity. The profound Mystery of this Number is revealed during the Initiation.

OM TAT SAT (*Sanskrit*) — a mantra signifying Supreme Absolute Truth. It is believed to be the most effective tool for purification and higher awakening. The utterance of a mantra brings into action the level of man's higher divine structures. It depends upon the energy of its utterer: the higher a person's energy, the more properties of the mantra are revealed.

OM or ***AUM*** — the most sacred and mystical of all words. It may be pronounced as two, three, or seven syllables, producing different vibrations. Its correct utterance, or rather, the intonation with which it should be pronounced, is a great secret, conveyed directly by the Teacher to His disciple. One who is able to pronounce it correctly draws close to the creative power of the Universe: *In the beginning was the Word, and the Word was AUM*. However, those who know how to use this Word, rarely turn to it, since they know that it evokes forces which they cannot control and which may destroy them.

AUM includes three components: Light, Colour, and Sound. These are the Three Fires or the Triple Sacred Fire in man and the Universe. According to popular belief, AUM symbolizes the three Vedas and the three Gods of Fire, Water, and Air. They also mean Creation, Preservation, and Transfiguration, personified by Brahma, Vishnu, and Shiva — or Buddha, Christ, and Maitreya. In esoteric philosophy, there are many interpretations of this three-lettered entity, which symbolizes the Trinity in One. Here are some of them:

"The letter A symbolizes Fire (Flame), the letter U Heat [Warmth], and the letter M Water."[43]

"A is Thought — the Foundation; U is Light — the Source; M is Mystery — the Innermost."[44]

---

[43] *Teachings of the Temple*, vol. 1 (Halcyon, CA: Temple of the People, 1925), p. 120.

[44] *Uchenie Zhivoi Etiki* [Teaching of Living Ethics], vol. 12, p. 67.

"A represents the Divine Agni, the Almighty Fire; U symbolizes the Light generated by it, going into M — Matter, which requires consecration by the Breath of Eternal Life."[45]

This word is usually placed at the beginning of sacred Scriptures and is prefixed to prayers, though it may serve in itself as a prayer. It is from AUM that the word *Amen* is derived.

TAT — all that is, was, or will be, all that the human consciousness is able to imagine.

In Egypt this was the symbol of stability, depicted as a cross. TAT relates to Nature and the Cosmos, representing the two principles of creation: the Masculine and the Feminine, Spirit and Matter, which are One in Eternity, being the Causeless Cause of All. It expresses the unity, interpenetration, and comprehensiveness of all creation.

SAT — the eternal Absolute Truth; the one ever-present Reality in the infinite world; the Divine Essence which is, but cannot be said to exist, since it is Absoluteness, the Essence of Being itself.

ONLY BEGOTTEN SON OF GOD — Christ, one of the Greatest Teachers of Humanity, the Teacher of Teachers, the Solar Hierarch, who has many Names. He was the first to sow the seeds of Divine Love in human hearts.

The ancient writings of the Initiates indicate that Christ is the Spirit of Sophia, the Power and Wisdom of God, and She is His Soul. He is the equivalent of the Central Spiritual Sun, whose Light gives life to all creation in the Solar System. The soul of every man is, first and foremost, the reflection or ray of this Light, clothed in the matter of the lower vibrations.

Being the Spirit of the utmost purity and fiery force, Christ can enlighten the purest human being with His Light, or Ray — and this may be justly considered to be His partial incarnation on the Earth. Such a man, born on the Earth, was Jesus — the incarnation of the one of the Great Teachers. However, it should be mentioned that He was not the Messiah promised in the ancient scriptures. He was a kind of

---

[45] *Uchenie Serdtsa* [Teaching of the Heart], vol. 4 (Moscow: Zvezda Vostoka, 2004), p. 367.

GLOSSARY

Precursor to prepare the Path for an even Higher Spirit, whose Advent is prophesied in all religions of the world. But in Jesus was manifested the Hypostasis of this Supreme Spirit, Christ, who illuminated him with His Light of the perfect knowledge of Sophia during the baptism in the River Jordan.

The physical bodies of the Highest Spirits who made human appearances on the Earth — such as Gautama Buddha and Jesus Christ — are only outwardly similar to the bodies of other people. The matter of immortality contained in their bodies is not yet a property accessible to humanity. Therefore, ordinary earthly parents could not build the body for a God. Esoteric Teachings say that the High Spirits came to earthly life as the future mother and father of Jesus Christ. Thus, His father Joseph was also the one of the Great Teachers. And His Mother was no less great than the Son: the Mother of the World was manifested in Her, having exchanged the consciousness of a Great Goddess for that of an earthly woman.

The chronology of the life of Jesus is quite inaccurate. Historians have found that Jesus was born earlier than commonly thought, namely between the years 7 and 2 BCE. From ancient scriptures it is known that He came in the year of the Tiger, which corresponds to 6 BCE.[46] Each of the Great Messengers, before beginning their Mission, is summoned into the Abode of Light, Shambhala, to restore spiritual knowledge. This is the reason that the twelve-year-old Jesus went to India. According to the ancient scrolls stored in the monasteries of Tibet,[47] for seventeen years He studied secret knowledge, visiting Greece, Egypt, Persia, the Himalayas and, most importantly, He studied with the Great Teachers of Humanity. At the age of 29, Jesus

---

[46] Helena Blavatsky and Mahatma Koot Hoomi stated that Jesus Christ lived a century before the time commonly thought. Therefore, the year 6 BCE is just an assumption; the Tiger year could actually be calculated according to a different time period.

[47] More information about these manuscripts can be found in *The Unknown Life of Jesus Christ* by Nicolas Notovitch, *Journey into Kashmir and Tibet* by Swami Abhedananda, and *Altai-Himalaya* by Nicholas Roerich.

left India and returned to Judea, where He began His sermon. Jesus Christ came to the people of Judea, but these people did not accept the Teaching of the Saviour and killed Him, thus determining their future for many centuries ahead. Therefore, Israel as a state arose only on the threshold of the Second Coming of the Messiah, having already redeemed most of its Karma.

After the death of His physical body, Jesus Christ managed to transform its matter so as to resurrect it, making it immortal. But it was the densified subtle body that became visible to the eye. This was a tremendous accomplishment for those times, for no one had been able to harness such a force of fiery energy on the Earth before. The Resurrection of the Teacher and His communication with His disciples afterwards made them true Apostles, who spread the Gospel of Love all over the world. Later, according to some researchers, Christ left Judea and continued His Mission in India, having lived nearly 80 years on the Earth.[48]

In crucifying God, humanity committed a most terrible crime which shocked the entire Universe. Every crime requires punishment according to Cosmic Laws, and the Earth was to be incinerated as unsuitable for further evolution. But Christ's Great Love saved the planet, along with His persecutors and enemies. In order to postpone the verdict signed by humanity itself, He changed the flow of Time by His Will, dividing it into two channels. One Time went into the evolutionary stream for those who have accepted Christ. The other Time designated a two-thousand-year probationary period for humanity to realize the whole gravity of the crime it had committed against God. And, through repentance in their hearts, people must redeem themselves with the same coin which God vouchsafed to them. He brought them only Love, and humanity can redeem itself before God solely by Love.

From 19 July to 11 August 1999, these two streams of Time joined, completing the probation period for those who have not accepted Christ. By this point everyone had already determined their place in the Universe — either Evolution or involution. The results have

---

[48] For further information, please see *Jesus Lived in India* by Holger Kersten.

GLOSSARY

already been summarized. Nevertheless, as a last chance, the Soul of Christ — Sophia — through Her Self-Sacrifice has allotted an additional brief period of 18 years, ending on 19 July 2017, for all those who persecuted and crucified Christ. And during this short timespan the giant stream of the Fire is being given to humanity in order to help, for the last time, those who have not yet accepted Love.

Today, there are many people who claim to be "Christs," "Maitreyas," or "Mothers of the World," and these have attracted many supporters. There are also those who do not claim anything of the sort, but people themselves feel the High Spirits embodied in them, sometimes considering them to be new incarnations of Jesus or Mary. This is because the Earth is the Messiah's lowest point of descent, and thousands of representatives and ambassadors of other worlds and civilizations have come here to meet Him. For example, the famous Anastasia of Siberia[49] and her son are High Spirits who came from a world of another dimension, a highly developed spiritual civilization, where they, may be said, are Gods. Such spirits, assimilating the Messianic Fire, return to their own worlds with the most elevated currents, each being a kind of Saviour for their respective people; thanks to them their spheres and strata will rise one step higher on the Ladder of Evolution. These people may not even realize who they really are, since the knowledge of the spirit has been obscured during their earthly incarnation.

All twelve Apostles are now incarnated on the Earth. All the people who were at Calvary two thousand years ago are gathered together, and Christ is testing everyone for Love.

PERIODS — the astrological combination of the rays of stars and Distant Worlds that strictly defines the time frame for the manifestation of certain events and phenomena, on both cosmic and individual scales. The Periods may have an impact on whole cycles and periods of Evolution.

In the Cosmos and Higher Worlds, time (in the earthly sense) does not exist, but there are Periods defined by inevitable consequences.

---

[49] Anastasia is described in the *Ringing Cedars Series* by Vladimir Megré.

Cosmic Periods are characterized by the sequence of events that allows a developed consciousness to take a specific event as a means of foreseeing all others.

When a deadline comes for a specific Period, nothing can delay its implementation. The Great Teachers merely watch to see that everyone and everything necessary is ready for the appointed time, otherwise the result might be disaster. It is better when everything is prepared in advance, but postponing it until the last moment need not cause significant damage. In this case, the Period's implementation proceeds with particular speed and intensity.

Certain dates in earthly time may not coincide with Cosmic Periods, since it is necessary to consider all seven sub-planes of the Seven Worlds, which could result in as many as forty-nine terrestrial dates. And so true prophets rarely mention specific dates of earthly time. The appearance or delay of a particular event depends on the combinations of the currents emanating from both the stars and the collective will of the Earth's humanity.

POISON — the black fire, called *imperil*, which is secreted by the human body from every negative thought, feeling, word, and action; it is also to be found in space and in the products of the darkness.

Dark phenomena and processes affect and destroy, first of all, their producer, since poison, after being deposited on the walls of the nerve channels, spreads from there throughout the body, infecting all human secretions. Hatred, irritation, fear, doubt, discouragement, gossip, self-pity, depression, and other vices, sins and passions, all secrete a poison that destroys accumulations of fiery energy, resulting in numerous diseases. Not only that, but the crystals of imperil emit an insensible and invisible fetid brown gas into space, poisoning their producer as well as others around him. In addition, whenever imperil accumulates, it attracts a rush of various evil entities of the Subtle Plane seeking to fortify themselves, and this further intensifies the effect of the poison.

Imperil is extremely contagious, and the products in which it is contained — such as alcohol, drugs, and nicotine — result in severe addictions. Moreover, imperil is also to be found in meat, since animals are known to have a premonition of their slaughter and are prompted by fear to take this poison into their blood and tissues.

No high achievements, refinement, or transformation of bodies are accessible to a person infected by imperil. If, during his lifetime on the Earth, a man has accumulated the crystals of this poison in place of fiery energies, he dooms himself to a painful existence in the Subtle World. For example, someone who hates allows themselves to be drawn into an evil environment in the company of the lowest and darkest spheres, and suffering is the result, for there it is even harder to rid one's self of harmful passions.

On the other hand, positive qualities such as love, calmness, patience, courage, confidence, optimism, silence, and others act as a strong antidote for imperil. But the cleansing of the body is not accomplished overnight.

Of course, in earthly conditions, a man with a dual nature finds it quite a challenge to purify himself of poisons completely, but it is important to demonstrate a significant preponderance of bright fires over dark ones. For this reason, all Teachings of Light contain certain commandments, obedience to which promotes the purification and transfiguration of the body. Even some religions decree or encourage fasting — or temporary abstinence from meat, alcohol, bad thoughts, and actions — to facilitate the extracting of imperil from the body.

POLARITY — the duality inherent in the manifested world. The denser the world, the more duality is manifested, while on the higher planes, polarity is expressed in chiaroscuro.

At the quaternary level the world is binary, while at the level of the Triad it is androgynous, or single. Hence *plus* and *minus*, *positive* and *negative* — are simply two sides of the same coin. Polarity gives man the opportunity to learn and improve, enabling a more rapid evolution. For the wise man, everything serves as a catalyst for ascension: enemies and friends, good and bad, and so on. Man can establish the balance, with power and control over each of the poles, but in his heart he must make the choice as to which focus to join: the Light or the darkness.

The present Solar System is binary, but the next one will be androgynous. For this, the two Principles — Masculine and Feminine, Spirit and Soul — will reunite. After all, man and woman are united at the level of their Triad, but at the quaternary level they are two halves of a single human being.

PRAYER — a bond with the Higher World; fusion with the Light. A prayer of the heart is the most powerful, for it is the fire of the heart in action. It can fly as far as its strength permits. Rhythmic prayer, which is never disregardable, is intensified manyfold in its force, inconspicuously transforming the human essence. Pure and sincere prayer for the good of the world and humanity attracts waves of spatial fire, contributing to the growth of the fiery crystal in the heart — hence the feeling of influx or restoration of spiritual forces. True meditation is also a prayer, which calls forth a responding fiery wave through its radiating love to the world.

A selfish prayer, aimed only at one's own desires, cannot fly far. In space, it meets other forms of the same selfish energy, which neutralize and destroy each other. The result is that none of these prayers reaches those who could possibly answer them; in other words, they bring no one any benefit. If one sends forth in one's prayer the strong energy of selfish desires, but without sufficient power to realize them, then the energy dissipates and the body which produced and sent it receives a boomerang blow, and is consequently weakened. Similarly, a mere mechanical repetition of words learnt by rote, devoid of the energy of love, does not bring any benefit to man.

United and collective prayer for the benefit of the entire world has immense power, although its effects may not appear instantly. It is especially needed when a major tragedy happens in the world, for the panic and fear of a large number of people can only strengthen the resulting negativity.

The Great Teachers are continuously praying for humanity and the Earth. Every day at 12 noon (in each time zone), when the Fire is at its zenith, a collective prayer of all the Forces of the Light takes place. And everybody can join in, sending forth a particle of their heart's fire into the world. There is no necessity for long prayers: the

GLOSSARY

most important thing is to be sincere. It may be the Lord's Prayer, the word *AUM* repeated three times, or just a brief thought "Good will to the world!" In other words, everyone may use the prayer which they find most familiar to them.

For those whose heart awaits the Messiah there is a short prayer, which is addressed to Maitreya (*Sanskrit*, "Love," "Saviour"), but anyone can change it to a Name that is closer to their hearts:

> In the Great Name of Maitreya,
> Let the Light of Sacred Faith,
> Let the Light of Divine Love
> Emblaze and permeate the Lord's World.

QUEST [50] — the assertion of the Light in life, bringing good to people in any form. A quest inevitably involves a sacrifice, sometimes even of one's life. People may not know many heroes personally, but their heroic deeds are recorded in the Scrolls of Akasha, and their consequences stay with heroes through all their lives. Thus heroic deeds abide in space, inspiring people to perform new such deeds.

One who has embarked on a lifelong path of heroism — a much more difficult challenge than a short-term heroic deed — is known as a servant of the Light. Quests may be great or small; however, all of them involve a process of intense growth of the heart's fiery crystal, which transforms not only its owner but also surrounding people and space. Consequently, the affirmation and development of light-bearing qualities in one's self is a constant quest. Truly, a heroic life consists in a continuous series of quests of different degrees, which then merge into a single brilliant chain of life.

The Greatest Heroic Deed ever accomplished on the Earth is the Quest of the Saviour of the World, including His Supreme Sacrifice.

---

[50] In the Russian original, it is *Podvig* — a word which cannot be translated by a single English word, signifying a highly spiritual achievement for the Common Good through self-perfection and heroic self-sacrifice in extremely difficult conditions, resulting in positive changes not only in one's personal destiny but also in a national or planetary destiny.

RACE — a stage of human evolution.[51] There are Seven Races in total, each of which has seven sub-races. Each Race develops a particular side or quality of man, densifying or rarefying the matter of the body. Since humanity, representing the appropriate Race, develops simultaneously on all Seven Globes of the Earth, moving from one World to another, the Fourth Round will finish with the Seventh Race.

People in the first two Races, as well as in the first half of the Third Race, did not have physical bodies — their bodies were of ethereal matter. Those people were genderless beings, not endowed with reason and never dying, for they did not have flesh. They had existed for 300 million years.

Eighteen million years ago, in the middle of the Third Race — i.e., the Lemurians — the separation of sexes took place, and people began to conceive their progeny. Humanity received dense physical bodies and began to reflect the Supreme Mind.

The Fourth Race — the Atlanteans — came into being approximately 4–5 million years ago. But only three sub-races of the Atlanteans evolved on the continent of Atlantis while the remaining four were in Egypt, Asia, and Europe.

The current Fifth Race, known as the Aryan,[52] originated about one million years ago in India. Its people are now to be found on each existing continent and all its seven sub-races have already formed. Nevertheless, the Third and Fourth Races are still represented on the Earth, too.

The formation of future Races does not require the millions of years needed by previous Races. Therefore, it may be said that the Sixth and Seventh Races will exist and develop simultaneously. Thus, since the beginning of the 20th century, in each country there have appeared the best and most spiritual and moral people, who are generating the next, or Sixth, Race. They are no different from others in their outward appearance, but they have loving hearts, strong energy, and

---

[51] Please note that this has nothing in common with racism.

[52] In the 20th century this term, as well as additional secret knowledge previously revealed by the Messengers of Light, was used by the dark forces to develop and circulate their anti-evolutionary theories.

GLOSSARY

often many abilities and talents. And in the present days the seeds of the Seventh Race are already showing themselves. At the end of this Race, many things that are now considered miraculous will become common, and the attenuation of the human body, as well as the matter of the planet, will reach the point prescribed by the Evolution for this Round and its last Race.

The farther one looks back into humanity's past, the more one can see of its future, for the past contains a projection of the future. Thus the first Races were ethereal — and matter slowly became solid. The last Races will be the same, but this time the matter will gradually rarefy. The end and the beginning are similar in form but distinct in expression. While the beginning was characterized by the absence of self-consciousness, the end is the pinnacle of self-awareness. The middle of the Fourth Round — the middle of the Fourth Race — marks the lowest point of the fall into matter, the densification of the human body, and the development of intelligence. The Fifth Race is on an ascending arc. Therefore, gradually the spiritual must achieve an ever-increasing preponderance over the material and the heart over the intellect, so that by the end of the Seventh Race matter is completely subordinate to spirit to the extent accessible to the Fourth Round of Evolution.

Humanity currently lives in a period of great responsibility — the time of the change of Races. This process is always accompanied by an extremely powerful influence of the Cosmic Fire, leading to a change in the inclination of the Earth's axis and magnetic poles, attended by natural disasters and climate change. Additionally, humanity is reaping what it has sown over this period of its development. As the time of the change of Races approaches, information is being imparted to the world (within permissible limits) through the Messengers of Light, with the aim of warning humanity of the forthcoming dramatic and earth-shaking changes.

Thus, Helena Blavatsky's works and the Mahatmas' Letters, along with other ancient writings, point out that during the change of Races, such continents as America and Europe are to be shaken by powerful earthquakes and submerge into the sea. Edgar Cayce, too, foresaw this scenario for the end of the 20th century. However, the development and collective will of humanity enabled the Hierarchy of Light to prevent such devastating cataclysms. But even they have the right to interfere in such cases only up to 50%; otherwise, humanity will learn nothing. The other half of efforts for salvation are to be made by Earth-dwellers themselves.

America and Europe may have a most beautiful future. Everything depends on people who must keep pace with Evolution, and that requires a revival of spirituality. Also it should be borne in mind that books, films, and other works of art which proclaim yet another "end-of-the-world" scenario and various cataclysms, promote — through human will — thought-forms that take on enormous proportions. Such energies may explode in space, resulting in huge disasters. So, North America finds itself on the Subtle Plane in a rather unstable condition since its population in the Physical World is constantly destroying its own cities and the entire continent — by the thought-forms contained, for example, in its entertainment films, which are distributed worldwide. It requires a tremendous effort on the part of all the colleagues of the Great Brotherhood to prevent such thoughts and the destruction they depict from coming true in reality. But it is also within the power of any conscientious citizen of any country. If someone can erect giant destructive structures simply through their thoughts, then by the same token a light-bearing individual is able to produce creative and positive currents — for example, by prayerful appeals to the Forces of the Light. And then the transfiguring Fire will descend into the lower spheres and mitigate the destructive influence of these negative formations.

Therefore, the manner in which the change of Races will actually take place depends upon everyone: whether through conscious evolution without tragic consequences or through constant upheavals.

RAY — creative power, energy; the focused Fire of space that creates and constructs all visible and invisible forms of life on all planes of existence. A ray is a material body, a form of expression of the Light, stretched out through space in all directions and saturated with the subtlest substance of matter, which contains a myriad of electrons.

GLOSSARY

The energy of the ray is creative, for it carries elements which combine among themselves and form compounds with elements of other rays by the Law of Magnetism and Consonance, thereby generating new types and combinations of matter and various orders of phenomena, along with whole new worlds. Thus, invisible and visible rays are mighty producers and movers of life, regulating the life of each specific organism and form.

The influence of the rays of the Sun and stars extends to all that exists on the Earth. Life has always depended on celestial bodies, for its elements are in the Universe and are sent to the Earth in the rays of their energies for the combination and generation of new forms. So, the rays of every planet took part in constructing man's physical body, whose elements are scattered in cosmic space around the corresponding stars. At a person's birth the rays intersect and develop the framework within which their physical, astral, and mental bodies are constructed. The form of each organ — heart, lungs, liver, etc. — depends on the combination of rays from appropriate stars at the moment of birth. The alignment of stars is always accurately defined and may be calculated for any given moment. Man is the concentration of the influence of rays, having gathered the crystals of cosmic energies in the Seed of his Spirit over billions of years. But rays and their combinations condition not only the life of individual man, but also that of peoples, planets, star systems, and so on.

The solar ray bears the essence of the structure and chemical composition of the Sun along with charges of powerful electromagnetic energy — bipolar in essence, threefold in manifestation, septenary in structure, and duodecimal in tonality. The visible solar ray is only one of its basest manifestations. The invisible rays of the solar spectrum, of course, are not limited to ultraviolet and infrared rays, but stretch out on both sides of the visible scale. This essence of a ray is natural not only to the rays of the Sun, but also to any star and to any centre of existence in either an actual or a potential state. And if the heart is the Sun of the body, then, consequently, every heart possesses the same qualities in its inexhaustible potential. Thus, everything radiates light, but this light varies in terms of both substance and extent.

Each Ray is a personified Being on some plane of Existence, and every person is a particle of a particular Ray. By the aforementioned analogy, one may assume that the One Solar Ray is personified by the Solar Hierarch, who is made manifest as the Great Masculine Principle — the Lord of Civilization or Sanat Kumara, but in essence He may also be called Christ or Maitreya, — while the Great Feminine Principle is the Mother of the World or Sophia. Sanat Kumara in His trichotomy is manifested as Buddha, Christ, and Maitreya; Sophia as Faith, Hope, and Love. The septenary nature of the Ray is represented in the Seven Great Teachers, each of whom personifies one of the Seven Rays, symbolizing the mastery of the corresponding stratum or type of matter. And each Teacher has a Spiritual Sister.

All the Lords pour the Light of their Rays into the world. They also use the Rays to communicate with their disciples. Every disciple is assigned a certain shade of their Master's Ray, through which they receive knowledge and information directly from Him. In this way, the Ray serves as a special tool for the translation of incomprehensible Cosmic Knowledge into what the disciple's consciousness is capable of perceiving. This helps to prevent gross distortions of Truth as well, since everyone can access the Ocean of Knowledge, but only a few are able to understand and convey it correctly to other people.

The current Era of Maitreya is the Era of the Synthesis of all Seven Rays, which together constitute the Colour White, but every two thousand years, a certain Ray, associated with one of the Seven Lords, dominates. Thus, the Ray of Christ has prevailed for two thousand years — the Age of Pisces. The next two thousand years will be the Age of Aquarius of the Master Rákóczi, also known as Saint-Germain, the Lord of the Seventh Ray. So, now the Violet Ray makes its appearance, alongside the White Ray.

Certainly, one cannot use the concept of *Time*, as it is the Periods that prevail here. The process of Transfiguration started in 1942, when the Age of Aquarius entered esoterically into force. However, it is impossible to pinpoint a definite moment at which something ends and something begins, because everything crosses over in a gradual

GLOSSARY

flow. For a while, the two Eras will overlap. Nevertheless, the Age of Aquarius is gathering momentum with every new day.

The sciences of the future, such as astrology, astrochemistry, astrobiology, astrophysiology, and astrophysics, will reveal the secrets of rays.

RHYTHM — the basic form of the manifestation of Cosmic Life in everything: from the pulsation of atoms to the movement of celestial bodies. Nothing is static; everything moves and vibrates. The aspect of various alternations is everywhere, but the length of interval is different, ranging from a millionth of a second to billions of years.

In ancient writings the essence of the Universal Law of Rhythm is expressed in the Great Breath, Inhalation and Exhalation, when the One Divine Principle "exhales" worlds, starting the active phase of their manifested life, and subsequently "inhales" them.

All the diversity of forms of matter and energy is the result of the varying speed of vibrations, or rhythmic variation. The higher the frequency of vibrations, the more perfect, refined, and energetically stronger will be the phenomenon.

There are the Great Rhythms of the Cosmos and the spatial Fire, called *Mahavan* (*Sanskrit*, "great rhythm") and *Chotavan* (*Sanskrit*, "small rhythm"). In Mahavan the stress is on the second and the last notes and on every third in the last bar; in Chotavan the stress is on the first and the last notes. These rhythms are the simplest, but there are more complex ones, which have an impact on the concept of *Time*, the planet, the Kingdoms of Nature, and so on. In essence Mahavan and Chotavan are the rhythms of the Fiery Heart of man, through which one can merge with the beating of the Great Cosmic Heart. Thus, in mastering these rhythms, man subdues the element of Fire and can even create whole new worlds. However, unless they interact with the fiery crystal of the heart, they will just be mechanical in nature and not lead to any results.

Rhythm conceals a great force. If man co-ordinated all his actions with rhythm, he would enjoy great success in every area of life, reaching the impossible, and at the same time, facilitating the achievement of any goal. Rhythmical actions create a process of gradual growth and enhancement of their effects. At a certain point the action begins to proceed on its own, by inertia, surmounting obstacles that seemed insurmountable.

ROUND — the life-cycle of Evolution of a different Time scale. So, the transition of humanity across all Seven Globes (or Spheres) of the Earth or any other planet through incarnation in each of the four Kingdoms of Nature — as mineral, plant, animal, and man — is known as the *Planetary Round*, or *Great Round*, or simply *Round*. The Great Round consists of the Seven Races, which evolve on the Seven Spheres of the planet. The development of the Seven Races on just one Globe of the planet is called a *Small Round*, or *Ring*. Also every Race involving human evolution within each of its seven sub-races may be considered a Small Round.

There are Seven Great Rounds in total comprising *Manvantara* — a period of active life. Although in ancient scriptures there are other divisions and expressions, this one is generally accepted at the present time. Between Rounds and Manvantaras there are *Pralayas* of different timespans — periods of rest, similar to slumber, which are equal in duration to the periods of activity. After passing through the Seven Rounds, humanity moves on to new planets, and so on *ad infinitum*.

As the current population of humanity, representing mainly the Fifth Race, we are now in the Fourth Great Round, which will come to completion in the Seventh Race. It is in this Round that humanity on the Earth has fully developed — earlier, it was referred to as *humanity* only for want of a more appropriate term. That which becomes man passes through all the forms and kingdoms during the First Round and through all human shapes during the two following Rounds. At the commencement of the Fourth Round, man appears on the Earth as a primeval form, being preceded only by the Mineral and Vegetable Kingdoms. Over the following three Rounds, humanity, like the globe on which it lives, will be ever tending to reassume its original divine form, except that humanity will become more and more self-aware. Like every other atom in the Universe, man strives to become first a God-man and then a God.

Every new Round always repeats the previous one in miniature before proceeding to a new level of development. The Mahatmas briefly revealed the human evolution in each of the Rounds:

First Round — Man is an ethereal being, non-intelligent, but super-spiritual. In each of the subsequent Races and sub-races and minor races of evolution he grows more and more into a compacted or incarnate being, but still essentially ethereal. And, like the animal and vegetable, he develops bodies corresponding to his coarse surroundings.

Second Round — Man is still gigantic and ethereal, but grows firmer and more condensed in his body as he becomes a more physical man. Yet still he is less intelligent than spiritual, for mind evolves with less speed and more difficulty than does the physical frame — i.e., the mind is not able to develop as rapidly as the body.

Third Round — Man has now a perfectly concrete or compacted body. At first it is the form of a giant ape, more clever (or, rather, cunning) than spiritual. For in the downward arc he has now reached the point where his primordial spirituality is eclipsed or overshadowed by his nascent mentality. In the last half of this Third Round his gigantic stature decreases, his body improves in texture and he becomes a more rational being — though still more of an ape than a man. The people of this Round had reached the physical state, but could not stay in it, causing a catastrophe, although on a smaller scale than in the subsequent Round. Some of them returned to their astral state, while others simply perished.

Fourth Round — The mental body and intellect experience an enormous development. The formerly mute races acquire human speech on the Earth, during which, starting with the Fourth Race, language is perfected and knowledge of physical things increases. At this point then the world teems with the results of intellectual activity and spiritual deterioration. In the first half of the Fourth Race, sciences, arts, literature, and philosophy are born, degenerating in one nation and reborn in another. Like everything else, civilization and intellectual development whirl through septenary cycles. Only in the second half of this Round does the spiritual essence begin the process of transmutation of body and mind to manifest its transcendental powers and accept the governing role of the heart.

Fifth Round — The same relative development and struggle continue, but with a new goal: the mastery of the subtlest Cosmic Energies. Plato and Confucius were representatives of this Round.[53] In this Round, the Supreme Mind reaches perfection. People have completely mastered thought; clairvoyance and clairaudience are available to almost everyone, but in varying degrees. Common language is replaced with the reading of thought. Evil in the form of a struggle against the Light does not exist, but there is imperfection at various stages of evolution. Science and art are highly appreciated; chemistry and other natural sciences are well developed.

Sixth Round — In this Round the human soul is fully developed. Humanity is so advanced that the qualities and abilities of the Greatest Master become the property of transfigured man. Gautama Buddha was a representative of this Round.

Seventh Round — Humanity becomes a tribe of Gods and animals are intelligent beings. It ends with the spiritualization of matter and the transition into subtly luminous forms. On the plane of ordinary visibility the Earth becomes invisible, but life remains, and its forms are manifested on the highest planes of invisibility. Everything is focused on spirit. Thought is the external expression of life, becoming a reality without a single limitation. But even these conditions are merely the preparation for a New Cycle of Evolution.

Thus, the chain of Rounds inevitably leads man towards a state of omnipotence, while each Round assigns a task for man to develop his bodies, principles, or any other abilities of his microcosm.

RULER OF THE EVIL EMPIRE — the Lord of the Darkness, the Prince of this World, the Fallen Angel, Lucifer (*Latin*, "Light-Bearer"). The ancient legend of the Fallen Angel, who rebelled against

---

[53] It should be understood that prior to their coming to the Earth, they were on another planet, which was already in the Fifth Round of development.

the Powers of Light and became Satan, reflects a real drama that took place on the Earth millions of years ago.

Lucifer was one of the Eight Great Spirits, who, in an act of self-sacrifice, left their worlds and came to the Earth in order to assist and edify humanity nearly eighteen million years ago. He quickly climbed up the Ladder of Evolution and achieved many triumphs in his World. Of all the Teachers, his Spirit was energetically the closest to the Earth, and had all the features of the composition of Saturn. This gave him the right to participate in the development of humanity, particularly its intellect. Like the other Great Teachers who had been incarnated and were interacting with people, he endowed them with reason and free will.

Being an expert on all the mysteries of the Earth, Lucifer had justifiably become known as the Prince of this World. But this also gave him a special attachment to the Earth, while the remaining Seven Great Teachers were subject to the attraction of the Higher Worlds and managed to preserve their purity. In this way, with every new incarnation on this planet, Lucifer's higher consciousness gradually darkened. Pride totally captured his mind and this led to his downfall and revolt against Cosmic Laws during the time of Atlantis.

Lucifer, having lost the right to bear this name, thought to limit the whole of humanity solely to the Earth, depriving it of a connection to the Higher and Distant Worlds. With his knowledge of all the mysteries of the planet and demonstrating the miracles of matter, he rapidly gained adherents, and these soon constituted a majority of the population of Atlantis. After all, the lack of development of human hearts meant that they were not impervious to temptations.

To achieve his goal of becoming the absolute and only god for Earth-dwellers, Lucifer directed all his efforts to demeaning woman, which always inevitably leads to the desensitization and degeneration of humanity. He destroyed the Cult of Spirit, creating instead a cult of personality: the Atlanteans began to build temples and monuments to themselves, and began to use their secret knowledge solely for their own benefit. So the application of black magic reached unprecedented proportions, directed against the Forces of the Light. However, nobody and nothing can go against Cosmic Laws, and Atlantis was effaced from the surface of the Earth.

With the beginning of a new stage of human development, the Fallen Angel founded and headed the black brotherhood, becoming a furious enemy of the White Brotherhood of Teachers for all time to come. But at this point, Lucifer decided to convince humanity that he did not exist, in order to deceive and enslave people more easily. His main goal was to put a stop to all of humanity's links with the Great Teachers. The servants of the darkness invaded the milieu of ministers of religions with the aim of distorting the simple and pure spiritual teachings of all peoples and ages beyond all recognition. This gave rise to dogmas and a terrible fanaticism, resulting in brutal intolerance and the persecution of all dissidents and infidels in the name of the Great Lords, who in fact instructed people only in Love and Compassion towards all living beings. The mass of humanity had become dark and ignorant, serving as an obedient tool for achieving Lucifer's perverted aims. And even the smallest reminder of the White Brotherhood was persecuted vigorously by humanity itself.

Nevertheless, the Messengers of Light succeeded in overcoming the situation — and this in the not too distant past. Then, realizing the nearness of his impending death, Lucifer decided to explode the planet in hopes of prolonging his life for a short while. In the 20th century, the Final Battle between the forces of the Light and the darkness occurred. And on 17 October 1949 the Great Lord of Shambhala exiled Lucifer to Saturn, where he will start his evolution anew under the extreme conditions of that planet.

Of course, Lucifer's rebellion against Cosmic Laws greatly slowed the evolution of the Earth. If it had not been for him, there would be no borders today between the physical world and the Higher Spheres, and humanity would not know such a thing as death. However, the Fallen Angel may become the Saviour of those souls that, just like him, had fallen to the ground, leading them high up the rungs of Evolution. After all, Saturn has every chance to develop at a much faster pace than the Earth.

GLOSSARY

SACRIFICE — the Law of Evolution, an awareness of which opens the boundless path of spiritual self-perfection.

The Existence of the Cosmos begins with sacrifice; life is supported by sacrifice; and it is through sacrifice that man achieves his perfection. In other words, each sacrifice offers the opportunity to obtain something new, to reach a new stage of development. True sacrifice is the conscious giving of one's own fire for the Common Good, but this is possible only for a loving heart.

The "Great Sacrifice" — this is the name often applied to the Great Lord who came to the Earth to save humanity when Lucifer's intention became clear.

SEAL — a special sign on the forehead, invisible to the physical eyes, which in accordance with Cosmic Laws determines the belonging of man to corresponding spheres, irrepressibly drawing him into their field of attraction. Also on the brow of one who has gone through the Initiation may be seen the Lighthouse of Eternity flaring. These signs of a particular colour indicate a level of spirituality and are usually represented as a shining star, but may take the form of some other symbol, too. A lilac-coloured star, for example, is a sign of very high achievement.

Extra-terrestrial technocratic civilizations which study man and his structure will never touch a man with a sign on his forehead indicating that he is following a spiritual path. They deal with the so-called biomass — people who have not yet made any kind of definite choice. The Cosmic Laws allow aliens to conduct all kinds of experiments with "nobody's" people like these: they might be taken aboard UFOs for research on their physical organs and suchlike. And hence this sign also designates personal inviolability.

SEED — a Divine Spark, or Ray of Eternal Light, a particle of the One Divine Principle in every manifestation of the world. This fiery Seed of the Spirit is referred to as *Monad* (*Greek*, "unity") in esoteric philosophy. It is indestructible, unchangeable, and eternal. It is the same for all existence as the unconscious basis of life. As a particle of the Divine Principle, this spark of life is inseparably linked with this

Principle. Its programme includes an aspiration to cognizing Divine Love and the eternal self-perfection of the forms it animates.

Besides, at the dawn of the Grand Cycle of Evolution, every Seed of the Spirit is begotten under the rays of a specific star or planet, which has its own Planetary Spirit, or Regent. Therefore, the Seed contains the same energies as this Spirit; in essence, the Lord of this star may be called the true Guardian Angel of the Monads conceived in His Rays, and the celestial body itself can be considered to be their Guiding Star for the whole Cycle. All Seeds engendered here are part of His own essence, although its vehicle — the human beings for whom He is Teacher and Cosmic Father — may never become aware of this fact. Similarly, the Great Masters of Wisdom have their Father, who has His own Lord, and so on — however, everything in the Universe is indissolubly connected with the Unknowable Divine Principle, who is the Primal Progenitor of all creation.

The more developed the Monad, the more advanced forms it embodies itself in. The levels of perfection correspond to the levels of the development of consciousness and are attained by an incredibly long evolutionary process. At the end of the Grand Cycle of Evolution, the Divine Spark returns to its Source, or point of origin, to begin a new cycle of development at a higher level. And so on *ad infinitum*, with neither beginning nor end.

The Monad is actually a duad: the union of Atma (*Sanskrit*, "Spirit") and Buddhi (*Sanskrit*, "Soul"). It is reincarnated in the lower Kingdoms of Nature — mineral, vegetable, animal — and gradually proceeds through them to man, clothing itself in appropriate forms. But upon entering the Human Kingdom, the principle of the Higher Consciousness, Manas (*Sanskrit*, "Mind"), joins the duad, forming the Divine Triad. It is Manas that transforms man into a rational and moral being, and this is what distinguishes man from ordinary animals.

Sixty billion Seeds were sown on the planet Earth, bearing the Divine Triad. All of them belong to the rays of various stars and planets, although they are all on the same temporary stop — the Earth. Of course, only seven billion are now incarnated in physical human

GLOSSARY

form, while others are in the Subtle and Fiery Spheres surrounding the planet.

The Divine Triad is in man's heart. From this fiery Seed germinates a special Flame, whose tongues create what looks like the folded petals of a Lotus. The higher the spirituality and morality of a man, the brighter and stronger will be the radiations of his heart's Flame. As a rule, there are three tongues, or petals, of the Flame — hence the threefold Flame. The first three petals are green, or emerald, the next three are rose, or scarlet, while the last ones are white. When man receives knowledge, the first three green petals of the heart-Lotus start to unfold. When he begins to love, then comes the time of the rose-coloured petals. Then appear the last three, the white ones, only of such a colour that is not accessible to the human eye.

Among humanity the vast majority are people with green petals of Knowledge, unfolded in varying degree. The rose petals of Love are revealed in a mere handful of people around the world — people who have reached the level of holiness. The white petals are possessed only by those who work with the Lords — the Adepts and the Initiates.

SENZAR — the language of the Sun, which is based on symbolism and closely associated with Sound, Light, Colour, and Number. This is the original language from which all other tongues are derived. In mythology it is often referred to as the language of the birds. Currently, Senzar is the secret sacerdotal language of the Great White Brotherhood, the Initiated Adepts, and their disciples all over the world. It is taught in Secret Schools in the Orient.

In earliest antiquity there was one knowledge and one universal language — Senzar. From the beginning of human evolution, this was transmitted from generation to generation. Yet during the times of Atlantis, when humanity fell into sin, this language, along with eternal knowledge, ceased to be available to posterity. All nations restricted themselves to their own national tongues and lost their connection with the Secret Wisdom, forgetting the one language. Humanity no longer deserved to receive such knowledge. So, instead of being universal, Senzar now became the possession of just a few. The biblical myth of the Tower of Babel and similar legends around the world symbolically testify to that enforced secrecy, narrating the story when the Lord had confounded the one original language into several, so that sinners could no longer understand one another's speech.

In present times, Senzar was discovered in the undecipherable inscriptions on stones and plants. For example, on the territory of the Buddhist monastery Kumbum in China there grows the sacred Tree of Great Merit, also known as the Tree of Ten Thousand Images. Legend has it that it grew out of the hair of the great Buddhist reformer Tsongkhapa. In the past, according to witnesses,[54] on each of its leaves in blossom a sacred letter or syllable appeared of such amazing beauty and perfection that no other existing letter could surpass them. Those mystic letters and syllables were written in Senzar, and in their totality comprised the whole Teaching of Buddhism and the history of the world.

SHAMBHALA (*Sanskrit*, "Place of Peace") — the Stronghold of Light, a legendary kingdom hidden in the heart of the Himalayas. It is known under different names in the myths and beliefs of various peoples of the world: Agartha, Belovodye, the City of Gods, the Garden of Eden, Mount Meru, the Pure Land, the White Island, and so on. Shambhala is the Imperishable Sacred Land, the first and ever-present continent of the planet Earth, which never shared the fate of the others, for it is destined to continue from the beginning to the end of the Grand Cycle of Evolution. It is the cradle of the first man and contains the sacral Source of all religions, philosophies, sciences, and esoteric teachings. This mysterious place, which preserves the Eternal Wisdom, lies at the intersection of the past, present, and future, as well as of the Physical, Subtle, and Fiery Worlds.

Shambhala was first mentioned in the Puranas. Information about it filtered into the world in different times. Back in the 9th century, one of the monks of Kievan Rus had been staying in the Ashram of the White Brotherhood for several days, however he was not allowed to

---

[54] See Évariste Huc, Chapter 2, in *Travels in Tartary, Thibet, and China, 1844–1846*, vol. 2 (London: Office of the National Illustrated Library, 1852).

GLOSSARY

talk about it, except upon his deathbed, to tell his story "from mouth to ear." It was not until in 1893, in fact, that this account was written down. In the 12th and 13th centuries, Popes Alexander III and Innocent IV both attempted to establish contact with Prester John, the head of the Secret Spiritual Brotherhood in the heart of Asia, who had sent letters to a number of Christian sovereigns: Constantine the Great, Manuel I Komnenos, Frederick I Barbarossa, Louis VII of France, and others. In the 17th century, the Portuguese Jesuit missionary, Estêvão Cacella, was the first to tell the Europeans of this mythical place, which he visited at the invitation of the Tibetans. In 1915, Albert Grünwedel published a German translation of the Guidebook to Shambhala, written by the famous Panchen Lama, Lobsang Palden Yeshe, in which the location of this legendary realm is indicated by a mass of symbols and complex geographical hints. And in 1925, in many newspapers all over the world, an extensive article by the Mongolian explorer, Dr. Lao Chin, appeared, telling of his journey to the Valley of Shambhala.[55] He was forbidden to write about the wondrous spiritual phenomena that take place there. However, Dr. Lao Chin mentioned that the inhabitants of the valley lived for many centuries, but looked like middle-age people, and they were characterized by clairvoyance, telepathy, and other higher abilities. Among other things, he saw how they levitated and even became invisible to the physical eye.

Shambhala is the Ashram of the White Brotherhood of the Teachers of Humanity, each of whom is a God, having become such for many nations and leaving the divine mark in human hearts as an equal among equals in the flesh. The work of the Mahatmas may be seen in three principal directions of research: the improvement of the earthly plane; methods of communication with the Distant Worlds; means of conveying the results of their research to humanity. The latter is indeed the most challenging of all.

The Shambhala of the Earth may be thought of as a spaceport from which messengers are sent to the Distant Worlds and where

---

[55] See "Strange Secrets of Thibet's Temple of Life," *The Atlanta Constitution*, 25 January 1925; "Mystic Colony Long Hidden in Valley of Tibet," *The Shanghai Times*, 16 March 1925.

ambassadors from the infinite Universe arrive. New ideas from other inhabited planets are tested in the laboratories of the Brotherhood; after being adapted to earthly conditions, they are in turn conveyed to scientists of the world as inspiration.

Here the most important decisions concerning the evolution of humanity and the planet are made. Once every hundred years, the Council of Shambhala is convened (1925, 2025); once every sixty years the Council of the High Initiates takes place. It is a real World Government, which has little in common with earthly regimes, but still it has often contacted them through its messengers. Indeed, the history of all times and nations records testimonies to the Assistance of the Great Teachers, which has always been secretly given at turning points in the history of every country. However, while the peoples of the East often accepted their advice, the West, as a rule, rejected them.

For example, in addition to the aforementioned information, it is known that warnings were received by the representatives of the Habsburg dynasty and the Norwegian King Cnut the Great. Charles XII of Sweden was warned not to start his fatal campaign against Russia. The repeated warnings to Louis XVI and Marie Antoinette of the impending danger to France and the French royal family are widely known. Napoleon was also warned not to go against Russia. A warning was given to Queen Victoria around 1850. And in 1926 the Mahatmas issued an austere warning to the government of the USSR, and the consequences of its rejection were indeed grave. Further, an unknown Tibetan lama passed a warning to Hitler through German zoologist Ernst Schäfer that he should not start a "great war." On the other hand, American Presidents George Washington and Abraham Lincoln listened to the advice of the White Brotherhood, which resulted in the powerful development of the United States. In the 1930s, however, when President Franklin Roosevelt was warned about the upcoming Second World War, he, unfortunately, did not take all the advice he was given to heart, otherwise there would be a United States of both Americas today.

A number of prominent people also visited Shambhala. As a rule, one or two candidates are admitted there each "century" (which consists not of a hundred years but sixty, according to the Kalachakra Calendar). For example, during their lifetimes this Stronghold of Light was visited by: Gautama Buddha, Jesus Christ, Lao-Tzu, Pythagoras, Plato, Apollonius of Tyana, Paracelsus, the Panchen Lama Palden Yeshe, Helena Blavatsky, Helena and Nicholas Roerich, and others — all of whom have played a significant role in the evolution of humanity. But not all the Great Spirits who had certain missions to fulfil visited the Brotherhood during their earthly life. Furthermore, anyone who visits this Abode of Light by an invitation resonating deeply in their heart takes a vow of silence, which may be broken only with the permission of the Great Lord of Shambhala. An uninvited guest will never find the right way to reach it.

Formerly, very little could be said about Shambhala, but still, something new has been revealed with each new century. Eventually, in 2012, at the Lesser Council of Shambhala, in addition to other important decisions for the planet, the Lords permitted the publication of a book entitled *Dialogues*, which Zinovia Dushkova wrote high in the mountains in 2004–2005. This work for the first time in human history unveils the inside story of the White Island: it tells how it is organized, what researches are conducted there, it talks about the life of the Teachers, about the Great Lord, and much more.

SMALL PLANET — a new planet, called *Urusvati* (*Sanskrit*, "Light of the Morning Star") by the Great Teachers, which should become a part of the Solar System in the future.

Today it is a comet that appeared more than once in the Solar System during the age of Atlantis. In present times, it was seen in November 1948 and is known as the Eclipse Comet (C/1948 V1). According to astronomers' calculations, the orbital period of this comet is approximately 85,000 years.

When the Cosmic Period comes, this comet will become a planet and settle in the Solar System. In those days, when passing near Saturn, Urusvati will disrupt its course and will knock it out of orbit by its powerful gravitational force. Thus, Saturn will leave the Solar System and its negative impact on all the other planets in the System will come to an end. And Urusvati, being slightly larger than the Earth, will take its place between the Earth and Venus and serve as a new home for a new humanity. The appearance of Urusvati will beneficially affect the entire Solar System, especially the Earth, accelerating its evolution. Under the influence of its rays, the Moon will also begin a new stage of development and, being covered by rich vegetation, will turn into a flourishing garden.

SOLAR SYSTEM — a planetary system with a Central Star, the Sun. The present Solar System consists of 14 planets, although some of them are not yet visible or are in the process of formation.

Every planet is inhabited, but they are at different levels of development. It is incorrect to assume that the farther a planet is from the Sun, the more primitive it is. Indeed, Uranus, Neptune, and Pluto are the most advanced planets of all; Venus is higher than Jupiter in its development; Mars and Mercury are currently undergoing a period of abatement, or a subsiding of manifested life, but their new cycle of evolution will be on a higher level than the present one of the Earth; Saturn is the lowest planet — there the process of creating conditions for life is just beginning.

According to esoteric tradition, Saturn was the firstborn son of Sirius and the twin brother of Uranus. Saturn became the Central Star, but it was not inhabited because of its lack of cosmic magnetism — which is essential for life and the proper development of the entire System — and was replaced by Uranus. The Sun subsequently appeared, first as a comet; through its tremendous force of magnetism it eventually became the Central Star, superseding Uranus.

There are evidently three Solar Systems in all. The task of the First Solar System was Knowledge, the formation of the physical body, intellect, and mind; this was the Masculine System. It ended with its dominant colour of green, the colour of Knowledge. Now we are experiencing the Second Solar System, which is Feminine, and its task is Love-Wisdom and the opening of the Heart. That is why all the Great Teachers worship and serve the Great Feminine Principle, the Mother of the World. Souls who were the best in the former System were the first to enter the Second Solar System. According to Cosmic Laws, evolution on a new stage always starts by repeating its forerunner,

GLOSSARY

therefore much Knowledge was imparted to humanity in the current System, and green is dominant in Nature. But two thousand years ago, the time came to start fulfilling the mission of Love-Wisdom, and Christ was the first to bestow such an opportunity on the Earth. The Third System will be Androgynous, when the two Principles — Male and Female, Spirit and Soul — will reunite; and its task will be the Divine Will and Divine Power. Only those will move there who succeed in properly developing their hearts and synthesizing Knowledge and Love into Divine Wisdom.

When creating the present Solar System, the number 7 was incorporated into its foundation as the energy code. Hence the sevenfold manifestation of the world, the structure of man and the planets. The next Solar System will be twelvefold — and this is why the number 12 plays a significant role in the current System as well.

SOUND — the vibration or rhythm of the Fire, accompanied by Light and Colour. This is one of the forms of existence and the basis of every manifested phenomenon and process. In Nature and the Cosmos, everything sounds and has its own note — and these notes are not limited to those known to humanity — along with its own unique melody. A sound generated in space never disappears, but remains there forever in the form of audio imprints in the Akasha Scrolls.

Sound is septenary in its structure and has seven aspects: the first four are sound, colour, smell, and magnetic wave; the other three aspects are not yet accessible to understanding by the Earth's humanity. This is because the secret meaning of sound is profound and sacred, full of ineffable power. Underlying any produced sound is either a positive or a negative force. In mastering the energy of sound, man comes closer to the source of cosmic power.

In the structure of the Universe, *music* occupies a most prominent place. Knowledge of music is the foundation of esoteric sciences. For one thing, it is needed to decipher the language of symbols and signs, which is based mainly on sound. Sound — music — is the most perfect language — the first section of the Mystery language, Senzar.

It is usually employed by the Initiates for intercommunication when the other elements of Senzar, such as colour, symbols, or speech, are inappropriate to use.

A magnificent musical symphony for the developed fiery consciousness represents an entire extravaganza of beautiful iridescent colours, arrayed in a host of fiery combinations and accompanied by the finest fragrances. The human body may be attuned to the acoustic wave of a song, for the condition of the human spirit is expressed in sound. And if a man sings with joy, and joy is expressed in his song, then the song in turn may arouse a particular feeling or emotion in him. A song for the heart is a powerful tonic. The song is a key to human hearts. Sound has a strong effect on the nervous system, which begins to vibrate in the key of the song playing, uniting listeners into a single whole. Thus, the song is a unifier and harmonizer of collective consciousness. For this reason, singing plays a vital role in all religions.

Thus, man possesses a powerful weapon — a voice that can either create or destroy. It is imbued with a tremendous power of magnetic influence. The voice sounds in consonance with the colours of the aura, because it expresses the whole essence of man. There is nothing in Nature richer in sounds than the human voice. But man has consciously mastered only a very few of its elements.

SPACE — just like Time, an indispensable condition for evolution, the cognition of Existence, or testing the true qualities of any creature.

The subtler and higher the matter, the less is the importance of Space and Time. Thus, in the Higher Worlds, space has no distances, and the human spirit may be in different places at the same time.

SPIRIT — the fire of life; super-rarefied matter; the Masculine Aspect of the Absolute, or the Primordial Fire. Spirit and Matter are the two poles of the One Divine Principle, Spirit and Soul, neither existing without the other.

Man has a spark in his heart, ignited from the Eternal Flame of Life, the Divine Principle, clothed in the Immortal Triad. The Seed of the Spirit, or Monad, is eternal and indestructible, being the crystalline light of stars, under which it was born at the beginning of the

GLOSSARY

Grand Cycle of Evolution, preserving the indissoluble spiritual and material bond with its Father.

Spirit is an eternal wanderer from planet to planet, from system to system. In the infinite evolution of forms, in which it consistently encases itself, all the experience it gains in every Kingdom of Nature is deposited and crystallized. The Seed of the Spirit remains unchanged, but the deposits of fiery energy in the form of crystals constantly grow. They result in the burning of the threefold Flame, and it is important that it not be extinguished. Every movement, thought, word, feeling, or act of man accumulates or wastes the crystals of this Treasure. Each established quality is a crystallized fire of varying degree and size. All aptitudes and personality traits are, in essence, the elements of crystallized energies, accumulated around the Seed of the Spirit. They impel the spirit to take on only those coverings that correspond to the energies of its crystals. And since the spirit is fire, its ascension on the Ladder of Evolution occurs through the growth of the fiery crystals that surround it. Hence the affirmation of positive qualities is the process of conscious design of man's fiery body, which accordingly gives shape to all the lower ones: mental, astral, and physical. When the Flame attains such a degree of power that it breaks through all coverings, its Light illuminates every sphere around, transforming not only its owner, but the whole environment as well.

Spirit is omnipresent, beyond dimensions, space, and time. Spirit has neither form nor covering, but can spiritualize and give life to any form, creating it from matter. To the spirit is given power over everything in which it manifests itself. Even the Seed of the Spirit has a form. But the One who dwells inside, without Name, incognizable in the manifested world, does not have form, but is self-existent. Man is the carrier of the Mystery of Immortality, the Mystery of Existence, the Mystery of Infinite Cosmic Life. His spirit combines within itself both Alpha and Omega, the beginning and the end of all that is, was, and will be.

STAR — an advanced form of conscious being that once lived and attained perfection in one of the worlds of a particular solar system. Therefore, man may be considered a future star in the firmament.

But stars, too, can assume human form as they are incarnated on different planets.

The human spirit has a property of divisibility which enables it to act consciously on various planes of existence, though this does not at all affect the quality of its manifestation or activity. The High Spirits have mastered this ability to perfection, and they may be on different planets in various worlds and even different systems at the same time. For example, all Seven Sisters of the Pleiades are manifested on the Earth in varying degrees, being the Sisters of the Great White Brotherhood. They can see their souls in Heaven. Still, they are here, but their bodies are composed only from the degree of the Fire which their physical earthly body is able to endure. Similarly, the Sun is one of the bodies of the united Christ and Sophia. That is why ever since ancient times the Sun has been considered equal to the Supreme God.

When the Teachings mention either a star or a planet, it can mean the same thing. Each creation has a sevenfold structure, and hence the fiery body of a planet is seen as a star. The Great Teachers call the Earth a *Dark Star* and also the *Cradle of Stars*.

The basic substance of the human body does not differ from that of the celestial bodies, therefore stars and people have a tremendous impact on each other. Every heavenly body corresponds to a certain metal. Metals are included in the structure of the human body as its constituent parts in various proportions and combinations. The presence of metals attracts the rays of planets which regulate human life. Thus a horoscope, or stellar map, may be seen as a diagram of the tonality of the human essence, which is capable of reacting to the influence of stellar rays in a particular way. Even the physical appearance of man is defined by his horoscope. But stars do not force, they only facilitate the development of the properties predestined by a given incarnation. That is, the free will of man contributes its own amendments to the stellar map and, to a certain extent (as determined by Karma), itself directs the course of life.

Astrology, astrophysics, and astrochemistry are the sciences of the future, where technological devices will enable scientists to

GLOSSARY

unmistakably identify the nature and properties of stellar rays and their influence on humanity.

SUFFERING — an earthly condition favouring the igniting of fires necessary for the highest achievements of man; a learning method that brings knowledge and experience. The causes of suffering are often earthly illusions and desires, and when man realizes this, suffering has a purifying and liberating property. Of course, this does not include self-torture or self-abasement, which are clearly anti-evolutionary and useless.

Suffering refines the heart and enlightens it with the great quality of empathy. Only the long-suffering heart is able to understand someone else's grief and suffering. Each instance of suffering creates a special substance that deposits fiery crystals in the heart. Those who have accumulated and increased this treasure have truly undergone much suffering in their lives. This in turn has given rise to that great quality of spirit known as *compassion*.

But one should not confuse *compassion* with *pity*, since these are completely different things, although the boundary between them is thin. One who pities immerses oneself into the feelings of another and gets bogged down in them, multiplying rather than dispelling the intensity of despair and gloom. This offers no real help for the object of pity, but the one who pities further darkens the radiations of one's own aura — thereby doubling the gloom in space. On the contrary, one who demonstrates compassion uplifts the condition of the sufferer, surrounding them with light, hope, cheerfulness, and joy. Thus, compassion is the acceptance and transmutation of the tribulation of one's neighbour through the fires of the heart, thereby completely excluding the possibility of infecting the helper with the darkened condition of the person in need of help. This quality requires a great degree of mastery of the radiations of one's own aura. Each Bearer of Light is thus a permanent transmutator of surrounding hearts. That is why it is so important for the Solar Stone of the heart to be always shining and only increasing in its power.

The highest form of suffering is the Sacrifice made by the spirit for the salvation of the world. The Great Sacrifice requires great suffering, too. The history of humanity has recorded the Sacrifices of the Great Spirits who have given their hearts to the service of the world. And the Lord whose name is Compassion gave people a great example of Love for humanity.

SUN — the Central Star of the Solar System, where the Supreme Fiery Beings reside. It revolves around the Central Star of another System, Sirius, being one of its sun-planets, though located a considerable distance away. The full passage of the Sun through its orbit takes at least a billion years.

The Sun appeared as a comet in the System at a time when Uranus was the Central Star. This comet had a strong magnetism and began to attract and absorb other comets, small planets, and various celestial bodies. And so, after assimilating a great number of energies, the Sun has become the Central Star of the System.

The Sun plays the role of the Heart of the Solar System, pulsating with a period of eleven years. Hence the Sun is the repository of the vital force necessary to all beings and planets of the System. Through it, from the invisible and far more powerful Central Spiritual Sun, passes a Cosmic Ray which contains all the elements and energies that are given to the planets by the Sun. Solar light is the reflection of the Spiritual Light — the Light of the Central Spiritual Sun. Further, the Sun receives the waste energies of the planets, transmutes them, and then sends them back into the System. The period of inhalation and exhalation of the Sun's vital energy ranges from four to five years.

Solar flares are intensified impulses which give off the necessary ingredients. If one of the planets is in need of additional life-giving energies, the Sun increases its activity. The disturbance of the harmony and balance of energy on a certain planet affects the general balance of the whole System. This means the Sun, along with other stars, needs to intensify its transmission of energy directed exclusively at that planet. Sunspots increase the chemical impact of the energy of rays, and this in turn affects the human nervous system. Sunspots and

GLOSSARY

explosions on the Sun cause contractions in the Earth's core, which give rise to earthquakes and floods and may even change the axial tilt of the planet. Solar rays contain all the ingredients of the Solar System. They exert a powerful effect on all life, acting as the regulator of the entire System. For example, studying the composition of solar rays can provide accurate information about weather for a month in advance.

High Spirits from other Systems enter and leave the Solar System through the Sun. So, in order for High Spirits from Sirius, for example, to be incarnated on the Earth, they travel through the Constellation of Orion, pass through the Sun, then through Pluto and all the other planets to Venus, and from Venus to the Earth. This is because the supreme Fiery Energies need to adapt gradually to the conditions of the planet during the descent of the High Spirits. If they went directly from Sirius to the Earth, the Earth would simply be burnt to ashes by the powerful intensity of the Fires.

In connection with the Age of Fire — the Age of the Heart, accompanied by the periods of the greatest activity of the Universal Fire — the Sun enters a phase of its highest activity as well, thereby exerting an impact on the higher human energy centres. The high-frequency vibrations come from the Fiery Core of the Sun and are directed into human hearts, thus contributing to the transfiguration of every human being.

THOUGHT — the Fire, or fiery energy, clothed by the will in a material form of certain firmness and durability, aspiring to realization. Thought is the basis of everything that exists in the Universe. It is limited by neither time nor space; its power knows no bounds. Still, it is restricted by Cosmic Laws. Therefore, every thought which has ever been generated — even thousands of years ago in previous lives, must sooner or later manifest itself in action.

Being the subtlest of the fiery energies, thought subordinates all the lower energies to its power and thus can shape the physical world. So, thought produces an image which is consolidated and encased in the flesh of the Subtle World, and is then embodied on the Earth as some particular consequence, appearing in a corresponding form of matter. But to shape dense matter, thought itself must take on clear and definite forms. The covering of thought is saturated with magnetic energy, which attracts other similar, consonant energies. Therefore, when a thought is sent forth into space, it accumulates kindred elements and grows like a snowball. As it grows in space, it returns periodically to its creator for affirmation or denial. In the former case, the thought intensifies, receiving additional energy, and then goes out once more into space, and so on until it achieves a full realization. In the latter case, if consciousness has already overtaken it or if the person lacks confidence or is unsure of themselves, the thought loses its power and continues to weaken until it is suppressed or destroyed. But at the same time, creating a strong, clear thought and then forgetting about it completely does not mean destroying it. It will again return to its producer and will eventually come to realization, possibly many centuries later. Thoughts and dreams always come true when the environmental conditions and the composition of its elements favour them, but not necessarily in the time or the way that people anticipate.

Dark thoughts are limited to the lifetime of the darkness and, therefore, doomed to perdition by the power of Cosmic Laws. Bright thoughts, on the other hand, are eternal and can grow limitlessly within Cosmic Laws. Thoughts directed to one's self pulsate close by, illuminating or darkening consciousness, either openly or invisibly. Every thought provokes a reaction in the body. Dark and vicious thoughts — thoughts of fear, doubt, and negativity — are like leeches, sucking vital forces out of the human aura. In destroying vital energies, such thoughts can cause various diseases. A person's health often depends on the balance of mental energy, and so the causes of illness can lie in the disequilibrium of thoughts. And vice versa: positive, optimistic, and joyful thoughts imbue the organism with the energies of life, increasing them in both man and the space surrounding him. Thought creates man's internal appearance, which is reflected to a certain extent in his physical body. Thus man is the reflection of his thoughts, and eventually becomes what and who he wants to be. Consequently, thought is an instrument for the self-perfection (or involution) of man. Similarly, the collective thought of humanity

GLOSSARY

powerfully affects the living conditions of the planet, making them better or worse depending on the general nature of thoughts.

It is incorrect to assume that the ability to think is the sole property of the human brain, for man without his physical body does not lose his ability to think. Thought can be governed by two centres: the brain and the heart — each in its own way, using particular types of energy of varying degrees of refinement. The currents of thoughts sent by the heart are especially effective; the thoughts of the brain are much weaker, and the radius of their action is much shorter. Thoughts can protect man, places, or things, as well as help someone else, instantly uniting with the object of aspiration. Their effect may last for either a long or a short time, depending on the assigned period or volitional order. They may also have an accurately defined and strictly limited purpose. Everything depends on the strength of the heart's energy or fire that is put into these currents. The most powerful thoughts are those created by the Power of Love — in fact, they are able to create entire worlds.

Discipline of thought is the principal condition for progress. Because of the concept of *Time* in the dense world, a certain period is required before anything shows its consequences. But in the Higher Worlds, time no longer has such power, therefore thoughts there become a reality instantly, and man reaps the fruits of his thoughts he produced during his life on the Earth. It is important now to learn how to control one's thoughts so as to avoid creating additional problems for one's self in the Subtle World.

The science of thought is the science of the future. The mastery of thought will lead to the mastery of many secrets of Nature and to the achievement of the might of the spirit.

THREADS — rays of connection. From the heart of one star a silver thread stretches to another, which in turn extends its radiant threads to other constellations. These binding ties between the stars also reach out to human hearts, which have close relations among one another, too. Thus, everything in the world is connected in a single vital network, through its bond with the Heart of Infinity.

THREADS — TIME

TIME — an illusion which is necessary for evolution; closely related to Space and the Cosmic Law of Cause and Effect. There is a Universal Time manifested in the entire Universe, which is defined Space, but it is connected with the Periods and has nothing in common with the earthly understanding of time. There is also *inner time*, characteristic of solar systems, planets, humans, etc.

The past, present, and future are the framework within which man comprehends the world. Causes create the future, proceeding from the past to the future. The past cannot be changed, while the future is changeable, for other causes may be created in the present which will influence it. Three times exist inseparably in space, therefore, people with a developed consciousness are able from the present time to penetrate both the past and the future for millennia to come. If it were not for the intervention of free will, the future, existing in space as a projection of past causes, would be fixed and immovable. But the will introduces its own corrections — that is why so many prophecies go unfulfilled. Nevertheless, the Law of Cause and Effect makes the plasticity of the future conditional on the causes which generate it, and determines the framework for the development of events.

Time is directly proportional to the density of matter. That is, the more attenuated the matter and the higher its vibrations, the more blurred is the concept of *Time*. In the Subtle World time loses its ordinary meaning, but there is still a sequence of things, events, and perceptions of consciousness. Dreams are the experience of this, when, in a few earthly hours or minutes, one can experience a mass of events in a dream. In the Fiery World, time does not exist either: everything occurs in the "here and now." Therefore, the spirit and human thoughts, having their origin in this World, are also beyond time.

Since the matter of the Earth under the influence of the Cosmic Fire has already started to gradually rarefy, one may notice that time does not pass at the same pace as it did in the 20th century: it seems to have accelerated.

GLOSSARY

TITANS — a race of giants of divine origin in Greek mythology.

Legends of the Battle of the Titans, or the Battle of the Gods, exist all over the world, telling about the time when a group of Gods opposed one dominant God. In fact, these myths reflect the events of the rebellion of the Sons of Light, the Titans of Shambhala, against the dictatorship of Lucifer and his evil sorcerers, which took place when the last islands of Atlantis remained, but the time of the current Fifth Race had already arrived. Compared with present-day human beings, the Atlanteans, like the first sub-races of the Fifth Race, were giants, as recorded in the legends. The victory of the Light over the warlock-giants of the last island of Atlantis, Poseidonis, occurred in 9564 BCE, when it plunged into the water.

TOWER OF CHUNG (*Senzar*) — the Central Tower of Shambhala. This multi-storey building is like a gigantic museum, which goes deep into the Earth as well as rises high above into the Subtle Spheres. All the works of art of all peoples that have ever existed on this planet are stored here. There is a large library of manuscripts and literary works throughout the ages, including those that have been considered lost or destroyed.

The Tower of Chung also contains absolutely all the exhibits of the Mineral, Vegetable, and Animal Kingdoms, all the patterns of Life that have ever existed on the Earth, including subterranean and ethereal inhabitants. They are immersed into centuries-old dormancy in special niches which are filled with certain gaseous substances to preserve life at the cellular level.

It is in the Tower of Chung that the Great Lord of Shambhala tirelessly keeps His Vigil for the good of all humanity.

TREACHERY — an indelible stigma for eternal ages; the gravest sin, for one who betrays once will always betray. Treachery may not only mean a breach of loyalty, betrayal of trust, slander, and malice, but also the belittling and suppression of Truth.

The roots of betrayal keep on growing for centuries, and cannot be extirpated by either words or persuasive arguments, or, indeed, by any other means. Even if there is a period of repentance and an attempt to atone for one's acts, the time will surely come when the betrayer is once again ready to dive into the darkness and surrender to evil. We should be more alert with friends than with enemies, for betrayal often comes through those closest to us. And while dark forces try with all their might to make a man betray, especially as he ascends the Ladder of Light, — the darkness, too, has no appreciation for traitors, but only uses them for its own purposes, since they are also capable of betraying the darkness itself.

Past sins are not an obstacle on the path towards the Light, unless marked with the stigma of betrayal of the Hierarchy. There is no worse crime than a deliberate betrayal of the Messenger of Light. Jesus Christ, even as He drew Judas closer to Himself, knew where his free will would lead him, for Judas had betrayed Him many times before. Other High Spirits were also aware of traitors appearing in their lives. For example, in the 1880s Helena Blavatsky was betrayed by Emma and Alexis Coulomb[56] with the aim of fabricating evidence for an accusatory report by the Society for Psychical Research. It was not until a hundred years later, in 1986, that the Society concluded that Blavatsky "was unjustly condemned."[57] Nicholas and Helena Roerich were betrayed by Louis and Nettie Horch,[58] whose slander damaged the reputation of the Roerichs in the United States, thereby putting an end to the wide circulation of *Agni Yoga*.

---

[56] When the Coulombs had financial problems, they appealed to Blavatsky for help and were offered a job at the Theosophical Society in India. Their betrayal was funded by Christian missionaries, who later did not even hide this fact.

[57] Incorporated Society for Psychical Research, "Madame Blavatsky, co-founder of the Theosophical Society, was unjustly condemned, new study concludes," press release, 8 May 1986.

[58] The Horchs were the closest colleagues of the Roerich family in the United States. They co-founded the first Roerich Museum and the Master Institute of United Arts, as well as other organizations dedicated to culture and art in New York City. Having being entrusted with all the financial aspects of Nicholas Roerich's activity, Louis Horch managed to acquire rights for all Roerich's paintings and other collections in the United States, which in fact had been presented by Roerich as a gift to the American nation.

GLOSSARY

One may wonder why, even though the High Spirits are aware of traitors, still, they always try to help them, despite the fact that their own lives might be in danger. Here is the answer which Blavatsky received from her Master, which begins with a rule from the *Book of the Golden Precepts*:

" 'If thou findest a hungry serpent creeping into thy house, seeking for food, and, out of fear it should bite thee, instead of offering it milk thou turnest it out to suffer and starve, thou turnest away from the Path of Compassion. Thus acteth the fainthearted and the selfish.' . . . Your two Karmas run in two opposite directions. Shall you, out of abject fear of that which may come, blend the two [Karmas] and become as she is? . . . They are homeless and hungry; shelter and feed them, then, if you would not become participant in her Karma." [59]

The Laws of Karma are complicated, and betrayers may appear owing to either a personal or collective Karma.

TREE OF EVIL — an actually existing creation of the dark forces in the lowest layers of the Subtle World, that is, those that are the closest to the dense spheres of the Earth. Its dangerous dripping poison can reach only those whose nature is susceptible to this infection, whose soul is correspondingly prepared for its venomous seed.

TRUTH — a concept of the world surrounding man, based on the Foundations, or Cosmic Laws. Secret Knowledge is built on them, and therefore is itself an aspect of Truth which is not transient through the ages, but is eternal.

One can find fragments of these Foundations in all great religions and philosophies — but only fragments, for Truth cannot be comprehended by human consciousness as a whole. It is accessible to High Spirits on a scale inconceivable to the human mind, yet even for them not entirely. For Truth is boundless, and is continuously revealing its infinite essence to the Greatest Cognizants of Cosmic Life. However, its Foundations remain the same at all times. They know neither

---

[59] Helena Blavatsky, *Collected Writings*, vol. 12 (Wheaton, IL: Theosophical Publishing House, 1980), pp. 587–588.

separation nor contradiction, for one of their inherent properties is monolithic integrity.

UNIVERSE — matter manifested within the framework of the Law. Nothing in nature vanishes, but everything is in a state of eternal formation, that is, in a process of constant, continuous transformation and transition from one form of expression to a different one. Likewise, the Cosmos is an integral whole, which is currently undergoing infinite development and expansion of all its life forms. And each form has its own mission. The end and disappearance of a form is not the destruction of the fiery principle that animated it, but only a step towards its manifestation in a new form. Every atom may be considered to be the Universe in miniature.

The plan of Creation may be represented symbolically as an equilateral cross. At the top of the cross are the Divine Worlds of the Absolute, the Higher Spiritual Worlds from where the High Spirits descend; at the bottom are the dark antiworlds. At one side are the technocratic civilizations that arrive on the Earth in UFOs to study the planet and human beings; while at the other side are the so-called "field forms" of life, such as elves, fairies, brownies — the Kingdom of Elementals. Each world has its own hierarchical structure.

Man may be pictured as though crucified on this cross. That which is above the heart — the higher centres, the higher vibrations — belong to the Divine World. Everything below the heart is inclined towards the lower worlds of the darkness. Man is under the close attention of all four sides represented as various forms of life, and he makes a free choice as to which side to take.

There are now representatives on the Earth of almost all the worlds — more than three thousand civilizations. Every world is interested in increasing its size. Each of them provides its own systematic worldview. If people are attracted to a particular magnet, if new societies or movements are founded and their collective thought nurtures the source whence the knowledge has been given, it means that the attracting world is thereby expanding and is bent on keeping as many people as possible drawn to its focus. Some worlds try to help, but some attempt to destroy. Hence man should be ever vigilant

GLOSSARY

in order not to fall into the attractive nets of the "ambassadors" of low-frequency worlds.

VOICE OF THE GREAT SILENCE — a single language consisting of all the vibrations produced by the Cosmos; it is the Voice generated by the beat of the Great Cosmic Heart. Nevertheless, there is no silence in the Universe, for the Silence is not voiceless. Indeed, some of these vibrations may be perceived by consciousness as sounds full of solemnity and beauty, as the harmony of the highest consonance, but these sounds are not like earthly ones — this is Cosmic Music.

Each heart has a command of this language. It does not require words, it knows no distances or obstacles. It is hard to hear the Voice of the Silence, uttered by the heart, in an instant. This is a special state of Grace that is accompanied by the emission of fiery currents. To hear the Voice of the Silence, one needs to abandon the hustle and bustle of chaotic thinking. One who learns the communication of the Silence will always be able to easily understand one's interlocutor without the aid of words.

VOLCANO — a connection channel between the Earth's core and spatial Fire.

At the very beginning of the formation of the planet, when its matter was still thin and pliant, the Highest Spirits descended on it. Buddha was the first, making the Seven Fiery Strides. As He walked, His feet "sank" into the ground. Hence these places became, as it were, closer to the underground fire. This is how volcano craters were formed — points for the Earth to breathe in the Fire of Heaven. In Japan, this page of the planet's history is symbolically reflected in the tradition of making and offering giant straw sandals called *waraji* — the sandals of Buddha — to Buddhist temples, and these sandals subsequently serve to adorn their walls.

The transition periods between different eras are marked with volcanic eruptions. This is one of the ways in which the infusion of the spatial Fire manifests itself, causing accelerated breathing in the Earth's core. Volcanoes, like barometers, testify to the intensity of the

Flame. They are the first to warn of impending danger. But so often volcanic activity is the result of human activity involving dissonance and destruction.

Nature always sends special signs into space before a volcano starts to erupt. For example, little red stars may appear in the air, indicating extreme tension in the atmosphere, along with the possibility of earthquakes. Many species of animals and birds notice them and, having a premonition of their impending doom, abandon those places. But, all too often, people take absolutely no notice of such warnings, and some stubbornly continue living at the foot of a volcano instead of moving to a safer place.

These days, when the Fire comes down to the Earth, an underground flame is activated: the earthly fire strives to unite with the Heavenly Fire, and many volcanoes awake and become active. But, through the power of his own thinking, man is able not only to silence volcanoes but also to subdue the spatial Fire to serve the needs of the Common Good.

WARMTH — magnetism, or hidden fire, which attracts and radiates the force of life. Warmth is the only kind of energy which can split any form of matter into constituent elements and then combine them with others, creating a new form of matter.

This power is generated from within the body and is expelled outside as a result of the constant interaction between internal and external fires. Consequently, magnetism — a third form of power radiating warmth — is the external manifestation of this interaction. When the inner fire holds the preponderance of power, the radiated energy of magnetism takes on a healing or life-giving force.

So it is with the Sun: its warmth, or magnetism, transmits a life-giving force to all creation. However, the emanating rays are neither hot nor cold until they encounter matter in space. Then the rays cause warmth through the resulting electric and magnetic interaction. The warmth then releases and unites elements in the atmosphere and elsewhere by changing their composition. And this in turn affects life on the planet.

GLOSSARY

WATER — deposited Light, being one with the Fire in its essence. Water itself is neutral in nature, but reflects everything that surrounds it, and serves as material for creating intermediate forms between the Fiery and Earthly Worlds.

Three basic states of water are known: liquid, solid, and gaseous. But further, as matter becomes subtler, water ascends to Light, and its projection penetrates all layers into the depths of the Waters of the Cosmos. This represents a special substance of the Light, consisting of the crystallized currents of the Great Feminine Principle. The interchange of Cosmic Waters with earthly waters goes on continually: it passes from one sphere to another, and its mass sets a certain direction for the development of life. This interchange with the Cosmos causes the growth of ozone holes. Waters on all manifestations of the Earth must have a definite interrelation with each other.

Now the Fire from the Cosmos is united with the water on the Earth. Every drop of rain is imbued with the sparks of the Fire. Thus, low temperatures, together with abundant rains and snowfalls, have a beneficial effect on the acceptance of the Fire by man, thereby facilitating a relatively painlessly cleansing of the Earth and the acceptance of Baptism by Water and the Celestial Fire.

WHEEL — one of the ancient symbols for the Sun, namely, the invisible Central Spiritual Sun, which is the source of life for everything in the Solar System, as well as in the Universe, since the physical Sun is only a reflection of its Supreme Spiritual Essence. All the suns of the Universe originate from the Spiritual Sun.

The image of the wheel may also be seen as a symbol of Evolution — continuous rebirth, renewal, and improvement — as movement repeats itself in a rotating wheel. Its rotations represent different cycles. The right to rotate the Wheel rests with the God-Hierarchs who have taken responsibility for the evolution of a certain world. Therefore, ever since ancient times, the Wheel has been an attribute of Chakravartin (*Sanskrit*, "One who turns the Wheel") — an ideal ruler who conceives conscious life and reigns according to Cosmic Laws.

WILL — a driving fiery force which awakens the energy concealed in matter. The will is the fire in action that forms matter. Man has power over all kinds of matter and energy, therefore the goal of Evolution is the development of the will right up to full control over the elements of all the Kingdoms of Nature. The human will is capable of overcoming everything, including Karma. Its power may be developed without limit.

Everything created in the Universe is created by the will, because thoughts and ideas govern the world, but both thoughts and ideas are governed by the fiery will. Will is the ability of the human spirit to control fiery energies, consequently, the mastering of the will is the mastery of fire. Everyone has fires, but some are able to master them, while others are not. Those who can handle their own fires, can handle others', too — that is, they can exert an influence on people, animals, plants, and so on.

Since the will is fire, the freedom of will is sacred, and no one has the right to destroy it, even if it leads into the darkness. After all, the will may be either bright or dark, but the evil will is doomed, as it violates Cosmic Laws. The weak will is headed for destruction because, without a strong will, people can easily fall victim to dark influences. Creatures with no will or a weak will cannot go forward, and so are unsuitable for evolution.

The will can be governed either by the brain or the heart of man. But since the heart is the centre of the fiery energy of the spirit, the will of the brain is correspondingly weak. A will that is affirmed and permeated by the fires of the heart is infinitely stronger than a will proceeding from the brain.

The will is not an abstract or invisible thing. It represents substance deposited in the heart over many lives, and consists of the crystalline formations of fire. Each victory, no matter how small, multiplies the fiery crystal of the will. Without such fiery accumulations, man is nothing.

The collective will of humanity is a frightful force. It is so strong that to destroy it — in case of disastrous errors — whole planetary catastrophes are required, as was the case with Atlantis. After all, it was the will of people that led the planet to this, in breach of Cosmic Laws. Even the stellar rays, which create favourable or neutralizing conditions for the establishment of certain phenomena in the earthly

GLOSSARY

world, do not control, but merely urge a particular course of action. Yet the most powerful — and often decisive — factor is the collective will of humanity. Hence, even though the transfiguration of the whole world depends on it, still, everyone can make themselves into whatever they desire.

WISDOM — Knowledge multiplied by Love. This is a necessary stage of evolution in fulfilment of the chief mission of the present Solar System. Since Love manifests itself solely in the heart, the path to Wisdom lies inevitably through the heart. Knowledge acquired throughout the ages but not imbued with the loving currents of the heart simply turns into information and eventually loses its significance.

According to the evolutionary plan, the Fifth Race must begin its spiritual ascent through the development of the mind of the heart — i.e., Wisdom. For this reason, part of Sacred Knowledge had already been given in the 1920s and 1930s by the Great Teachers in the Ray of Love-Wisdom, thereby paving the way from the intellect to the heart. And all subsequent Knowledge was to be given solely through the prism of Love-Wisdom along with inner intuition, with human hearts as its focus.

The Masters of Wisdom are wise, not because they know everything, but because they have a passionate love for the whole suffering world. Everyone knows that a drowning person must be rescued, but not everyone will throw themselves into deep water. Therefore, heartless people cannot enter the Era of the Heart and Wisdom, even if they happen to be founts of knowledge.

WORD — a covering of thought, its seeming physical form, regardless of whether it is expressed in the form of sound or symbol. The word is inseparable from thought, which means it is a carrier of the Fire, either bright or dark. Hence each word contains within itself either constructive or destructive power. The World was created by the Word. Therefore, the word is a powerful force, if used conscientiously.

Each letter, by virtue of its vibrational key, affects the human nervous system through its corresponding vibrations. Not only that, but it also awakens as yet unmanifested forces in space. Vowel sounds are fiery in nature, while consonants are perishable and earthly. Indeed, one can evoke healing energies from space through a particular combination of vowel sounds, whereas the low-frequency, hiss consonants are capable of causing rockslides, tornadoes, and other destructive phenomena, including earthquakes. Also, every pronounced word represents fiery energy — transmitted, or radiated, by the body through mouth. During all this, the affected nerves flare up like wires with fiery currents and cause an external flash in the form of fiery formations. Words fly in space like colourful balls of fire. Every letter creates fiery discharges. Even ordinary conversation can be imagined as an exchange of fires or coloured rays. Thought encased in words is cast into the surrounding sphere, and either remains there, influencing the environment long after the words are spoken and forgotten, or flies to its destination.

Words are the channels of magnetic attraction from space of what their essence expresses. None of the energies, once put into action, disappears completely, but each brings its own consequences, depending on its nature and especially its producer, for the crystal of such energy remains in their aura. Thus, these energies are forever connected with their creator by a magnetic thread. They are their spatial property, which will not leave them until the magnetic force of these words is exhausted on themselves. The energies again return to them in order to be neutralized, in order that the disturbed balance might be restored. Hence one must be accountable for every word one utters. The dense conditions of the Earth often prevent the completion of this process, but after death, the process of neutralizing one's own created energies continues freely and unhindered in the Subtle World, until it consumes everything — bad or good — that one has generated on the Earth.

Since words are external symbols of the thoughts behind them, the repetition of any word calls into being the latent energy within it, which affects the man and the surrounding space. Even the mental repetition of words which affirm high and positive qualities is beneficial. In this way, through words one may bring one's self or anyone else into a harmonious or an inharmonious state. The power of verbal prayer, for example, has been known since ancient times.

GLOSSARY

The mystery of perfection in speech and text lies in the absolute harmony of form and content. The vibrational keys of words, their sound and tonality, the colour of the thoughts concealed in them, should be in full consonance and harmonization. Provided there is such an accord, spoken and written texts can be expressed in any rhythm and tonality. Words can be short and abrupt if the rhythm requires, and sentences may feature peculiar constructions, since the power of influence resides not in the external form, but in the consonance between the words and the essence therein expressed. A properly and harmoniously constructed rhythm of speech or text has a tremendous invisible impact. This is why the creations of some writers and poets are considered to be great, and why some scriptures are honoured as sacred.

For the reasons cited above, all Teachings emphasize *discipline* in word and speech. After all, it is better to be silent than to experience the blows of spatial energy upon one's self. Silence is golden: man does not squander his precious fiery energy in vain. Many people are sick because they waste their strength through their own talkativeness. Besides, great harm is done by idle chatter when one should really remain silent. For example, if one has made an important decision or special plans, one should not advertise this to anyone prematurely, since disembodied evil entities populating the near-Earth space may overhear it and do everything in their power to hinder those plans. It easier to hide thoughts than words from subtle beings, for not all disembodied entities are capable of mind-reading. Moreover, foul language is inadmissible, being the antipode of prayer. Scientists have already discovered that "impure words" uttered with a loud or quiet voice (or even a whisper) have equally destructive effects on the living cells of one's body.

In the future, humanity will not send shockwaves into space through the sounds of its speech. Instead, communication will be mental, or telepathic. Until then, one should be careful in using the great power of the word and employ it only for good. It is worth attempting to follow, where possible, the wise precept of Christ:

"But let your communication be, Yea, yea; Nay, nay: for whatsoever is more than these cometh of evil."[60]

WORLDS — various states, or planes, of Cosmic Matter. For the present Solar System, there are Seven Worlds, each of which has seven sub-planes, according to the degree of rarefaction and refinement.

Four Worlds are available to humanity and the Earth in the Fourth Round:

1. ***The Physical World, the Dense World***, or ***the Material World***. It is the Earth itself, where physical humanity lives.

2. ***The Subtle World, the Astral World***, or ***the Ethereal World***. This is the world where everyone goes during their sleep. It encircles the Earth, and is much more spacious than the dense world. It has many layers, from the lowest to the highest, to which everyone is drawn by consonance. Everyone assumes an appearance corresponding to their inner essence, and reaps what they have sown on the Earth. Its matter is pliant and instantly becomes the expression of the thoughts of the spirit which the individual really is. Everything is created and moved by thought. Illumination comes from the radiation of people's subtle bodies, hence the lower spheres which bad people are drawn to are dark. All earthly emotions and habits remain in a considerably intensified state, so if man has not overcome his lower desires on the Earth, here he will painfully suffer from the absence of a physical body to satisfy them. The lower areas of the Subtle World are the closest to the Earth, therefore people there often use Earth-dwellers to satisfy their desires — hence their obsessions. For good people, not bound by physical aspirations, the Subtle World provides limitless freedom of the spirit; they can fly, endlessly create and contemplate creativity in all domains of life, study and explore everything they want. Souls may stay in this world for thousands of years.

3. ***The Mental World***, or ***the World of Thoughts***. Its contents are comprised by the products of the mental creativity of thinking creatures: mental forms or thought-forms. Its layers are determined by the

---

[60] Matt. 5:37.

GLOSSARY

affinity of thought emanations composing the content of the form. The line of attraction is determined by the way one's consciousness is attuned. The tuning process may be subconscious, or it may also be by order of the will. Then the will chooses the desired direction and establishes the necessary control. Whereas on the Earth people travel by cars, trains, etc., in the Mental World they travel in the vehicle of thought. Consciousness enters thought like a passenger enters a railway carriage, and the vehicle of thought brings it to the mentally chosen sphere.

4. ***The Fiery World**, **the Spiritual World**,* or ***the Empyreal World***. Its matter is so subtle, perfect, and imbued with energy that it causes fiery luminosity everywhere, hence the name. There is neither time nor distance in the earthly sense; everything happens "here and now." The beauty of this world is incredibly magnificent. Especially amazing are flowers, which are everywhere; they move and flutter, giving off marvellous fragrances and melodies. The elevated forms of matter and energy which compose the world create an atmosphere of Joy and Love. However, not everyone is able to get into the Fiery World, because for this they need to have their immortal fiery body developed. This happens when the individual follows a spiritual path on the Earth.

When the Worlds are enumerated, the Mental World is often omitted. It is the link between the Subtle and Fiery Worlds, belonging more to the latter, for thought does not exist without the Fire. Hence one might come across statements to the effect that there are Three Worlds accessible to humanity, and that the Fiery World is the World of Thought and vice versa.

The planet Earth exists in all these Worlds, and it is represented in each of them by its corresponding globe. All Four Worlds are combined concentrically one inside another, forming the complex septenary body of the planet. Thus, the Earth consists of dense physical matter, penetrated by the spheres of subtle and fiery matter. All Seven Spheres of the planet in the Four Worlds are inhabited. The dwellers of one World do not see or sense the other Worlds. But they are continually moving from one World to another; dying in one, they are reborn in another, moving either upwards to the next higher planes or downwards once more to the Earth. In this way, man passes through the Round of incarnations within the Planetary Chain.

Each of the bodies in which man lives in turn a conscious and full life, is restricted by the world and sphere to which he belongs, and is subject to its laws. All the Worlds have their boundaries and limitations, restricting man in some measure by the properties of their matter. All ancient Teachings prescribed certain norms of behaviour, diets, and so on, aimed at the purification, or refinement, of the matter of all human bodies. The crude astral body, weighed down by crude habits, cannot rise higher than the lower layers of the Astral World, which are in perfect correlation with the astral body's composition. Having been released from the dense body, only the individuals that have purified their coverings from dense particles on the Earth, may succeed in soaring on high. In the Subtle World every disembodied person undergoes a process of cleansing, and yet, for all that, they cannot ascend higher than the height they themselves have attained. The Law of Consonance is just and does not make mistakes.

The planet Earth has already passed the lowest point — or the greatest density — of its evolution, and so it is now on a course of ascent. As a result, the convergence of the Dense and Subtle Worlds is now gradually taking place, and the planet is rising one step higher than before. Hence the Subtle World is advancing on the Dense World, expanding the spheres of its own influence, thanks to the addition of properties that rarefy the matter of the Earth; the Physical World, in turn, is harmoniously flowing into the layers of the Subtle Spheres. Similarly, the planet's Subtle World in its higher layers blends with the Mental World, and the Fiery World ascends into an even Higher World. Thus, in the Fifth Round, Five Worlds will be accessible to the Earth and humanity, where the Physical World will resemble the lowest layer of the Subtle World — that is, without such a sharp demarcation as evident in the present days.

RECOMMENDED READING

There is an ancient law that enjoins the Great Teachers of Humanity to make an attempt to enlighten the world in every century, at a certain specified period of the cycle. Thus, since time immemorial, the Mahatmas have, either directly or through their messengers, imparted a religion, philosophy, science, or needed advice to each country at a particular turning point in its history.

Below are listed a number of publications originating from the Masters of the Ancient Wisdom in the 19th and 20th centuries, when the time had come to reveal to humanity more than had ever been previously allowed. Almost all these works have gone through multiple reprints and editions, and now may be found in electronic form, free of charge.

MASTERS OF WISDOM

In the 1880s, for the first time since Atlantis, the Lords of Shambhala openly contacted the general public, sending hundreds of letters to their correspondents which were later transcribed and published. These letters, mainly from the Mahatmas Koot Hoomi (*left*) and Morya (*above*), constitute the most important source for understanding the role and meaning of the Great White Brotherhood in the life of humanity.

Letters from the Masters of the Wisdom. Compiled by C. Jinarajadasa. 2 vols. Adyar: Theosophical Publishing House, 1919–1925.

The Mahatma Letters to A. P. Sinnett. Compiled by A. Trevor Baker. London: T. Fisher Unwin, 1923.

HELENA BLAVATSKY
(1831–1891)

In the middle of the 19th century, the Sages of the Himalayas gathered in the lamasery of Ghalaring-Tcho, near Shigatse (Tibet), to discuss the question of choosing a Messenger for the West. However, by an almost unanimous decision, they concluded that the arrogant and unbelieving people of the West, who cared for nothing but power and material well-being, had lost all possibility of receiving and understanding the true Secret Doctrine, and there was no point in sending Messengers to those who had no desire to welcome them. Nevertheless, the voices of the Mahatmas Morya and Koot Hoomi were raised in favour of obedience to the instructions contained in the ancient law. They accepted the responsibility for selecting the Messenger of Shambhala to the West, and Helena Blavatsky was chosen. She took upon herself the hardest labour of all — sharing with people the Ageless Wisdom in the form of two capital works: *Isis Unveiled* and *The Secret Doctrine*, both written in Western countries in the Rays of the present Great Lord of Shambhala. Aimed at the human intellect, Blavatsky's writings were to bring about a fundamental shift in the ossified consciousness of humanity.

RECOMMENDED READING

Isis Unveiled: A Master-Key to the Mysteries of Ancient and Modern Science and Theology. 2 vols. New York: J. W. Bouton, 1877.

The Secret Doctrine: The Synthesis of Science, Religion, and Philosophy. 2 vols. London: Theosophical Publishing Company, 1888.

The Key to Theosophy: Being a Clear Exposition in the Form of Question and Answer of the Ethics, Science, and Philosophy for the Study of Which the Theosophical Society has Been Founded. London: Theosophical Publishing Company, 1889.

The Voice of the Silence: Being Extracts from the Book of the Golden Precepts. London: Theosophical Publishing Company, 1889.

Gems from the East: A Birthday Book of Precepts and Axioms. London: Theosophical Publishing Society, 1890.

Transactions of the Blavatsky Lodge. 2 vols. London: Theosophical Publishing Society, 1890–1891.

From the Caves and Jungles of Hindostan. London: Theosophical Publishing Society, 1892.

Nightmare Tales. London: Theosophical Publishing Society, 1892.

The Theosophical Glossary. London: Theosophical Publishing Society, 1892.

The Letters of H. P. Blavatsky to A. P. Sinnett. Compiled by A. Trevor Baker. London: T. Fisher Unwin, 1925.

The People of the Blue Mountains. Wheaton, IL: Theosophical Press, 1930.

Collected Writings. Compiled by Boris de Zirkoff. 15 vols. Wheaton, IL: Theosophical Publishing House, 1950–1991.

The Durbar in Lahore: From the Diary of a Russian. The Theosophist (August 1960–March 1961).

The Secret Doctrine Commentaries: The Unpublished 1889 Instructions. The Hague: I.S.I.S. Foundation, 2010.

RECOMMENDED READING

FRANCIA LA DUE
(1849–1922)

After the demise of Helena Blavatsky, the Great White Brotherhood chose Francia La Due to continue her mission in America. In 1898 she founded the Temple of the People under the direction of the Master Hilarion in Syracuse, New York; the Temple was later relocated to Halcyon, California. Together with the Mahatmas Morya and Koot Hoomi, Hilarion revealed through Francia La Due a new section from the secret *Book of Dzyan* and imparted marvellous Teachings, which were first published in the *Temple Artisan*, the official magazine of the Temple of the People.

From the Mountain Top. 3 vols. Halcyon, CA: Temple of the People, 1914–1985.

Teachings of the Temple. 3 vols. Halcyon, CA: Temple of the People, 1925–1985.

Theogenesis. Halcyon, CA: Temple of the People, 1981.

NICHOLAS ROERICH
(1874–1947)

During his lifetime, Nicholas Roerich, the Messenger of Beauty, created approximately 7,000 paintings, some of which are now stored in the Nicholas Roerich Museum in New York. All of his paintings are prophetic, but they are coded. The creation of these masterpieces of art, which conceal the mystery of Colour, Light, and Sound, involved the participation of the

RECOMMENDED READING

four Greatest Spirits of the Hierarchy of Light. The colours in his paintings, radiating invisible and inaudible sound, have a direct influence on the higher centres of a person's thought and awaken their creativity. It is no accident that some people are healed just by looking at them, or that later they start to write or draw. Being well acquainted with Oriental philosophy and with the same sacred sources from which Helena Blavatsky obtained her knowledge, Nicholas Roerich also left a literary legacy.

Violators of Art. London, 1919.

Adamant. New York: Corona Mundi, 1922.

Altai-Himalaya: A Travel Diary. New York: Frederick A. Stokes Company, 1929.

Flame in Chalice. New York: Roerich Museum Press, 1930.

Heart of Asia. New York: Roerich Museum Press, 1930.

Shambhala. New York: Frederick A. Stokes Company, 1930.

Realm of Light. New York: Roerich Museum Press, 1931.

Fiery Stronghold. Boston: Stratford Company, 1933.

To the Woman's Heart. New York: Woman's Unity of Roerich Museum, 1933.

Roerich Essays: One Hundred Essays. 2 vols. India, 1937.

Joy of Art. Amritsar: Art Society, 1942.

Beautiful Unity. Bombay: Youths' Art and Culture Circle, 1946.

Himavat: Diary Leaves. Allahabad: Kitabistan, 1946.

Himalayas: Abode of Light. Bombay: Nalanda Publications, 1947.

The Invincible. New York: Nicholas Roerich Museum, 1974.

RECOMMENDED READING

HELENA ROERICH
(1879–1955)

The Mother of Agni Yoga, Helena Roerich, proclaimed the dawn of the New Era and the future Resurrection of Spirit and Love in the world. From 1920 to 1947, she recorded another cycle of the Divine Wisdom from the Great Teachers — *Agni Yoga*, also known as the *Teaching of Living Ethics*. It was written for the most part in the Orient, in the Rays of the Lord M., the King of Shambhala. Aimed initially at the mind, this Fiery Teaching paves the way to the heart and points out Infinity in the Cosmos and Life. Moreover, the Heroic Achievement of Helena Roerich consists not only in delivering the Teaching to humanity but also in the fact that she offered herself for the Fiery Experiment — the influence of spatial energies upon an incarnated person. This Experiment has helped the Instructors of Humanity find ways to minimize the sufferings of the world in the present day, as it is these cosmic energies that started affecting all humanity and the planet Earth in 1999. By strictly following the canons and principles of the secret science, Roerich succeeded in the mastering of the spatial Fire, and reached the highest condition of spirituality possible on the Earth.

Agni Yoga. 17 vols. New York: Agni Yoga Society, 1923–2004.

Foundations of Buddhism. New York: Roerich Museum Press, 1930.

On Eastern Crossroads: Legends and Prophecies of Asia. New York: Frederick A. Stokes Company, 1930.

Letters of Helena Roerich. 2 vols. New York: Agni Yoga Society, 1954–1967.

At the Threshold of the New World: Dreams, Visions and Letters of Helena Roerich. Prescott, AZ: White Mountain Educational Association, 1998.

FOR FURTHER INFORMATION ON
WHERE TO ORDER OR DOWNLOAD
THE RECOMMENDED BOOKS, PLEASE VISIT

www.dushkova.com/en

INDEX

Page numbers appearing in *italics* refer to pages with illustrations.

NUMBERS

3rd Panchen Lama, 184, 186
6, number of Earth and Life, 25, 158
7
   basis of colour spectrum, 82
   basis of Earth and Solar System structure, 91–92, 187–88
   basis of human maturation and structure, 146–48
9, converting 6 to, 159
9th Panchen Lama, 78
12, number of next Solar System, 188
14th Dalai Lama, 78
19, number of the new world, 159
666, number of the beast, 158–59
777 leaders of humanity, 151
999, number of God, 159
144,000
   high spirits, 91
   types of fiery radiation, 112

A

abstinence, 166
addictions, 165
adepts, xii–xiii, 63, 111, 147, 182
advents, 97, 101–7, 119
affirmations, xv, 89, 118, 158, 168
agape, 4–6, 52–54, 63, 97, 161
Agapegenesis (Dushkova), xvii–xviii
Agartha. *See* Shambhala
ageing, 129–30, 134, 146, 149
agency, 81–82, 90, 142–43, 191
Agni (God of Fire), 40–41, 45, 63–64, 161
Agni Yoga (H. Roerich), 120, 122, 151, 157, 199
Agni Yoga, Leaves of Morya's Garden (H. Roerich), 102
air, 113, 117, 153
akasha, 64, 127, 153
Akasha Chronicles, xiv, 64, 65, 188
Akbar the Great, 116
alertness, 17–18, 64–65, 91, 99
Alexander III, 184
all-seeing eye, 27, 54, 65
Anastasia of Siberia, 164
Anaxagoras, 116
Ancient of Days. *See* Great Lord of Shambhala
anger, 19, 33, 48, 49
animal kingdom, 75, 138
Anthropogenesis (Blavatsky), xvii
apes, 141, 176
Apollonius of Tyana, 186
apostles, twelve, 108, 164
Aquarius, Age of, 173–74
archangels. *See* high spirits
argo coefficient, 110–11, 113
Armageddon, 45, 65–66
aromas, 4, 20, 66–67, 114, 189
Arraim, 131
art, 37, 67–68, 171, 198

INDEX

Arthur, 116
ascent
   evolutionary, 138, 206, 211
   path of, 81, 106, 131–32
   spiral, 28, 96, 145–46
ashrams, xi, 68, 184
Athena, 97, 116
Atlantis, x, 68–70, 178–79, 182–83
auras, 70–71, 143
avatars, 115–16, 120
Avesta, 157

B

Babel, Tower of, 182–83
balance, 17, 21–22, 38, 71–73, 139, 195
Balance, Law of, 71
baptism, fiery, 28–30, 53, 100–10, 154, 159
baptism of Earth, 28–29, 204
beacons, 26, 30, 49, 51–52
   sons of God, 14–15, 20, 53
beauty, 35–39, 68, 73–74
Belovodye. *See* Shambhala
betrayal, 47, 150, 198–99
Bhagavad-Gita, 157
Bible, 157
biorobots, 75, 117
black brotherhood, 74–75, 87, 179
Blavatsky, Helena, 151, 186, 199, 214, 214
   Anthropogenesis, xvii
   Cosmogenesis, xvii
   Secret Doctrine, The, xvii, 78, 120, 151, 157
   Voice of Silence, The, 78
blindness, 11, 27
blood, 26, 74–76, 125
bodhisattvas. *See* high spirits
bodies, mental, astral, and physical, 147–49, 172, 190, 211
Böhme, Jakob, 116
Book of Dzyan, x–xviii, 78
Book of Fiery Destinies, xiv–xv, 78

Book of Golden Precepts, xiii, 78, 200
Book of Maitreya Buddha, xiii, 78
Book of Secret Wisdom. *See Book of Dzyan*
books, ix–xi, 76–78
brain, 30, 78–80, 196, 205
   See also mind
brotherhoods, xi, 80–81
   black, 74–75, 87, 179
   white, 66, 121–22, 150, 182, 184, 213–14
brownies, 201
Bruno, Giordano, 116
Buddha, 104, 116, 154, 162, 177, 186, 202
bullets, 75

C

Cacella, Estêvão, 184
calendars, 106–7, 133, 185–86
calls, 22, 30, 36, 40, 81
Canis Major, 90
catastrophes, natural, 69, 104, 142, 170–71, 207
cause and effect, 89, 95
   karma, 124, 133–34, 149, 200, 205
Cause and Effect, Law of, 85–86, 88, 133, 197
   See also Law of Karma
Cayce, Edgar, 102, 104, 121–22, 170
celestial fire, 63, 204
cells, 26–27, 129–30, 208
chain, planetary, 91–92, 210–11
chain of evolution, 96, 106
Chakravartin, 119–20, 204
chalice, 87, 107, 132, 137
   See also fiery heart
Charles XII, 185
chiaroscuro, xv, 83, 92, 166
choice, 81–82, 90, 142–43, 191
   final, 11, 22–23, 44, 82, 103, 108
Christ, 63, 100–5, 119, 131, 173
   teachings, 86, 121
   See also Only Begotten Son of God

INDEX

circle, 63–64, 105
City of Gods. *See* Shambhala
City of Golden Gates (Atlantis), 69
civilization, cycles of, 141–42, 176–77
climate change, 170, 204
Cnut the Great, 185
codes, 103
colour, 28–29, 82–83, 108, 182, 189
Coma Berenices, 90
comets, 186, 187, 193
Commensurability, Law of, 139
Communicating Vessels, Law of, 139
communication, xii–xiii, 53, 188–89, 202, 208–9
Community of the Seven Messengers of the Distant Worlds, 80
compassion, 123–24, 179, 192–93, 200
condemnation, x, 21, 83–84
Confucius, 116, 177
conscience, 80, 124
consciousness, 72, 84–85, 147, 195, 209–10
    diminishment of, 157–58
    expansion of, 94, 114, 128
    planes of, 86, 92, 181
    refinement of, 68, 70, 73, 76–78, 99
Consonance, Law of Magnetism and, 140, 142–43, 172, 211
consonants, 207
Constantine the Great, 184
Correspondences, Law of, xviii
cosmic fire, 104, 142, 149, 170, 197
cosmic knowledge, 135, 136, 157, 173
cosmic right, 85–86
cosmic scales, 106–9
Cosmogenesis (Blavatsky), xvii
Coulomb, Emma and Alexis, 199
Council of High Initiates, 185
councils of Shambhala, 185, 186
creativity, 37, 68, 76, 209
Creator, Preserver, and Transfigurer of the Solar System, The. *See* Great Lord of Shambhala
crosses, 29, 86–87, 161, 201

crucifixion, 125, 201
Cryptograms of the East (H. Roerich), 119
crystals, 113, 190, 207
    of the heart, 93, 94, 110–11, 137, 167, 168

D

Daitya, Island of, 69
Dalai Lama, 14th, 78
darkness, 5–12, 87–88
    and blood, 51, 74
    and destruction, 16, 33–34
    evils of, 26, 27, 35, 41, 99
    and labour, 15–16, 137
    and light, 28–29, 49, 143–44
    and poison, 48, 165–66
    See also evil
Dark Star. *See* Earth
death, 16, 23, 47, 88–90, 129, 130, 148
deceptions, 26, 41, 98–99, 144
denial, 157–58
dense world. *See* physical world
descent, 29
deserts, xi
destiny, xiv–xv, 47, 67, 79, 90
dhyan chohans. *See* high spirits
Dialogues (Dushkova), 186
disasters, natural, 69, 104, 142, 170–71, 207
discernment, 11, 14, 30, 64–65, 84
disciples, xi, 150–51, 173
distant worlds, ix, xi, 69, 90–91, 141
    and solar systems, 186, 193–94
    See also planets; stars
divine currents, 20, 30, 33, 42
divine love, 4–6, 52–54, 63, 97, 161
Divine Love, Law of, xviii, 139
Djual Khool, 149
doctrines, three, 119–22
doubt, 30, 41, 91, 165, 195
dreams, 89, 131, 195, 197
Dushkova, Zinovia
    Agapegenesis, xvii–xviii

223

INDEX

Dialogues, 186
Teaching of the Heart, The, 106, 122
dwarfs, 117
dzyan, 91
Dzyan, Book of, x–xviii, 78

E

Earth, 3–6, 91–93, 158
  baptism of, 28–29, 204
  element of matter, 113, 117, 153
  heart of, 28, 49–50
  and solar systems, 66, 80, 209–11
  transformations of, 20–21, 24–25, 44–45, 130, 170–71
earthquakes, 203, 207
Easter Island, 140, 142
Eastern Brotherhood, 80–81
Eclipse Comet, 186–87
Egypt, 69–70, 80, 109, 159
eighth sphere, 47, 93
electricity, 112
  as spatial fire, 85, 153, 174, 202–3
elixir of life, 33, 93–94
elves, 117, 201
empathy, 31, 192
empowerment, 174–75
energies, xvi–xvii, 63, 110, 142–43
  and alertness, 64–65
  and auras, 70–71, 143
  and balance, 71–72
  and creativity, 67–68, 114–15
  and fire, 111–12
  and spirit, 189–90
  of thoughts and words, 99, 194–96, 206–7
energy centres, 104–5, 114
energy units, 110–11, 113
enlightenment, 31, 55, 116
Equality of Principles, Law of the, 139
equilibrium, 17, 21–22, 38, 71–73, 139, 195
esoteric, 95
eternity, 3, 42, 46, 95
  See also infinity

Euryale, 25–26
evil, 14, 23–27, 36, 47–48, 67
  See also darkness
evolution, 96, 181
  chain of, 106
  and death, 129
  and the heart, 131–32
  of humanity, ix–x, 14–15, 37, 43, 140–41, 175–77
  and karma, 134
  ladder of, 125, 144, 190
  of planets and the Universe, 93, 95
  and self-consciousness, 84–85
Evolution, Law of, 180
exoteric, 96
Expediency, Law of, 139

F

fairies, 201
faith, 96–97, 98
Faith, Hope, and Love, 41, 97–98
  See also Sophia
falsehoods, 26, 41, 98–99, 144
fanaticism, 36, 73, 179
fasting, 166
fear, 37, 91, 99, 165, 195, 200
feelings, 15, 30, 67, 89, 124, 149
female deities, 116
feminine principle, 107, 116, 139, 173, 187
fiery baptism, 28–30, 53, 100–10, 154, 159
fiery cross, 29, 87
fiery experience, 100, 121
  See also fiery experiment
fiery experiment, 154, 218
fiery heart, 3, 15, 41, 174
  See also chalice
fiery-white core, 84, 110–11, 142
  of the heart, 44, 93–94
  and the Law of Love, 52
  solar stone, 192
  of the sun, 28, 42, 49

224

INDEX

fiery world, 40, 89, 91–92, 125, 210–11
fifth race, 169, 175, 198
   dominant colours, 83
   and great choice, 82
   and wisdom, 170, 206
final battle, 23–27, 65–66, 179
final choice, 11, 22–23, 44, 82, 103, 108
fire, 46–50, 111–13, 194
   celestial, 63, 204
   cosmic, 104, 142, 149, 170, 197
   and the heart, 43, 124–25, 155, 167–68
   and love, 53, 144
   spatial, 85, 112, 153, 174, 202–3
   spreading of, 18–20, 35, 54–55, 206
   See also light
Fire, God of (Agni), 40–41, 45, 63–64, 161
First Ray of Will and Power, 83
flowers, 4, 12, 28, 67, 113–14, 210
form, 114–15, 126, 190, 201
14th Dalai Lama, 77
fourth race, 68, 169, 170, 176–77
fourth round, 105, 169–70, 209–11
fragrances, 4, 20, 66–67, 114, 189
Francis of Assisi, 116
Frederick I, 184
free will, 81–82, 90, 138, 139, 142–43, 191
Free Will, Law of, 138, 139
fruit, ix, 12
future, 28, 30, 37–43, 54

G

Garden of Eden. *See* Shambhala
genies, 117
gloom. *See* darkness
God, 63, 115, 163, 191
God of Fire (Agni), 40–41, 45, 63–64, 161
gods, xii, 14–15, 27, 50–56, 115–16
   and destiny of man, 145, 149, 159, 175
golden age, 101, 119

golden fleece, 24, 116
Golden Gates, City of (Atlantis), 69
golden path. *See* balance
Gorgons, 25–27, 117
government, 88, 185
great ghoice, 82
Great Lord of Shambhala, 117–23, 173
   and fiery baptism, 107–10
   and ladder of hierarchy, 138
   and Lucifer, 66, 101, 179
   from Sirius, 159–60
   and Tower of Chung, 198
Great Sacrifice, 118, 180, 193
great teachers, 69, 91, 111, 118, 136, 153, 167
   masters of wisdom, 149–52, 206, 213–14
   seven great spirits, 55, 116, 173
greed, 26, 30, 37, 41, 145
Grünwedel, Albert, 184

H

habits, 113
hatred, 21, 41, 123–24, 165
   and Tree of Evil, 48
healing, 67, 77, 114, 132–33, 203, 207
heart, 7–9, 31–34, 124–25
   and brain, 64, 72, 78–80, 85, 170
   chalice, 87, 107, 132, 137
   crystals, 93, 94, 110–11, 167, 168
   of the Earth, 28, 49–50
   fiery, 3, 41, 174
   hardened, 25, 27, 43, 99
   language of, 15, 37, 53, 67, 81, 91, 202
   and love, 3–6, 22–27, 31–34, 46–50, 47, 192
   silence of the, 19–20, 41, 79
   and song, 35, 189
   and thought, 30, 196
Heart of Asia (N. Roerich), 121
heaven, 40, 89, 91–92, 125, 210–11
Hermes Trismegistus, 116, 131
heroism, 24–25, 168

225

INDEX

hierarchy, ladder of, 55, 85–86
Hierarchy, Law of, 140, 201
hierarchy of light, 71, 82, 104, 115, 137
higher worlds, 88–90, 130, 189, 196
high spirits, 67, 87, 115–16, 200–1
   and discernment, 84, 97
   on Earth, 91, 146, 164, 194
   gods, xii, 14–15, 27, 50–56
High Wheel of Eternity, 27, 55–56
Hilarion, 149
Himalayan Brotherhood, 80–81
Hitler, Adolf, 185
Holder of the Wheel of the Law. *See*
   Great Lord of Shambhala
Horch, Louis and Nettie, 199
horoscope, 191
human experiments, 180
human hands and feet, 21, 125–26
humanity, stratification of, 11, 29, 36, 82
human kingdom, 75, 105, 138, 181

I

ice, 92
ideas, 23, 121, 126–27, 205
idleness, 137
ignorance, 10–11, 18–19, 23, 27, 51,
   127–28, 157
illumination, 30–31, 52–54, 128,
   143–44, 195
Immaculate Conception, 104–5
immortality, 16, 54–56, 93–94, 114,
   128–30
imperil, 14, 48, 165–66, 200
implosion, 54, 130
indifference, 72, 82, 90
Inexhaustible Chalice, The (icon), 107
infinity, 89, 96, 138, 146
   See also eternity
initiates, 78, 111, 130–31, 182
initiations, 63, 130–31, 156, 159–60
Innocent IV, 184
instincts, 15, 131–32
intolerance, 179

intuition, 15, 80, 132
Ishtar, 97, 116
Isis, 97, 116, 159
Island of Daitya, 69
Island of Poseidonis, 69
Island of Ruta, 69
Israel, 75, 122, 163

J

Jacob's ladder. *See* hierarchy of light
Jesus, 97, 126, 161–63
Jesus Christ, 108, 116, 154, 186
   teachings, 67, 72, 90
Joan of Arc, 111
John the Apostle, 116
Joseph, 116, 162
Joshua, 116
joy, 9, 44–45, 132–33, 189
Judas, 199
Jupiter, 66, 90, 101, 109, 187

K

Kalachakra, 55–56
Kalki Avatar, 100, 119
Kalki Rudra Chakrin. *See* Maitreya
karma, 124, 133–34, 149, 200, 205
   cause and effect, 89, 95
Karma, Law of, 84, 139, 147
   See also Law of Cause and Effect
keys, xvi, 134–35
kingdoms of nature, 75–76, 84, 138,
   175, 181
   animal, 146
   human, 105
   mineral, 4, 84, 145–46
   plant, 67, 146
knowledge, 86, 135–37, 157
   in the beginning, 10, 141, 182
   cosmic, 135, 136, 157, 173
   of the heart, 7–9, 64, 96–97, 128, 132
   and human progress, x, xv, 38, 69,
      80–81, 176–77
   and supreme mind, 132, 147, 154–55

INDEX

Koot Hoomi, 116, 120, 149, *213*
Krishna, 116

L

labour, 15–16, 19, 54, 132, 137
ladder of evolution, 125, 144, 190
ladder of hierarchy, 55, 85–86
ladder of light, 33–34, 37–38, 55–56, 137–38
La Due, Francia, xvii, 216, *216*
  Theogenesis, xvii
Lakshmi, 97, 116
language, 176, 182–84, 202, 206–8
  of the heart, 15, 37, 67, 81, 91
  of love, 32–33, 53
  and numbers, xiii
  of scriptures, xiii, 100, 161
  Senzar, xii–xiii, xvii, 188
  and sound, xiii, xv, 135
Lao Chin, 184
Lao-Tzu, 116, 186
Last Judgement. *See* final choice
Law, Wheel of, 117, 119
Law of Balance, 71
Law of Cause and Effect, 85–86, 88, 133, 197
  See also Law of Karma
Law of Commensurability, 139
Law of Consonance, 142–43, 211
Law of Correspondences, xviii
Law of Divine Love, xviii, 52, 139
Law of the Equality of Principles, 139
Law of Evolution, 180
Law of Expediency, 94, 106, 139
Law of Free Will, 138, 139
Law of Hierarchy, 140, 201
Law of Karma, 84, 139, 147
  See also Law of Cause and Effect
Law of Magnetism and Consonance, 140, 142–43, 172, 211
Law of Reincarnation, 140
Law of Retribution, 144
Law of Rhythm, 140, 174

Law of Sacrifice, 140
Law of Unity of All Things, 140
laws of the Universe, 52, 63, 138–40
laziness, 137
Lemuria, ix, 140–42
Leo (constellation), 109
Lesser Council of Shambhala, 186
Lha. *See* gods
libraries, x–xi
life, 8–9, 42–43, 142–43, 172
  elixir of, 33, 93–94
  missions in, 134, 150
Life, Wheel of, 3–9, 13–14, 42, 45, 56
light, 5, 36, 143–44, 204
  and beauty, 72
  and darkness, 10–11, 21–27, 30, 40, 52
  and discernment, 37–38, 48–50, 65
  ladder of, 33–34, 55–56, 137–38
  servants of, 168
  See also fire; rays
Li Hong, 119
Lincoln, Abraham, 185
Lipikas. *See* lords of destiny
Lord of Civilization. *See* Great Lord of Shambhala
Lord of the White Flame. *See* Great Lord of Shambhala
Lord of the World. *See* Great Lord of Shambhala
lords of destiny, 3–6, 144
lotus, 182
Louis VII, 184
Louis XVI, 185
love, 10–13, 30–34, 56, 63, 144–45
  and brotherhood, 80–81
  fire of, 46–50, 105, 111
  and the heart, 43, 125
  karma of, 29, 74, 87, 134
  language of, 53
  resilience of, 18–22
  and wisdom, 35–39, 45, 132, 187–88, 206
Lucifer, 48–49, 65–66, 69, 123, 177–79
Luxor, Brotherhood of, 80–81

INDEX

M

magic, 24, 26, 69, 117, 145, 178
magnetism. *See* warmth
Magnetism and Consonance, Law of, 140, 142–3, 172, 211
Maha-Chohan, 118
mahatma, 145
Mahdi, 100, 119
Maitreya, 78, 100, 107–8, 118–19, 156–57
   See also Morya
Maitreyavyakarana, 108–9
malice, 19, 21, 33, 198
man, 7–9, 145–49, 176–77
   born again, 27, 36, 41–43, 46, 51
   and discernment, 37–38, 48–49, 154–55
   free will of, 21, 32–33, 44, 142–43, 204–6
   seed of, 10, 85, 172, 189–90
   and time, 16–17, 54–55, 130
Manuel I Komnenos, 184
manvantaras, 175
Marie Antoinette, 185
Mars, 91, 109, 187
Mary, 97, 116, 162
masculine principle, 107, 116, 139, 187
masters of wisdom, 118, 136, 149–52, 206, 213–14
   great teachers, 69, 91, 111, 153, 167
   seven great spirits, 55, 116, 173
materialism, 26–27, 143
Materia Agidya-Mani, 153
Materia Lucida, 153
Materia Mai-Ga-E, 154
Materia Matrix, 64, 127, 153
matter, 25–26, 139, 152–54
   changing of earthly, 45
   primeval, 3–5, 64, 127
Matthew, Gospel of, 102
meat, 76, 165–66
meditation, 42, 167
Medusa, 25, 117

Melchizedek, 116
memory, 78
Menes, 116
mental world, 89, 91–92, 148, 209–11
Mercury, 109, 187
Messiah, 100, 104–6, 119, 154
metals, 75, 191
middle path. *See* balance
migration, 80
mind, 14–17, 147, 154–55, 181
   heart and, 7–8, 31–32
   See also brain
mineral kingdom, 4, 75–76, 84, 138, 145–46, 175
missions, 43, 95, 125, 201
   of Earth, 3, 59
   in life, 134, 150
   of love, 19, 23, 125, 206
   See also quests
monads. *See* seeds
monsters, 25, 117
Moon, 91, 101, 109, 146, 187
Morya, 102, 116, 149, *213*
   See also Maitreya
Moses, 116
Mother of the World. *See* Sophia
mountains, xi, 131
Mount Kailash, 107
Mount Meru. *See* Shambhala
Muhammad, 116
music, 188–89
mysteries, 42, 125, 131, 157
   of nature, x, 69, 87, 117, 141, 145, 158
Mystery, 56, 155

N

names, 26, 97, 101, 118, 155–57, 168
Napoleon, 185
natural disasters, 69, 104, 142, 170–71, 207
nature, 64, 83, 107, 203
   beauty of, 28–29, 73
   mysteries of, x, 69, 87, 117, 141, 145, 158

INDEX

negation, 41, 43, 91, 157–58
Neptune, 187
Nostradamus, 101
   Vaticinia Nostradami, 119–20
Numa Pompilius, 116
numbers, 73, 82, 102–3, 158–60
   associated with entities, 25, 27, 110, 151
   and fire, 112
   in language, xiii, 182
   and solar systems, 146, 188
numerology, 125, 135, 158–59
nymphs, 117

O

omnipotence, 85, 113, 177
Om Tat Sat, 160–61
Only Begotten Son of God, 25, 56, 161–64
   See also Christ
ores, 75
Origen, 116
Orion, 90
Orpheus, 116
ozone, 204

P

Palden Yeshe, 184, 186
palmistry, 79
Panchen Lama, 3rd, 184, 186
Panchen Lama, 9th, 78
Paracelsus, 186
Paul, 116
perfection, 130, 132, 145–46, 180, 181, 190
   of self, 55, 67, 95, 96, 125, 138–40, 195
Pericles, 116
periods, 10–13, 16, 34, 164–65
   of the advent, 103–4, 106, 109
   cosmic, 102, 142, 173–74
   of the Solar System, 54–56, 186–87
   See also time
persecution, 18–22, 118, 179

Perseus, 117
philosopher's stone. *See* fiery-white core
physical world, 92, 107, 148, 155, 194–96, 209–11
Pisces, Age of, 173
pity, 192
planetary chain, 91–92, 210–11
planets, 71, 95, 109, 137–38, 152–53
   small, 54, 186–88
   See also distant worlds; stars
plant kingdom, 67, 75, 138, 146, 175
Plato, 116, 126, 177, 186
Pleiades, 90, 191
Pluto, 90, 187
poison, 14, 48, 165–66, 200
polarity, 16–17, 21–22, 72, 88, 90, 166–67
Poseidonis, Island of, 69
pralayas, 175
prana, 148
prayer, 35, 145, 167–68, 207
Prester John, 184
Puranas, 157
Pure Land. *See* Shambhala
purification, 34, 38, 41, 43–44, 52, 94, 166
pyramids, 66, 102, 109, 131, 159
Pythagoras, 116, 186

Q

quests, 29, 116, 168
   See also missions
Quran, 157

R

races, 68–70, 81–82, 140–41, 145, 169–71, 175–77, 198, 206
Rákóczi. *See* Saint-Germain, Count of
Rama, 116
Ramesses II, 116
rays, 11–12, 83, 104, 171–74, 180–81
   individual, 71
   of knowledge, 81, 136

INDEX

of love-wisdom, xvii–xviii, 59, 206
of Sophia, 97–98
See also light
reading, 76–78, 135, 136
of thoughts, 177, 208
refinement, 34, 38, 41, 43–44, 52, 94, 166
regents of planets. *See* high spirits
Regulus, 109
Reincarnation, Law of, 140
reincarnations, 128, 145–46, 148, 181
restraint, 64–65, 166
resurrection, 4, 56, 86–87, 108, 163
Retribution, Law of, 144
Revealer of Mysteries. *See* Sophia
Rhythm, Law of, 140, 174
rhythms, 68, 140, 174–75, 208
of the cross, 87
of matter, 152
and sound, 77, 188, 208
of the Universe, 30–31, 33, 54–55
Rigden Dragpo Khorlocan. *See* Maitreya
rings, 175
rishis. *See* high spirits
Roerich, Helena, 100, 102, 120–21, 151, 186, 218, *218*
Cryptograms of the East, 119
Roerich, Nicholas, 186, 199, *216*, 216–17
Heart of Asia, 121
Signs of Christ, 126
Roosevelt, Franklin, 185
rounds, 175–77
fourth, 105, 169–70, 209–11
and identity, 125
new, 7, 11, 42, 45, 83, 211
seven, 93, 145–47
Ruler of the Evil Empire. *See* Lucifer
Russia, 121–22
Ruta, Island of, 69

S

sacrifice, 41, 149, 168, 180
Lucifer's, 123, 178
of self, 98, 116, 164
See also Great Sacrifice
Sacrifice, Law of, 140
Saint-Germain, Count of, 94, 116, 149, 173
Salsk Celestial Code, 103
salvation, 11, 40, 49, 56, 159
Sanat Kumara, 117–23, 173
and fiery baptism, 107–10
and ladder of hierarchy, 138
and Lucifer, 66, 101, 179
from Sirius, 159–60
and Tower of Chung, 198
sandals, 202
Saoshyant, 100, 119
Saturn, 66, 87, 93, 179, 186–87
saviours, 53, 104, 164
scales, cosmic, 106–9
scents, 4, 20, 66–67, 114, 189
Schäfer, Ernst, 185
scriptures, 77, 89, 115, 208
ancient, 161–62, 175
language of, xiii, 100, 161
Scrolls of Akasha, xiv, 64, 65, 188
seal of immortality, 47
seals, xii, 29, 47, 48, 73, 87, 180
Secret Doctrine, The (Blavatsky), 78, 120, 151, 157
Secret Wisdom, Book of. *See Book of Dzyan*
seeds, 10–16, 89, 142–43, 180–82
of love, 23
monads, 128, 146
of the spirit, 84–85, 148, 172, 189–90
selfishness, 132, 133, 145, 155, 167
self-knowledge, 114, 128
self-mastery, 17, 64–65, 113, 125–26, 170
self-perfection, 55, 67, 95, 96, 125, 138–40, 195
Senzar, xii–xiii, xvii, 182–83, 188
Serapis, 118, 149
Sergius of Radonezh, 116
seven fiery strides, 202
seven great spirits, 55, 116, 118, 173

INDEX

great teachers, 69, 91, 111, 136, 153, 167
masters of wisdom, 136, 149–52, 206, 213–14
seven rays, 151–52
seventh race, 70, 81, 170
Shambhala, xi–xiv, 70, 107, 133, 183–86
Tower of Chung, xiii–xv, 103, 198
Signs of Christ (N. Roerich), 126
silence, 53, 124, 166, 186, 208
of the heart, 19–20, 31–32, 33, 41, 79
Silence, Voice of the Great, xiii, 53, 202
Sirius, 108, 159, 193
sixth race, 70, 81, 169–70
sleep, 54, 110, 158, 209
and death, 88–89, 130
solar eclipses, 101, 103, 153
Solar Hierarch, 117–23, 173
and fiery baptism, 107–10
and ladder of hierarchy, 138
and Lucifer, 66, 101, 179
from Sirius, 159–60
and Tower of Chung, 198
solar stone, 110, 192
solar systems, 130, 152, 167, 187–88
and distant worlds, 90–91, 186, 193–94
and Earth, 66, 80, 91–92, 209–11
Solomon, 116, 117
song, 188–89
sons of fire. *See* high spirits
sons of God, 14–15, 20, 53
as beacons, 26, 30, 49, 51–52
sons of heaven. *See* high spirits
sons of light, 14–15, 26, 53
sons of reason. *See* high spirits
Sophia, 97, 107, 116, 155, 161–62, 164, 173, 187
See also Faith, Hope, and Love
souls, 147, 189
essence of, 65, 88, 110
and light, 10, 31, 36, 40, 46, 161
and love, 9, 32, 53

path of, 92, 134, 146, 159, 176–77, 187–88
and stones, 5, 19–20
sound, 188–89
and beauty, 73
and colour, 82
and fire, 111–12, 143
and the heart, 31, 33, 52, 70, 93, 124
and joy, 132
and language, xiii, xv, 135, 182, 202, 206–8
and matter, 152
and names, 155–56
and numbers, 158
and rhythms, 77, 188, 208
and scents, 66
and thought-forms, xii
space and time, 104, 110, 189, 190, 197
spatial fire, 85, 112, 153, 174, 202–3
spiral ascent, 28, 96, 145–46
spirit, 147, 189–90
spirit and soul, 97, 131, 147, 167, 187–88, 189
spirits, 27, 59, 76, 81, 139
and aromas, 67
and auras, 70–71
Stalin, Joseph, 148
stars, 23, 44, 54, 190–92, 193–94
See also distant worlds; planets
Stheno, 25–26, 117
stones, 4, 5, 11–12, 19–20, 44
subtle plane
battles waged on, 66, 92
and creativity, 76
and forces of darkness, 70, 74, 92, 165, 171
and magic, 145
subtle world, 67, 123–24, 166, 197, 207, 209–11
and the brain, 78–79, 154–55, 194–96
transitions to, 88–89, 91–92, 110, 143, 148, 158
suffering, 149, 166, 192–93
suicide, 89

231

INDEX

Sun, 187, 191, 193–94, 204
  bearer of love, 3, 9
  and light, 8, 42
  renewal of, 54–55
  solar rays, 20, 28, 172
supreme mind, 132, 147, 154–55
supreme triad, 101, 148, 154–55
swastika, 87, 88
symbolism, xii–xiii, 76–77, 109, 134–35, 158–59, 160–61
  of an all-seeing eye, 65
  and circles, 63–64
  and codes, 103
  and crosses, 86–87, 201
  of death, 90
  of the golden fleece, 116
  and language, 182–84, 207
  and sandals, 202
  and spirals, 96
  and wheels, 204
Syria, 75

T

Tao Te Ching, 157
Tara, 97, 116
Teacher of Teachers. *See* Great Lord of Shambhala
Teaching of the Heart, The (Dushkova), 106, 122
temperance, 64–65, 166
Thebes, 80
Theogenesis (La Due), xvii
third eye, 27, 54, 65
third fire, 105
third race, 68, 140–41, 169
Thomas à Kempis, 116
thought, 126–27, 177, 194–96
  darkness of, 37, 43, 48–49, 165–66
  and destiny, 79, 144
  development of, 14–15, 23, 28, 30, 37
  and dreams, 89
  and energy, 73, 76, 99
  -forms, xii–xiv, 171, 209–10
  power of, 67, 70–71, 113, 144–45, 158

  and word, 206–9
threads, 20, 24–25, 142, 196
three doctrines, 119–22
Thutmose III, 116
time, 3, 197
  and intervals of fire, 49
  passage of, 23, 28, 31
  and rhythm, 174
  and thoughts, 196
  two streams of, 163–64
  See also periods
Time, Wheel of, 22, 133
time and space, 104, 110, 189, 190, 197
Tishya, 101
titans, 24, 198
Tower of Babel, 182–83
Tower of Chung, xiii–xv, 103, 198
transmutation, 176–77
  of disciples, 150–51
  and fiery baptism, 100
  of instinct, 15
  and polarity, 90
  of tribulations, 192
treachery, 47, 91, 198–200
Tree of Evil, 48, 200
Tree of Great Merit, 183
Tree of Knowledge, ix
Tree of Ten Thousand Images, 183
trinity, 63, 160
truth, 200–201
  and comprehension, 14, 26, 42, 88, 157
  discerning of, 64
  sources of, 125, 128, 135–36, 173
Tsongkhapa, 116
Tutankhamun, 116

U

UFOs, 180, 201
Ukraine, 75
undines, 117
Unity of All Things, Law of, 140
Universe, the, 201–2
  creation in, 4, 153, 172, 205

INDEX

and eternity, 95
and fire, 111–12, 144
laws of, 52, 63, 138–40
planets and stars in, 90–91
rhythm of, 54–55
spirits of, 144
Uranus, 90, 187, 193
Urusvati, 186–87

V

Vanga, 122
Vaticinia Nostradami (Nostradamus), 119–20
Vedas, 157
Vedic Trimurti, 63
vegetable kingdom, 67, 75, 138, 146, 175
Venus, 66, 90, 91, 109, 187
vibrations. *See* rhythms
Victoria (queen), 185
Violet Ray of Transfiguration, 83
Virgo, 109
Voice of Silence, The (Blavatsky), 78
Voice of the Great Silence, xiii, 53, 202
voice of the heart, 7–8, 15, 91, 124, 132
volcanoes, 24, 202–3
vowels, 207

W

war, 23, 26, 36, 74–75
warmth, 3–5, 32–33, 41, 47, 203
Washington, George, 185
water, 19, 38, 113, 117, 153, 204
Western Brotherhood, 80–81
wheel, 30, 38, 44–45, 50, 54, 204
Wheel of Eternity, High, 27, 55–56
Wheel of Law, 117, 119
Wheel of Life, 3–9, 13–14, 42, 45, 56
Wheel of Time, 22, 133
White Brotherhood, 66, 121–22, 150, 182, 184, 213–14
White Island. *See* Shambhala
will, 204–6
wisdom, 31, 35–39, 137, 206
word, 206–9

worlds, 43, 95, 209–11
World War I (1914–1918), 66
World War II (1939–1945), 66

Z

Zoroaster, 116

DATES

19 July, 159
9564 BCE, 69
6 BCE, 162
1568, 101
c.1850, 185
1878, 107
1881, 120
1884–1888, 120
1888, xvii
1893, 184
1898, 216
1899, 65–66, 78
1906–1918, xvii
1914–1918, 66
1915, 184
1920, 81, 120
1920–1947, 218
1924, 118, 119, 126
1924–1947, 121
1924–1955, 100
1925, 184, 185
1926, 185
1929, 119
1931, 66
1932
  29 July, 102
  30 June, 102
  29 November, 121
1933
  25 August, 121
1934
  23 June, 102
1935
  12 April, 102
  11 October, 102–3

233

INDEX

1936, 66
1939–1945, 66
1942, 100, 173
1943
  1 August, 101
1944
  22 June, 121–22
1948
  November, 186
1949, 65–66, 101, 179
  17 October, 66, 101, 179
1954, 65–66
  10 October, 121
1977, 65–66
1978, 122
1986, 199
1989
  15 September, 103
1994, 119
1995, xvii, 122
1997, 81
1998, 102, 103, 107, 121–22
1998–2000, 106
1999, 65–66, 101, 102, 218
  19 July, 82, 103
  19 July to 11 August, 163–64
  11 August, 103
2004–2005, 186
2005, 130
  19 July, 107
2012, 108, 110, 186
  19 July, 108, 130
2015, 108
2017, 108–9
  19 July, 82, 108, 164
2025, 185

ABOUT THE TRANSLATOR

Zinovia Vasilievna Dushkova, Ph.D., is a Russian author, poet, philosopher, historian, and traveller. She has been honoured with a number of awards, prizes, and commendations for her contribution to the spiritual development of society and for merit in the domain of scientific research in the ecology of consciousness. She is a Fellow of the European Academy of Natural Sciences (*Europäische Akademie der Naturwissenschaften*) and the European Scientific Society (*Europäische Wissenschaftliche Gesellschaft*), both based in Hanover, Germany.

Dr. Dushkova's interest in the history of world religions and philosophy, along with a desire to realize and fulfil her mission in life, led her first to the wisdom of prominent philosophers and thinkers, and subsequently to the works of Helena Blavatsky and the Roerichs, which changed her life radically. It is said in Oriental teachings that when the disciple is ready, the Teacher will appear — thus, in 1992, the Master came to her. After three years of intense training and probation, in 1995 she embarked on her first trip to India — the land of ancient teachings. There, at the foot of the sacred Himalayas, in the Buddhist Ghoom Monastery — where Madame Blavatsky in 1882 and Helena Roerich in 1923 met with the Master M. — the path of Zinovia Dushkova began.

The mysterious paths — leading into the heart of the Himalayas and the Blue Mountains, in the vicinity of Mounts Kanchenjunga,

ABOUT THE TRANSLATOR

Kailash, Everest, and so on — brought Dushkova to the secret Abodes of Light, from where the Call had sounded. Much like a hermit monk, her soul started poring over the sacred pages of Life from the archaic manuscripts that have been preserved in the most hidden corners of Sikkim, Ladakh, and other unexplored places of India, as well as those of other countries in Asia, Africa, Europe, and North America. She has braved the most dangerous paths through impassable mountains, wild deserts, and unknown caves so that now — having embraced the unembraceable and collected treasures of Ageless Knowledge and Wisdom in her heart — she may tell people, once again: "Love!" This is the only power capable of transforming the life of humanity and the entire planet.

Dr. Dushkova has devoted more than twenty years of her life to the study and acquisition of hidden esoteric wisdom, which she is now sharing with people through her books. She is the author of approximately forty works, published in Russia, Ukraine, Moldova, and France. These works of an ethical and spiritual nature reflect a synthesis of science, religion, history, and philosophy. Underlying her poetry and prose, fairy tales and legends, is a worldview full of wisdom and the cultural heritage of both the East and the West.

Zinovia Dushkova's major works, *The Teaching of the Heart*, *The Fiery Bible*, and *The Secret Doctrine of Love*, have called forth a wave of social movement in Russia, Ukraine, and Kazakhstan, centred around the development of culture, science, and education, all of which contribute to the progress and prosperity of society. Her award-winning philosophical children's book, *Fairy Tales for the Saviour*, has been given a ringing endorsement by teachers working with problem children in orphanages and juvenile detention centres.

Reigniting hope where it has disappeared, illuminating love where it has died away, and adding delight to life where its meaning has been lost — this is the goal which Dr. Zinovia Dushkova strives to attain in all her writings.

VISIT THE AUTHOR'S OFFICIAL WEBSITE AND
SIGN UP FOR A NEWSLETTER AT:

www.dushkova.com/en

FOLLOW THE AUTHOR AT:

www.facebook.com/ZinoviaDushkova

www.twitter.com/ZinoviaDushkova

www.goodreads.com/ZinoviaDushkova

LETTER TO THE READER

DEAR READER,

The Great Lord Buddha said: "Do not believe me simply because I, Buddha, told you so, but believe only when this resonates with your heart." Everyone is endowed with the divine free will; and no one has the right to dictate where you must go and what you must do. Listen to your heart alone. People are not slaves, but Gods — thus said Christ.

Therefore, believe what is written throughout the pages of this book only as it resonates with your heart. And when you feel the words which are voiced here in the depths of your own soul, you may listen to yourself and trust what is said.

I do not offer any new religion and the idea of forming a society that creates idols is absolutely foreign to me. My "religion" is — Love. And the only aim of all my books, addressed to human hearts, is to show and explore the infinite facets of Love, endeavouring to affirm them in my own life as well. While devoutly believing that Love is the Supreme Law of Creation, and that by honouring this Law everyone is capable of becoming a true luminary of the Universe, I still cannot urge you to follow this Path, but only to show it, as did the Greatest Teachers throughout the entire history of humanity.

If you find it difficult to accept something new, this is not a problem. Whichever Teaching of Light you are devoted to, all of them are given for eternity and will never lose their actuality. For each one represents a facet of the One Truth, whose Name is Love, and therefore the sincere study of any Sacred Scripture will inevitably lead you solely towards Love. And if it should turn out that what is written in *The Book of Secret Wisdom* is not consonant with your heart, please do not be hasty to dispose of the volume. It would be better to show it to

LETTER TO THE READER

your relatives, friends, or colleagues, or donate it to a nearby library. There are people who will most certainly be thankful to you for this.

You are welcome to send me your thoughts, commentaries, or suggestions at *contact@dushkova.com*. And while I personally will not be able to read, let alone answer all of your letters, my assistants will certainly review them and, if necessary, respond. You might have questions for which exhaustive answers are already available in the recommended literature or in future English translations of my books. But please do not become upset if you do not receive an answer to your question right off. Do bear in mind that in our binary world, when you have a question, you have immediately an answer to it, for the one does not exist without the other. And, sooner or later, you will most certainly find what you are looking for.

I would be cordially grateful for any review of *The Book of Secret Wisdom* you would care to share. After all, it might be useful for others, who, like you, are seeking for Truth. The success of the mission of this book is in the hands of every reader.

I am infinitely thankful to you for letting your heart penetrate the essence of the unspoken, for letting it perceive and carefully pour the Immortal Wisdom of the Ages into the treasury of your spirit. Everyone who is enkindled with new Fires of Love brings Light and Good into this suffering world, imperceptibly changing for the better thousands of people around.

To your grateful heart is dedicated every new work, wherein Love always reigns supreme, and my declaration of Love to you will be eternal. Blessed be your Path of Love! And if you need a loyal travelling companion, my heart and spirit will always be with you.

In sincere gratitude,

Zinovia Dushkova

Search not for the things foreign to you,
Follow the path that is untrodden, but clear.
Whatever you come across along the way,
With kindness in your eyes and warmth in your hands,
Give away for the good of the pilgrims who come after you.

ALSO BY ZINOVIA DUSHKOVA

THE TEACHING OF THE HEART

For the first time in history, the Masters of Wisdom have opened their treasury of secret knowledge to reveal the highest Teaching. This Teaching will empower you to transform yourself and the world through awakening the omnipotent power hidden in your heart.

Existing since time immemorial and called *Surya-Vidya* in antiquity, this Teaching taught the most worthy people about the sacred meaning of the heart as the sun of their universe — an inexhaustible source of perfect wisdom and divine power. However, humanity was not ready to accept the prevailing role of the heart. Therefore, the Teaching of the Heart has been kept secret and remained the prerogative of only the chosen few — those spiritual teachers who have proclaimed the omnipotence of the pure and loving heart.

The time has come to awaken humanity to the almighty treasure we possess because its infinite possibilities can radically change not only individual lives, but also the entire suffering world for the better. This mission has been undertaken by the Greatest Teacher known as the *Great Heart* — the Lord of Love and Compassion, the King of the legendary kingdom of Shambhala hidden in the Himalayas. He is Maitreya for some, Christ for others, and the Mahdi for many more — He is the promised Messiah of all religions. Before coming into the world, He has given *The Teaching of the Heart*, making it accessible to everyone for daily use in modern life.

ALSO BY ZINOVIA DUSHKOVA

Employing a *spiral approach*, the inspirational and uplifting books of *The Teaching of the Heart* series will reveal your heart's secret powers and cover a wide range of topics from everyday life to travels within the Universe.

The Teaching of the Heart was written by Zinovia Dushkova through a unique creative process called the *Fiery Experience* in three cycles of manifestation of the Ray of Love-Wisdom:

I
Leaves of Maitreya's Garden
The Call of the Heart
The Illumination of the Heart
The Heart of the Community
The Heart of Infinity
The Fiery Hierarchy
The Fiery Heart
The World of Fire
The Prayer of the Heart
Brotherhood

II
Flowers of Maitreya's Garden
The Sun of Love
The Joy of the Heart
The Rainbow of Fire

III
Fruits of Maitreya's Garden
The Fruit of Love

ALSO BY ZINOVIA DUSHKOVA

PARABLES FROM SHAMBHALA

This inspirational little book will help you comprehend the greatest ancient truths of the East through twelve short and profound parables containing the universal Laws of Existence. These truths will be revealed to you through the juxtaposition of opposites: spirit and body, good and evil, freedom and slavery, life and death, and so on. In this way, the spiritual lessons of *Parables from Shambhala* will enable you to make the right decisions in your daily life and to respond with wisdom to the events happening around you.

The parables were left as a heritage to humanity by the Mahatmas, the Great Souls of the East, and written down by Zinovia Dushkova. During her trips across Tibet, India, Nepal, and Mongolia, she has stayed at numerous monasteries — those open to the public as well as those hidden within high mountains and caves. She has been honoured to communicate with representatives of different religions, elderly monks and hermits who have generously shared their secret knowledge with her. In 2004, one Himalayan Master of Wisdom narrated legends and tales originating from the mysterious kingdom of Shambhala. This experience inspired the author to write down the stories in this book of parables under the canopy of the gigantic deodar cedars on the summit of the Himalayas.

Parables from Shambhala will be your loyal companion during your journey of self-improvement and spiritual growth, revealing its symbolism and depth as your consciousness expands.

COPYRIGHT

The Oldest Book in the World and Its Sacred Language: Contains translated and edited excerpts used by permission from the following works: *Bratstvo. Nadzemnaia Obitel'* © 1998, 2000 by Zinovia Dushkova; *Uchenie Serdtsa* © 1998–2000, 2001, 2004 by Zinovia Dushkova; *Dialogi* © 2012 by Zinovia Dushkova.

Agapegenesis: Twelve Stanzas from the *Book of Dzyan*: Represents translation of *Stantsy Liubvi* © 2001 by Zinovia Dushkova; *Epilogue* © 2015 by Zinovia Dushkova.

Glossary: Compilation and translation © 2015 by Alexander Gerasimchuk. Based on the public domain works in Russian of the Masters of Wisdom, Helena Blavatsky, Francia La Due, Nicholas Roerich, Helena Roerich, and Boris Abramov, as well as on the works of Zinovia Dushkova, which are used by permission. Scripture quotations are from the Authorized (King James) Version; rights in the Authorized Version in the United Kingdom are vested in the Crown; reproduced by permission of the Crown's patentee, Cambridge University Press. Edgar Cayce quotations are from Edgar Cayce Readings © 1971, 1993–2007 by the Edgar Cayce Foundation; reproduced according to permission guidelines.

Letter to the Reader © 2015 by Zinovia Dushkova.

THANK YOU FOR READING!

If you enjoyed this book, please consider leaving a review, even if it is only a line or two. It would make all the difference and would be very much appreciated.

Sign up for our newsletter to be the first to know when new books by Zinovia Dushkova are published:

www.dushkova.com/en/sign-up

Made in the USA
Coppell, TX
14 May 2020